Science Fiction and Anticipation

Science Fiction and Anticipation

Utopias, Dystopias and Time Travel

Edited by Bernard Montoneri

LEXINGTON BOOKS
Lanham • Boulder • New York • London

Published by Lexington Books
An imprint of The Rowman & Littlefield Publishing Group, Inc.
4501 Forbes Boulevard, Suite 200, Lanham, Maryland 20706
www.rowman.com

86-90 Paul Street, London EC2A 4NE

British Library Cataloguing in Publication Information Available

Library of Congress Cataloging-in-Publication Data

Names: Montoneri, Bernard, editor.
  Title: Science fiction and anticipation : utopias, dystopias and time
    travel / edited by Bernard Montoneri.
  Description: Lanham : Lexington Books, [2022] | Includes bibliographical
    references and index. | Summary: "Science Fiction and Anticipation
    focuses on American and European influential works of science fiction
    published between the 18th and 20th century. The book explores how
    writers presented in this book envisioned the future of their country,
    and it discusses issues such as ethics, censorship, racism, sexism, and
    slavery"-- Provided by publisher.
  Identifiers: LCCN 2022026868 (print) | LCCN 2022026869 (ebook) | ISBN
    9781666918137 (cloth) | ISBN 9781666918144 (ebook)   Subjects: LCSH:
  Science fiction--History and criticism. | Future, The, in
    literature. | Utopias in literature. | Dystopias in literature. | LCGFT:
    Literary criticism. | Essays.
  Classification: LCC PN3433.5 .S323 2022 (print) | LCC PN3433.5 (ebook) |
    DDC 809.3/8762--dc23/eng/20220608
  LC record available at https://lccn.loc.gov/2022026868
  LC ebook record available at https://lccn.loc.gov/2022026869

Contents

Preface   vii

Introduction   1

Chapter One: Mercier's *The Year 2440*, a Dream and a "Thought
    Experiment"   9
    Bernard Montoneri

Chapter Two: Origins of Hard Science Fiction: An Approach   31
    Fernando Darío González Grueso

Chapter Three: Beyond Utopia: The Dystopian Capitalist Society in
    Paris in the Twentieth Century (1863)   45
    Murielle El Hajj

Chapter Four: With Second Sight and Afro-pessimism: The Im/
    Possibility of Black Utopia in Martin R. Delany's *Blake; or,*
    The Huts of America   67
    Michaela Keck

Chapter Five: The Phenomenon of Human-Animal Hybridization in
    Russian Science Fiction of the 20th Century   91
    Anna Toom

Chapter Six: Barjavel, Ravage: *roman extraordinaire* (1943)   119
    Bernard Montoneri and Murielle El Hajj

Chapter Seven: Dystopia as the First-Person World: Rereading
    E. M. Forster's *The Machine Stops* as a Pandemic Novel of a
    Global Society   145
    Akiyoshi Suzuki

Chapter Eight: Orwellian Themes and Echoes in Today's World—A
    Perspective   171
    Beena Giridharan

Chapter Nine: The 19th Century American Socialism: A Vision of a
    Future Utopia   183
    Majed S Al-Lehaibi and Bernard Montoneri

Chapter Ten: *The Invention of Morel*, a Projection on Dreams and
    Immortality   211
    Miguel Ángel González Chandía

Appendix: Non-exhaustive List of Titles in Science Fiction, Utopias
    and Dystopias   233

Index   245

About the Editor and Contributors   249

Preface

Dear Readers,

It is our great pleasure and my personal honor as editor to introduce this book titled *Science Fiction and Anticipation: Utopias, Dystopias and Time Travel*. It is a selection of ten chapters on science fiction, with a special focus on utopias and dystopias set in the future.

When I was a teenager, I had the chance to have great professors of literature. After I graduated, I spent around 25 years to teach History, Literature and Languages. Nowadays, in France, high-school students study Barjavel's *Ravage* (1943; *Ashes, Ashes*). When I was around 14, our teacher spent several weeks to study *La Nuit des temps* (1968; *The Ice People*). I quickly read all of Barjavel's novels, and I wished for years I could meet him. Sadly, he died in 1985.

My consolation is that he met with many students and some of his interviews are now on the Internet (http://barjaweb.free.fr/SITE/documents/chalais.html). A few years ago, I became more familiar with Louis-Sébastien Mercier and his novel, *L'An deux mille quatre cent quarante, rêve s'il en fut jamais* (1771; *The Year 2440: A Dream If Ever There Was One*). I began to think about editing a book on Science Fiction because I wanted to share my thoughts on *Ashes, Ashes* and *The Year 2440*. I discussed my project with Ms. Holly Buchanan, Acquisitions Editor at Lexington Books. This is my third work in collaboration with Lexington Books. The first one was a chapter called "Modern Renaissance Education in Taiwan's Departments of Foreign Languages" I wrote in a book co-edited by Professor Patricia Haseltine and Professor Sheng-mei Ma titled *Doing English in Asia: Global Literature and Culture* (April 2016). The second one was as the editor of a book titled *Academic Misconduct and Plagiarism: Case Studies from Universities around the World* published in November 2020.

I am grateful to Ms. Holly Buchanan and to Ms. Megan White, Assistant Acquisitions Editor at Lexington Books. I would also like to thank my friends and colleagues who accepted to write a chapter in this book and who trusted me with their valuable work. Please note that all the chapters in this book have been peer-reviewed and proofread by the contributors of this book and by several professors and researchers, including:

Ms. Jillian Marchant, PhD candidate (PhD to be conferred on the 28th of July, 2022), James Cook University, Australia.

Dr. Iryna Morozova, full professor (Doctor of Philological Sciences, Grand PhD) at Odesa Mechnikov National University.

Dr. Alyson Miller, Lecturer in Writing and Literature at Deakin University, Australia.

Dr. Ellie Gardner, Literary Studies and Children's Literature at Deakin University, Australia.

Dr. Yoriko Ishida, PhD on African American literature and culture from the viewpoint of gender consciousness, Oshima College, Japan.

Ms. Mary B. Patrovic, Self-Employed Editor and English Language Instructor at Suffolk County Community College, New York.

We appreciate their valuable feedback, and we would like to thank them for their support and feedback.

Best regards,

Dr. Bernard Montoneri, associate professor, independent researcher, Taiwan

About the cover pictures:

The first one at the top is a bird view of London by Daniel Tomlinson. The second one at the bottom is a Provence-style photo by Michelle Silke. Many thanks to them for their beautiful work.

This book cover is inspired by Barjavel'*Ashes Ashes*, by his autobiography *La charette bleue* (*The Blue Cart*; Barjavel 1980) and also by my personal experience in Paris and London and the ten happy years I spent to study in Provence.

Introduction

It is not an easy task to define what science fiction is and when it first appeared. "Science fiction can be defined as that branch of literature which deals with the reaction of human beings to changes in science and technology," wrote famed writer and professor of biochemistry at Boston University, Isaac Asimov (1920–1992), in *How Easy to See the Future!* (Asimov 1975, 62). Science fiction editor David Hartwell (1941–2016) wrote that "Science fiction's appeal lies in combination of the rational, the believable, with the miraculous. It is an appeal to the sense of wonder" (Hartwell 1985, 42).

According to Brian Aldiss (1973), works published prior to 1818 *Frankenstein or, The Modern Prometheus* by Mary Shelley (the "mother of science fiction," as she "gave her story an air of scientific plausibility"; Britannica 2022) can be considered proto science-fiction. Science fiction is considered to be a modern literary genre, probably really beginning with French writer Jules Verne (1828–1905), "the inventor of science fiction." Hugo Gernsback (1884–1967) coined the term "scientifiction" in 1926 to refer to the "Jules Verne, H. G. Wells and Edgar Allan Poe type of story—a charming romance intermingled with scientific fact and prophetic vision" (quoted in Stableford, Clute, & Nicholls 1993, 311–314). Gernsback then coined the term "science fiction" in 1929 (Latham 2014).

According to Britannica (2022), science fiction "formally emerged in the West, where the social transformations wrought by the Industrial Revolution first led writers and intellectuals to extrapolate the future impact of technology." However, many science fiction tropes can be found in ancient literature, notably in India. Johnson (2019) made a list for Barnes and Noble of the "25 Greatest Science Fiction Tropes; number 11, cloning, may be the most ancient trope: the Sumerian story of the supreme god Marduk, patron deity of the city of Babylon, consulting with the god of wisdom Ea, decided to create human beings" (EnÛma Eliš, tablet 6; Heidel 1951, 9), literally "cloning mankind from the blood and bone of the renegade god Kingu" (Menadue & Cheer 2017, 1).

A story from India mentions some form of cloning when, in *Śrīmad-Bhāgavatam* (an epic philosophical and literary classic written in Sanskrit thousands of years ago), King Nimi died, a new baby was created from his dead body (process known as 'Mantha': "the sages 'churned' Mahārāja Nimi's material body, from which, as a result, a son was born"; Canto 9 "Liberation," chapter 13, text 12, see https://vedabase.io/en/library/sb/9/13/12).

Trope number two on Johnson's list (2019) is time travel. The oldest time travel story occurs in the Sanskrit epic and longest poem ever written, *The Mahābhārata* (ten times the length of *The Iliad* and *The Odyssey* combined; 1.8 million words). Benevolent King Kakudmi (or Raivata) and his young daughter Revati went to meet with Brahma on Mount Meru. The king was in search of a suitable groom worthy of the princess. But Brahma told them that during the short time they spent in Brahma-loka (the creator's plane of existence), 108 yugas (27 catur-yugas; length of the yugas varies considerably depending on the sources, see for example Gupta 2010, 7) had already passed on earth, meaning that they went back home millions of years later. The *Śrīmad-Bhāgavatam* also tells the story (Canto 9 "Liberation," chapter 3, text 32: "Twenty-seven catur-yugas have already passed. Those upon whom you may have decided are now gone, and so are their sons, grandsons and other descendants"; see https://vedabase.io/en/library/sb/9/3).

British science fiction and fantasy novelist Adam Roberts considers that science fiction begins with the "voyages extraordinaires" of the Ancient Greeks; he uses the Vernean phrase on purpose as he considers it to be "the most supple and useful descriptor for these sorts of texts" (Roberts, 2006, preface, vii). One of the oldest examples of extraordinary voyages would be Greek satirist Lucian's *Trips to the Moon* (Lucian was born AD 120 in Samsat, Turkey). Roger Bozzetto and Arthur B. Evans described modern science fiction as follows:

> Between the end of the 17th and the 19th centuries, what would later be called SF begins to take shape as an autonomous fictional domain as concerns its materials, themes, and narrative formats derived from varying sorts of merveilleux, utopias, imaginary voyages, and texts of scientific popularization (Bozzetto & Evans 1990, 3).

American science fiction writer and scholar James Edwin Gunn's definition is probably the closest to the themes (time travel, utopias and dystopias, failure of modern technology, post-apocalyptic stories) our book is discussing: "Science Fiction is the branch of literature that deals with the effects of change on people in the real world as it can be projected into the past, the future, or to distant places. It often concerns itself with scientific or technological change, and it usually involves matters whose importance is greater than the individual or the community; often civilization or the race itself is in danger" (Gunn 1977, 6).

This book presents ten chapters discussing several themes related to time travel, utopias and dystopias in science fiction novels published in America and in Europe between the 18th and the 20th century, such as social progress, freedom and human rights, technological advances, and the issues of ethics, racism, sexism, censorship, and slavery.

Chapter 1 presents proto science-fiction in France in the 18th century and in particular *The Year 2440* (1771) by Louis-Sébastien Mercier (1740–1814). It is not only one of the first works of science fiction, but also one of the first utopias set in the future. In the story, the protagonist wakes up in Paris in the year 2440; he carefully writes down everything that he can observe in the streets of the French capital. Because the novel describes a secular future, it was banned by the Holy See in 1773. This chapter will discuss the various issues related to the publication, censorship, and English translations of *The Year 2440*. It will present the story and the protagonist who constantly compares 25th-century Paris to his 18th-century capital, as well as two former places of absolute power: the Bastille prison and the Palace of Versailles. Despite some social progress such as the abolition of dowries, the right to divorce and the end of forced/arranged marriages, Mercier's vision of women's rights is surprisingly reactionary and very conservative. Mercier's take on slavery and colonization is more prophetic and the narrator of the novel is overjoyed by their abolition and interdiction in the future; the last section will finally assess the legacy and influence of Mercier's incredible thought experiment on later authors such as Restif de la Bretonne, Vladimir Odoyevsky, Faddei Bulgarin, Mary Griffith, and many others.

Chapter 2 deals with the key role played by the Argentinian writer Leopoldo Antonio Lugones Argüello in creating the Hard Science Fiction subgenre with six published short stories, compiled some years later in the book *Las fuerzas extrañas* (1906). By exploring themes, motifs, scientific models, and even the rhetoric, the author demonstrates that Lugones is one of the first writers to adhere to the hard form of this style, for his stance in a group of short stories and to show the form in pure state, from the beginning to the end of every text. In order to justify this view, the author employs structural, formalistic, and comparative literature methods and approaches, making use of studies of reputed authors such as Rabkin, Scholes, Suvin, or Harwell, among others.

This subgenre presents science as the main element of the plot, and places all its emphasis on descriptions of technology and/or a very advanced science, with realistic and rigorous scientific and technical descriptions. After the eight pages of his *Voyage au center de la Terre* [1868], by the master

Jules Verne, Lugones establishes a model for future generations of writers. Sadly, political situations, which influenced many Hispanic critics, unreliable translations, and even appropriations of authorship, placed him next to Bioy Casares and Borges as one of the most famous writers of Neofantastic and Weird Literature in their time, forgetting, maybe, his most relevant contribution to literature.

Chapter 3 examines the vision of Paris in Jules Verne's dystopian fiction titled *Paris in the Twentieth Century* (or *The Lost Novel*). Written in the 1960s, this futuristic novel is a description of Paris during the twentieth century with technological predictions. The latter include electric streetlights, gas-powered vehicles driven on asphalt roads, computers, fax machines, and the electric chair, among many others. The novel is also the story of Michel Jérôme Dufrénoy, a student of literature and an aspiring poet and dramatist, who lives in this high-tech world where arts and creativity have fallen into a state of terminal idleness. In this chapter, the author discusses the transition from utopia to dystopia in *Paris in the Twentieth Century*, the impact of technological advances on society, and the emergent dangers of a utilitarian culture, as well as the philistine culture of capitalism. The discussion concludes that *Paris in the Twentieth Century* is an anti-utopian fiction that depicts the dark, dystopian, and depressive world in which we currently live.

Chapter 4 presents *Blake; or, The Huts of America*, by Martin Robinson Delany (1859–1862), which envisions the struggle for a future free Black society. Commonly cited as the first Black utopian and/or science fiction novel, *Blake* highlights the major predicament of Black utopia, which is the sheer impossibility to escape the dystopian aspects of Black lives and bodies even when devising ways for a better life. Indeed, this study contends that Delany's utopia, which imagines pathways to the im/possible freedom of Black people, does not resolve the tension between a hopeful vision of Black emancipation and a pessimistic sense of ongoing racial violence. Understanding Black utopia as the desire for and imagination of alternative worlds yet inseparable from the Black dystopia of enslavement and its afterlife, this chapter aims to contribute to the recently emerging scholarship on Delany's Black utopia. *Blake*, the author argues, desires and imagines the Black journey to freedom as a process of expanding the awareness of the racialized condition of African Americans into what W. E. B. Du Bois (1903) calls the gift of second sight in order to devise ways of organizing a better world and ways of being Black in this world. However, alongside the vision of Black self-ownership and self-reliance, as well as the emergence of a distinct future Afro-diasporic society and identity, *Blake* also anticipates the contemporary Afro-pessimist insistence on Black people's enduring social death. In the final part of this chapter, the author addresses the question of the im/possibility of a narrative of Black redemption.

Chapter 5 studies two Russian science fiction works: the novel *The Amphibian Man* by Alexander Belyaev and the story *Heart of a Dog* by Mikhail Bulgakov. These works appeared in the 1920s as a response to similar life-events. The young Soviet society, overwhelmed by the idea of revolutionary transformations, developed a tendency to transform everything: from social processes and hierarchies to human nature. Like a few real-life researchers-pioneers in the field of genetic engineering of that time, the main characters of these literary works, prominent scientists and practicing surgeons, experimentally created human-animal hybrids. Belyaev's Doctor Salvator turned a human being into an ichthyander capable of living on land and in the ocean, and Bulgakov's Professor Preobrazhensky managed to humanize a dog. Ichthyander and Sharikov, these "products of scientific experiment," are diametrically opposite—they have different personalities, interests, styles of behavior, and relationships with their creators and environments. However, with all the dissimilarities one thing is invariable—the story's tragic end. The creators of these hybrids are punished in one way or another, and their creations forever leave the human world, in which they are not destined to get along.

Chapter 6 introduces René Barjavel (1911–1985), a French author and journalist more famous in the speaking-French world than in Anglo-Saxon countries, despite the fact that he was one of the pioneers of science fiction and time travel (the grandfather paradox in *Future Times Three*; French: *Le Voyageur imprudent*, 1944). *Ashes, Ashes* (French: *Ravage*, 1943) is a science fiction novel set in 2052 France. The protagonist, 22 years old François Deschamps, leads a small group of survivors after the sudden disappearance of electricity that causes chaos and destruction in France. This chapter introduces Barjavel and his works, describes Paris in 2052 before the apocalypse (technology/society), and discusses several themes, including censorship and population control (comparison with *Fahrenheit 451*), the technocratic hubris and the collapse, the creation of a patriarchal society in New Provence, tribal war and the infernal machine, the issues of racism and sexism, and durability of love.

Chapter 7 proposes to read E. M. Forster's short science fiction *The Machine Stops* (1909) allegorically as a warning to the world of today, a global society of coronavirus pandemic. In order to come to that conclusion, firstly, the author reads the story from the perspective of both utopia and its negative mirror, dystopia, in light of Forster's thought and the society of the time in which he wrote the story and consider the significance of warning of *The Machine Stops* from the viewpoint of the function of utopian and dystopian novels, that is, social and political criticism. This argument identifies *The Machine Stops* as a dystopian novel. The dystopian nature of the society in the story is that the machines have created an equal society and isolate people to protect them from mortal danger by giving them in the house all kinds of things they need, such as food, communication, study, and books, but simultaneously they divide people, make them lonely, and treat others as objects. This is a representation of the society of today with the development of information and communication technology and with the spread of infectious diseases as well. The protagonist Kuno aspires for the society where respecting an individual with flesh and blood, all individuals coexist in harmony. In the end, this reminds us of the ideal that "we are all in this together" as Rieux emphasizes in Albert Camus's *The Plague*, but this is also the contemporary significance of the warning in *The Machine Stops*.

Chapter 8 discusses Orwellian themes and echoes in today's world. It is undeniable that George Orwell's *1984* (1949) has left a lasting legacy among readers, and that whenever modern democratic countries spring surprises in the form of seemingly autocratic leaders, the educated populace turn to the famous dystopian novel to search for meaning. The events that had occurred in George Orwell's life had led him to develop strong beliefs against totalitarianism and to stand firmly against it and inspired him to write novels like the *Animal Farm* (1945) and *1984* (1949), through which he sought to foster democratic socialism. Today, the books are deemed to be reminders that democracy is not failsafe, and that it is possible for governing systems and better selves to show deep cracks even in well-developed democracies in the developed world.

Animal Farm reminds us that totalitarianism and hypocrisy are rife to the human condition. Orwell contends that if lower classes are not educated and not empowered, society will constantly default to tyranny. Orwell demonstrates how powerful language and propaganda are used to control people in *Animal Farm,* and how songs and slogans are used to evoke emotional responses that reinforce the animals' loyalty to the state authorities.

Seaton, Crook & Taylor (2017) draw parallels between key messages in *1984* and Brexit, and Trump's propaganda language which seeks to limit human consciousness, confuse human conscience, and control range of thinking in people using "alternative facts" and deliberate untruths. This chapter attempts to highlight the rise of distortion of facts by leaders of the free worlds both in developed and developing worlds, and propaganda policies used to oppress free thought among average middle-class citizens. It draws comparisons and analysis between characters and events in Orwellian novels, *1984* and *Animal Farm*, to modern-day democratic government actions and measures, to raise awareness and understanding of the "Big brother is watching" concept and the rise of tyranny in democratic countries.

Chapter 9 presents Bellamy's utopian novel *Looking Backward: 2000–1887* (1888). *Looking Backward* was a best-seller in its time; Bellamy refers to his project as "nationalism" rather than socialism. His project gave rise to 165 nationalist clubs throughout the United States to spread his ideas. From the publication of the novel to the end of the century, 46 new utopian stories were published in America. Many writers around the world were also influenced by Bellamy's futuristic utopia, notably in Germany, China and Russia. Bellamy worked as a journalist and published hundreds of editorials during his career. He wrote twenty-three short stories between 1875 and 1889 and several novels. This chapter presents *Looking Backward* and discusses several themes, including Bellamy's utopia and Social Darwinists, the labor question and the workers' condition, the Great Trust, competition versus cooperation, and Bellamy and Millennialism. Before he died, he published a sequel to *Looking Backward* titled *Equality* (1897). The book sold quickly and famous authors and intellectuals, such as John Dewey, praised the sequel.

Chapter 10 wanders through the interpretation and narration of Adolfo Bioy Casares (1914–1999) and his work titled *Morel's Invention*. A novel published in 1940. Without a doubt, Bioy Casares offers us a journey into the future; where time and technology are dimensions that both intersect. In the same manner, his main character, Morel, tries to narrate and represent history as an essential process to bring the human being to his perfection. In this way, to the author, history and technology are also a prediction about regarding the advancement of science today. Perhaps, the possibility of reaching a destination that is the dream of centuries: immortality. However, in this development, it is required to introduce a type of supernatural power that can rationalize the existence of immortal characters. *Morel's Invention* describes an inventor, who manages to create eternity by conceiving a recording machine. That is, an artifact that justifies the abstract idea of perpetuity, loneliness, life, death, and dreams. In short, it is the recreation of technology and its perfection which do not predict the achievement of a brave new world.

We hope this book will be of interest to undergraduates, graduate students, as well as teachers and scholars who love and study science fiction.

REFERENCES

Aldiss, Brian W. 1973. *Billion Year Spree. The True History of Science Fiction.* New York: Doubleday.

Asimov, Isaac. 1975. "How Easy to See the Future!," *Natural History.*

Bozzetto, Roger, & Evans, Arthur B. 1990. Intercultural Interplay: Science Fiction in France and the United States (As Viewed from the French Shore) (Des liaisons équivoques: la science-fiction en France et aux États-Unis (une vue des côtes françaises)). *Science Fiction Studies, 17*(1), 1–24. http://www.jstor.org/stable/4239968.

Britannica. 2022. *Science fiction, Literature and Performance*. The editors of Encyclopaedia Britannica. Article added to new online database: Jul 20, 1998. Retrieved March 5, 2022 from https://www.britannica.com/art/science-fiction.

Gunn, James. 1977. *Road to Science Fiction. Volume 1: From Gilgamesh to Wells*. New York: Mentor / New American Library.

Gupta, S. V. 2010. "Ch. 1.2.4 Time Measurements." In Hull, Robert; Osgood, Jr., Richard M.; Parisi, Jurgen; Warlimont, Hans (eds.). *Units of Measurement: Past, Present and Future. International System of Units*. Springer Series in Materials Science: 122. Springer: 6–8.

Hartwell, David. 1985. *Age of Wonders*. New York: McGraw-Hill.

Heidel, Alexander. 1951. *The Babylonian Genesis. The Story of Creation*. Second Edition. Chicago: The University of Chicago Press.

Johnson, Ross. 2019. "The 25 Greatest Science Fiction Tropes." Barnes and Noble. Retrieved March 24, 2022, from https://www.barnesandnoble.com/blog/sci-fi -fantasy/the-25-greatest-science-fiction-tropes-ranked.

Latham, Rob. 2014. *The Oxford Handbook of Science Fiction*. New York: Oxford University Press.

Menadue, Christopher Benjamin, & Karen Diane Cheer. 2017. Human Culture and Science Fiction: A Review of the Literature, 1980–2016. *SAGE Open*, 1–15. https: //doi.org/10.1177/2158244017723690.

Roberts, Adam. 2006. *The History of Science Fiction*. New York: Palgrave Macmillan.

Stableford, Brian, Clute, John, & Nicholls, Peter. 1993. "Definitions of SF." In Clute, John; Nicholls, Peter (eds.). *Encyclopedia of Science Fiction*. London: Orbit/Little, Brown and Company.

Chapter One

Mercier's *The Year 2440*, a Dream and a "Thought Experiment"

Bernard Montoneri, Independent Researcher, Taiwan

This chapter presents one of the earliest and most successful works of proto science-fiction (before 1818 *Frankenstein or, The Modern Prometheus* by Mary Shelley, according to Aldiss 1973) written in France in the 18th century: *The Year 2440* (1771) by Louis-Sébastien Mercier (1740–1814). It is not only one of the first works of science fiction, but also one of the first utopian novels set in the future; some earlier futuristic fictions might include 1733 *Memoirs of the Twentieth Century* by Samuel Madden, 1644 *Aulicus, His Dream of the King's Sudden Coming to London* by Francis Cheynel and 1659 *Epigone: Story of the Future Century*, by chaplain and adviser to King Louis XIV Michel de Pure, aka Jacques Guttin. Mercier's time travel novel tells the story of a Parisian who wakes up hundreds of years in what the author and his hero consider to be a utopia: the French capital has become clean, orderly, and moral. Technology and science play a discreet but vital role in the novel; for example: scientific standards are applied to run hospitals, surgery is seldom performed as medical treatments are highly efficient, the city uses transparent stonework and lights that burn forever.

In the story, the protagonist carefully writes down everything that he can observe in the streets of Paris. Because the novel describes a secular future, it got banned by the Holy See in 1773. This chapter will discuss the various issues related to the publication, censorship, and English translations of *The Year 2440*. It will present the story and the protagonist who constantly compares 25th-century Paris to his 18th-century capital, as well as two former places of absolute power: the Bastille prison and the Palace of Versailles. Despite some social progress such as the abolition of dowries, the right to divorce and the end of forced/arranged marriages, Mercier's vision of women's rights is surprisingly reactionary and very conservative. Mercier's take on slavery and colonization is more prophetic and the narrator of the novel is overjoyed by their abolition and interdiction in the future; the last section will finally assess the legacy and influence of Mercier's incredible thought experiment on later authors such as Restif de la Bretonne, Vladimir Odoyevsky, Faddei Bulgarin, Mary Griffith, and many others.

MERCIER, HIS LIFE AND WORK

Louis-Sébastien Mercier (1740–1814) is a French writer and dramatist; he was born in Paris and came from a lower middle class family. His father, Jean-Louis Mercier, was a skilled artisan and furbisher of weapons. He came from Metz and had lost his first wife, Claude Galloy. He then married Élisabeth Andrée Le Pas in 1739 in Paris. Louis-Sébastien was born on June 6, 1740; he had two brothers: Charles-André born in 1741 and Jean-Baptiste one year later. Their mother died in 1743. Jean-Louis then married his third wife, Charlotte Spol, and they had a daughter together named Anne Charlotte. While Jean-Baptiste died in the cradle, Charles-André lived, eventually married, and had a daughter named Louise. Charles-André had a longstanding friend called Thomas Holcroft (1745–1809), an English dramatist, miscellanist, poet, and translator. Holcroft was sympathetic to the early ideas of the French Revolution. After nine years as a widower, Holcroft married his fourth wife, Charles-André's daughter Louise Mercier (1779 –1853), in March 1799. From this marriage came four sons and two daughters (Holcroft; Hazlitt 1852).

Despite his modest origins, Louis-Sébastien received a decent education, studied Latin, and entered the 'collège des Quatre-Nations' (College of the Four Nations; Mercier dedicates chapter XII of *The Year 2440* to his school in Mercier 1771, 58–68). Notable students of the collège include the chemist Antoine-Laurent Lavoisier (1743–1794), the painter Jacques-Louis David (1748–1825), and the encyclopedist Jean le Rond d'Alembert (1717–1783). Suppressed during the Revolution, the collège became part of the Institut de France in 1805.

Mercier discovered for himself a passion for the French theater. He was a prolific writer (more than 60 plays), with a special interest in drame bourgeois (middle-class drama). He began his career by writing heroic epistles, plays, poems and pamphlets. His first published work is a héroïde titled *Hécube à Pyrrhus* (published in 1760. *Hecuba to Pyrrhus*; 'héroïde': letter in verse, written under the name of a hero). He also published several 'éloges' (praise, tribute), including one to René Descartes (1596–1650) in 1765.

L'An 2440, rêve s'il en fut jamais published in 1771 made Mercier quite famous, even though for years, the novel was released anonymously. It is a "work of prophetic imagination" (Encyclopaedia Britannica 1998), an "exceedingly popular Proto SF [science fiction] tale" (Forsström 2021). In 1786 came a second and expanded edition in three volumes, followed by an allegorical text: *L'An 2440, rêve s'il en fut jamais, suivi de l'Homme de fer* (literally*: The Year Two Thousand Four Hundred and Forty, Followed by The Iron Man*). During the 1770s, Mercier wrote many plays. The drama *Jean Hénuier, évêque de Lizieux* (*Jean Hennuyer, of the Bishop of Lizieux*), printed in 1772, was written by Mercier, but "accidentally published under the name Voltaire [1694–1778], a mistake that favored this minor writer," according to Nielsen (2006, 280). In 1773, he published *Du théâtre* (*On Theater*), in 1775, a social comedy, *La Brouette du vinaigrier* (*The Barrel-load of the Vinegar Merchant*) and in 1788, a comedy in five acts, *La Maison de Molière* (*The House of Molière*).

Mercier notably became friends with Claude-Prosper Jolyot de Crébillon (called "Crébillon fils"; 1707–1777), novelist and son of a famous tragedian and member of the Académie française. In his *Tableau de Paris* (12 volumes published from 1782 to 1788), Mercier describes the father and the son in the chapter titled "Les deux Crébillons" (Mercier & Desnoiresterres 1853, 355–361). Mercier's *Tableau de Paris* is a monumental work with more than one thousand chapters. From 1781 to 1785, he stayed in the principality of Neuchâtel (in Romandy, an associate of the Swiss Confederation from 1034 to 1848) because he was afraid of being prosecuted for his controversial essays. In a 1787 letter to James Madison, Thomas Jefferson wrote:

> I put among the books sent you, two somewhat voluminous, & the object of which will need explanation; these are the *Tableau de Paris* & *L'espion Anglois*. The former is truly a picture of private manners in Paris, but presented on the dark side & a little darkened moreover. But there is so much truth in it's ground work that it will be well worth your reading. You will then know Paris (& probably the other large cities of Europe) as well as if you had been here years (Jefferson 1787).

From 1789, Mercier collaborated with several newspapers, including the *Annales patriotiques* (*Patriotic Annals*), of which he was one of the founders. During the Revolution, he became a moderate member of the Convention (1792–1794). He voted in favor of the detention of Louis XVI, but opposed the death penalty for the king, executed in January 1793. Imprisoned during The Terror (1793–1794) because he protested against the arrest of the Girondins, Mercier escaped death and was released after the execution by guillotine of Maximilien Robespierre in July 1794. Mercier then became a member of the Council of Five Hundred (1795–1797) and a member of the National Institute (from 1795; section II, *moral*, along with Bernardin de Saint-Pierre and L'abbé Grégoire; Academie des sciences morales et politiques 2021, 7).

According to Encyclopaedia Britannica (1998), Mercier was an admirer of Rousseau; he was heavily influenced by his philosophy and an enthusiastic promoter of his ideas. But he was mocked for it and nicknamed "Le Singe de Jean-Jacques" ("Jean-Jacques' Ape"). In 1791, for example, Mercier wrote *De Jean-Jacques Rousseau considéré comme l'un des premiers auteurs de la Révolution* (*About Jean-Jacques Rousseau considered one of the first authors of the Revolution*).

According to Cloutier (2009), Mercier was quite popular and several of his works were sold and translated in Europe. He could feed his family and live decently. However, he wrote that life was difficult and he often had to choose quantity over quality, lacking time and money to polish and refine his writings:

> Je n'ai que cette plume pour subsister; elle m'a déjà gagné cent-quarante mille livres, et m'a mis en état d'entretenir décemment moi, et les miens. Je souhaiterais qu'une rente médiocre me mît, comme vous en état de mÛrir mes productions; mais je suis en telle situation, qu'il m'importe beaucoup plus d'écrire vîte, que de bien écrire (Varot d'Amiens 1825, 31–32).
>
> Personal translation: I have only this pen to subsist; it has already earned me a hundred and forty thousand pounds, and enabled me to support my family and I decently. I would like a small income to put me, like you, in a position to mature my productions; but I am in such a situation that it is much more important to me to write quickly than to write well.

Mercier went to prison for his political views; he also had to suffer, much like contemporary French playwright Beaumarchais (1732–1799), attacks against his writings and repeated attempts to censor his work. "L'acharnement contre *Le Mariage de Figaro* est l'une des dernières grandes affaires de censure sous l'Ancien Régime" (Montoneri 2018, 34. Personal translation: "The relentlessness against *The Marriage of Figaro* is one of the last major cases of censorship under the Ancien Régime"). It should be noted that it is Thomas Holcroft who translated Beaumarchais' play into English: *The Follies of a Day-Or The Marriage of Figaro* got even played in London, at Covent Garden in 1784–85, small world indeed (the original translation is available at https://www.gutenberg.org/files/64953/64953-h/64953-h.htm). Actually, Beaumarchais and twenty-two authors wrote a complaint in 1777 about the fact that writers were at best very poorly remunerated for their work. Because of his connections and also thanks to the commercial success of *The Barber of Seville* (1775), their cause got heard and during the Revolution, "in 1791, Louis XVI ratified the first law on authors' rights" (Montoneri 2018, 6). However, less famous or not so well-established writers like Mercier continued to be treated with disdain, mocked and viciously criticized. Mercier belonged to a group of authors who were both "populaires et dédaignés" by some (Monselet 1885; "popular and despised"):

> Quelques excentriques, comme Delisle de Salles, Mercier et Carra, osèrent demander des pensions, mais n'obtinrent rien [. . .] La racaille littéraire tendait la main, mais le gouvernement réservait ses aumônes aux écrivains bien placés dans le "monde" (Darnton 1983, 13).
>
> Personal translation: Some eccentrics, like Delisle de Salles, Mercier and Carra, dared to ask for pensions, but obtained nothing [. . .] The literary scum held out their hand, but the government reserved its alms for writers well-established in the "world."

In 1792, Mercier moved in with Louise Marie Anne Machard (born in 1768). In 1797, he became history professor at the 'écoles centrales' (public educational institutions established in 1795). In 1798, he published *Le Nouveau Paris* (*The New Paris*; six volumes and 271 chapters) and decided to stay away from politics. He finally married the mother of his three daughters, Louise Machard, on February 9, 1814. Héloïse was born in 1792, Sébastienne in 1794, and Pauline in 1796. Mercier died on April 25, 1814, and was buried in Père Lachaise Cemetery, Paris, in the company of Jean de la Fontaine (1621–1695), Molière (1622–1673), and Beaumarchais.

L'AN 2440, A "THOUGHT EXPERIMENT"

Literally, *L'An 2440, rêve s'il en fut jamais* means "The Year 2440: A Dream If Ever There Was One," but it was translated and published as *Memoirs of the Year Two Thousand Five Hundred* (Mercier 1772; Hooper's translation) or *Astraea's Return, or The Halcyon Days of France in the Year 2440: A Dream* (Mercier 1797; Harriot Augusta Freeman's translation). In a letter to John Adams' wife and closest advisor, Abigail on January 11, 1817, Thomas Jefferson wrote: "Mercier has given us a vision of the year 2440." He also mentions that Napoleon is "in the cage of St Helena, like a lion in the tower" (Jefferson 1817). Jefferson had a French edition published in London in 1771. As to George Washington (1732–1799), he owned Hooper's English translation (Mercier 1772). Wilkie (1984) considers that *L'An 2440* was one of the best sellers of the 18th century and surely Mercier's most famous and popular work. Wilkie also believes that the book was published "so late in 1770 that it was dated 1771" (Wilkie 1984, 8). Despite being ridiculed by some when it was published, *L'An 2440* quickly became recognized as a prophetic work because of how many of its predictions became true during the Revolution.

During the first years after its publication, relatively few people knew that Mercier was the author and the book often got attributed to other writers, even to Rousseau or Voltaire, two of Mercier's favorite authors (Wilkie 1984, 23). No doubt Mercier published his novel in Amsterdam anonymously to help avoid France's strict censorship laws. According to Léon Béclard, "*L'An 2440* parut sans nom d'auteur en 1770 à Amsterdam chez van Harrevelt" ("*The Year 2440* appeared without an author's name in 1770 in Amsterdam by van Harrevelt"). He also adds: "Plus le livre nouveau était prohibé, plus on le rechercha naturellement. Et les contrefacteurs se mirent à l'œuvre" (Béclard 1903, 90; "The more the new book was prohibited, the more it was naturally sought after. And counterfeiters got to work"). Not surprisingly, the fact that the novel was anonymous and forbidden or criticized made people curious and everybody wanted a copy of it. The English translator of *The Year 2440*, William Hooper wrote that he didn't know who the author was ("Who the author of this work is, we will not pretend to determine") and that he made only one change, the year, preferring "a round number" (that is, *Two Thousand Five Hundred*; Mercier 1772, IV). The novel got quickly translated into several languages, including English, Dutch and German, even though it was condemned and banned by the Inquisition. According to Breña & Puga (2019), enlightened philosophers, especially the French ones, were considered as the "new heretics" (358). University of Otago (2010) notes that *L'An 2440* was considered to be "potentially seditious, the Church authorities put the book on the 'Index' in 1773, and in 1778, it was judged heretical in Spain, banned and reputedly burned by the King himself" (ironically, Charles III, reign 1759–1788, was hailed as an Enlightenment king). Breña & Puga (2019) give a translation of the original edict of 1778, which notably states that *L'An 2440* is "impious, reckless and blasphemous, promoter of Deism, very slanderous against the Supreme Pontiff" (358). The edict was published by the Inquisition in Madrid and Mexico (General Inquisitor Felipe Bertrán. July 4, 1778); it attacks an edition of the novel published in London in 1776 that is anonymous, luckily for Mercier (Block 2016; the article online contains a copy of the original edict).

L'AN 2440, A UCHRONIA AND A DREAM

Mercier's novel is a uchronia (Delon 2017, 143), that is, a fictional time period, in this case, set in the year 2440, more than 670 years after the publication of his book. Though not the first one, *The Year 2440* is certainly the most famous and the most influential uchronia. Earlier futuristic fictions include 1733 *Memoirs of the Twentieth Century* by Samuel Madden, 1644 *Aulicus, His Dream of the King's Sudden Coming to London* by Francis Cheynel and 1659 *Epigone: Story of the Future Century*, by chaplain and adviser to King Louis XIV Michel de Pure. His story is recognized as the first true uchronia (Michel de Pure 2005). The French term 'uchronie' was coined by philosopher Charles Bernard Renouvier (1815–1903) in his novel *Uchronie* (1876). He calls it a "utopie dans l'histoire" ("utopia in history"). It is a neologism based on the term created by Sir Thomas More (1516), replacing τόπος 'place' by χρόνος 'time'; the term is a pun on the Greek οὐ 'no/not' and εὖ 'good'; in fact, eutopia means 'good place' while utopia means 'no place'; as to the term dystopia, δυσ-and τόπος 'bad place,' it was coined in 1868 by English philosopher and Member of Parliament John Stuart Mill in one of his Parliamentary Speeches. *L'An 2440* was one of the first novels in history to use utopian tropes and a story happening in the future. The 19th century began to see an increasing number of novels and short stories set in the future instead of on an unexplored island, as the world had already been thoroughly explored. The idea to use a machine to travel in time was not entirely new when H. G. Wells (1866–1946) wrote his highly influential novel *The Time Machine* (1895): for example, Edward Page Mitchell published *The Clock that Went Backward* in 1881. It was first published anonymously in *The Sun* newspaper and went unnoticed. Wells probably did not hear about it. Interestingly, he did not use his time machine idea again and went back to follow like Mercier the "sleeper awakes" convention, notably in *When the Sleeper Wakes* (1899; revised version in 1910: *The Sleeper Awakes*), a dystopian science fiction novel: the protagonist, an Englishman living in London in 1897 named Graham falls into a coma and wakes up in 2100. In *A Connecticut Yankee in King Arthur's Court* (1889), Mark Twain's take is quite funny as his hero, a Yankee engineer named Hank Morgan, receives a blow to the head, loses consciousness and is transported in time and space to 6th century England. He wakes up underneath an oak tree near Camelot; this is clearly one of the most famous examples of accidental travel, that is, an accidental time travel plot device also called a time slip. One of the first famous examples of this plot device just after Mercier died was Irving Washington's 1819 *Rip Van Winkle* (a villager falls asleep and wakes up 20 years later, having missed the American Revolution). In this type of story, the protagonist generally comes home, the same way they left, or sometimes gets stuck in the past or the future, with no control or understanding of the process. In December 1771, Madame d'Épinay mentioned *L'An 2440* and its story of a man who wakes up in a futuristic Paris and wrote: "C'est une rêverie perpétuelle que cet ouvrage, rêverie si rêverie qu'on n'a pas la consolation d'espérer qu'aucune de ces belles institutions puisse jamais se réaliser" (Béclard 1903,

90; "This work is a perpetual reverie, a reverie so reverie that one does not have the consolation of hoping that none of these beautiful institutions can ever be realized"). She considered Mercier's uchronia to be a beautiful dream, probably too good to be(come) true. As such, it should be called a euchronia or a beautiful time period, at least in the eyes of Mercier . . .

THE YEAR 2440, GENERAL PRESENTATION

According to Darnton (1996),

> Despite its self-proclaimed character of fantasy . . . *L'An 2440* demanded to be read as a serious guidebook to the future. It offered an astonishing new perspective: the future as a fait accompli and the present as a distant past. Who could resist the temptation to participate in such a thought experiment? And once engaged in it, who could fail to see that it exposed the rottenness of the society before his eyes, the Paris of the eighteenth century? (Darnton 1996, 120).

Short Summary: An Unnamed Hero in an Anonymous Book

For the sake of clarity, the quotes from the various editions of *The year 2440* are modernized in this chapter (for example: "Le tems préfent" is rendered as "Le temps présent"). The first edition of *The year 2440* featured the following epigraph, a reference to Leibnitz's determinist theory of human behavior, on the cover of his anonymous novel (Mercier 1771, page 9 in the PDF): "Le temps présent est gros de l'avenir" ("The present is big with the future"; a quote from *Principles of Nature and Grace Based on Reason*, by Leibnitz 1646–1716; Leibnitz 1714, 6). The uchronia tells the story of an unnamed man who falls asleep after listening to an old Englishman complaining about France and contemporary life and wakes up several hundred years later in Paris, in the 25th century. He visits the futuristic capital as well as the ruins of the Palace of Versailles. France is ruled by Louis XXXVI, a constitutional monarch who applies the laws voted by the Senate. The future king is made aware of his role at age 22 and must retire when he turns 70. French culture is studied and emulated worldwide, including in Japan and in China. Colonialism and slavery have been abolished and former colonies are all independent. In France, the Bastille prison doesn't exist anymore and has been replaced by a Temple of Clemency. Merit has replaced privileges, science and state are separated and much social progress has been made, such as the abolition of the dowries, the legalization of divorce and the interdiction of arranged marriages. After 24 hours of guided visit of Paris and the ruins of Versailles haunted by the ghost of Louis XIV, the protagonist, bitten by a snake, wakes up.

The Protagonist

In the 1771 original version of *The Year 2440*, there are 44 short chapters, heavily footnoted by Mercier. The protagonist is also the narrator of the story. He is an unnamed man who falls asleep around midnight after a long conversation with a very critical English visitor ("Your affairs compel you to frequent a quarter of the town, where there exhales a foetid and mortal vapour; thousands of mankind are forced to breathe that poisoned air," Mercier 1772, volume 1, 7; "I am disgusted with Paris as with London"; 12) and then wakes up in 2440, transformed into an old man ("my forehead was furrowed with wrinkles, and my hair was white," chapter II, 15).

While chapter II in the 1774 version begins with the title "J'ai sept cents ans" ("I am seven hundred years old"; Mercier 1774, 12), the narrator then points out that he has slept for "six cent soixante-douze années" (672 years, that is, assuming Mercier began to write his story in 1768; Mercier 1774, 14). Meanwhile, the English title of Mercier 1772 in chapter II (15) is "1 am seven hundred and sixty years old." It should be noted than Mercier later denied being the author of the 1774 version (Forget 2002, 187–188). A "man of letters" offers the protagonist to be his guide in chapter III (Mercier 1772, 20) and together, they visit the city during a day, constantly comparing the old and the new capital.

The Bastille Prison

The prison doesn't exist anymore in 2440:

> On me dit que la Bastille avoit été renversée de fond en comble, par un Prince qui ne se croyoit pas le Dieu des hommes, et qui craignoit le Juge des Rois; que sur les débris de cet affreux château, si bien appellé le palais de la vengeance, (& d'une vengeance royale) on avoit élevé un temple à la Clémence (Mercier 1771, 39–40).
>
> Personal translation: I was told that the Bastille had been dismantled from top to bottom, by a Prince who did not believe himself to be the God of men, and who feared the Judge of Kings; that on the ruins of this frightful castle, so aptly called the palace of vengeance (& of a royal vengeance) a temple to Clemency had been erected.

The Bastille prison was originally a massive defensive doorway built to protect one of the entrances of Paris, Porte Saint Antoine, during the 14th century. 'Bastille' is a corruption of the French word 'bastide' (fortification). Cardinal Richelieu (1585–1642), Louis XIII's chief minister, was the first to use the fortification as a state prison. During the 18th century, prohibited books were also stored in the prison which received many famous guests, such as Voltaire, twice, in 1717–18 for eleven months and then again in 1726 (Fitzpatrick 2000, 64). In his *Tableau de Paris*, Mercier wrote:

> La Bastille, c'est un "gouffre", un tombeau dont les secrets sont "couverts d'un voile impénétrable". Les embastillés, d'ailleurs, à leur sortie de prison, comme condition de libération faisaient voeu de silence concernant tout ce qu'ils avaient vu et vécu à l'intérieur de la forteresse (cited in Mulryan 2016, 58).
>
> Personal translation: The Bastille is an "abyss", a tomb whose secrets are "covered with an impenetrable veil". The imprisoned, moreover, on their release from prison, as a condition of release, took a vow of silence concerning everything they had seen and experienced inside the fortress.

Actually, there were already talks about demolishing the building because it was too expensive to maintain, but in 1784, that is, many years after the publication of *The year 2440*. According to professor and historian Raymond Trousson (2006, 90),

> [. . .] dans *L'an 2440*, si la Bastille a été démantelée, ce ne fut pas par l'insurrection, mais par un "prince philosophe" instaurateur d'une monarchie constitutionnelle [. . .] Tout cela reflète surtout les aspirations du temps, non un programme révolutionnaire [. . .] si la société de Mercier est meilleure, elle le doit, non à un profond changement structurel, mais à la diffusion des lumières et aux progrès de l'éducation morale—moins xxve siècle que xviiie siècle amélioré.
>
> Personal translation: [. . .] in *The Year 2440*, if the Bastille was dismantled, it was not by insurrection, but by a "philosopher prince" who founded a constitutional monarchy [. . .] all this above reflects the aspirations of the time, not a revolutionary program [. . .] if Mercier's society is better, it owes it, not to a profound structural change, but to the diffusion of enlightenment and to the progress of moral education—less 25th century than an improved 18th century.

In fact, there were only seven prisoners left in July 1789 when the people of Paris stormed the infamous symbol of absolute power. In 1781, Louis XVI said about Beaumarchais' play *The Marriage of Figaro*: "il faudrait détruire la Bastille pour que la représentation de cette pièce ne fut pas une inconséquence dangereuse" (Montoneri 2018, 34. Personal translation: "the Bastille would have to be destroyed so that the performance of this play would not be a dangerous inconsistency"). Not only the play was published and performed in public in 1784 (Benjamin Franklin attended an early showing; Bronowski 1990, 268), but Beaumarchais witnessed the storming of the infamous prison from his magnificent mansion nearby and managed to save some of the archives (Lambert 2010, 4).

Palace of Versailles

The Palace, symbol of the centralization of power, became the de facto capital of the kingdom when Louis XIV (reign: 1643–1715) moved the government to Versailles in 1681. After his death, Louis XV's regent, Philippe II, Duke of Orléans, neglected the palace which slowly lost its cultural power under Louis XV (reign: 1715–1774) and Louis XVI (reign: 1774–1792). The various treaties known as the Peace of Paris signed in Paris and Versailles in 1783 ended the American Revolutionary War. On 14 July 1789, Louis XVI and Marie-Antoinette were at the Palace, isolated there as the anger was growing in Paris. In October 1789, several thousand people marched to Versailles, forced Louis and his family to return to Paris, and the Palace was closed. In 1792, paintings and sculptures were transferred to the Louvre, which became a museum in 1793. In 1799, when Mercier finally signed his name on the third official edition of *The Year 2440* after 1771 and 1786 (Béclard 1903, 91), he wrote: "Je suis donc le véritable prophète de la révolution" (Delon 2017, 143; "I am therefore the true prophet of the revolution"), even though he was horrified by how quickly and surprisingly to him the Revolution turned violent and bloody.

The Year 2440 ends with chapter XLIV (Mercier 1771, 414–416), with the protagonist's visit to Versailles. According to Mayer: "Mercier also closes his novel with ruins and death. His narrator journeys out from Paris to Versailles. These ruins are haunted by their own apparition, the spirit of Louis the Fourteenth" (1998, 14). The protagonist finds out that the Palace is not only in ruins, but haunted by the ghost of the Sun King ("now that I am Lewis XIV who [built] this rueful palace"; Mercier 1772, 248).

A king alone in his empty palace, a monarch crying, and a snake biting the protagonist who then returns home . . . this should sound familiar to readers of *The Little Prince* (1943). There are some interesting commonalities between the two stories and as famous as *The Year 2440* was, Antoine de Saint-Exupéry (1900–1944) must have heard about it or read it. *The Little Prince* is a novella by French writer and military aviator Saint-Exupéry, who first published his most famous work when he was in the United States with Reynal & Hitchcock in April 1943. *The Little Prince* is a fantasy science fiction novel written in the form of a modern fable. Chapter XX tells the story of the Little Prince's visit to the King, a lonely and powerful king without subjects. The prince is quite amazed by the king's grandiosity and showiness (a reference to Louis XIV? It is also probably a reference to Louis XVI's powerlessness and ineffectiveness). Mercier and Saint-Exupéry both seem to scorn monarchs' obsession with wealth, power ("Sire—over what do you rule? Over every-thing, said the king, with magnificent simplicity"; Saint-Exupéry 1943, 24) and show the pointlessness of vanity ("they who abuse a momentary power, only discover their weakness to future generations"; Mercier 1772, 248) and pride ("How transient are the moments of pride!" 248).

In Chapter XX, the Little Prince is crying alone on the ground after seeing a garden full of roses: he realizes that his rose is not unique and that he is not such a great prince after all ("That doesn't make me a very great prince . . . And he lay down in the grass and cried"; Saint Exupéry 1943, 44). As to the ghost of Louis XIV, feeling lonely and disconsolate, he "shed a flood of tears" (Mercier 1772, 248).

Finally, at the end of the novella, the Little Prince believes the only way for him to return home is to be bitten by the snake. In chapter XVII, the snake is even prouder than the king: "But I am more powerful than the finger of a king, said the snake" (Saint Exupéry 1943, 40). Then, the snake offers to help the Little Prince and send him home: "You move me to pity [. . .] I can help you, some day, if you grow too homesick for your own planet. I can—" (Saint Exupéry 1943, 40). According to Alkon (1987), in Versailles, "the site is swarming with adders, reminiscent perhaps of Louis's courtiers. One of these snakes bites the narrator, who then, we are told in the book's last sentence, wakes up to find himself again in the eighteenth century" (118).

Another commonality with *The Year 2440* is certainly the issue of censor-ship. Even though Antoine's novella had little to fear from the Inquisition, his writings got banned (Schiff 2000), ironically, not only in occupied France (by the Germans and Vichy Regime), but in Free France and all the French colonies (by General Charles de Gaulle because Saint Exupéry refused to support him; Hastings 1994).

WOMEN'S RIGHTS IN *THE YEAR 2440*

Despite some social progress and a few advances (Mercier 1772, 157: "People marry only to be happy" and have the right to divorce if they are not), Mercier's generally progressive and modern views about human rights don't seem to apply to women in the chapter he dedicates to them around the end of the novel (Chapter XXXVIII, "Des femmes," Mercier 1774, 315–330; chapter XI, "The Women," in the English translation, Mercier 1772, volume 2, 151–168).

Mercier worries about the "dangerous 'disharmony' in the balance of power between men and women" and believes women should not be rivals to men (Evans 2003, 131, citing Riikka Forsström, 140–141). Mercier's solu-tion is quite surprising and reactionary and many sentences in this chapter can feel like a cold shower: one might be happy about the fact that "women have no portion" anymore (Mercier 1772, volume 2, 151), that is, dowries don't exist in 2440. The shocking part is why: "Tout homme nourrit la femme qu'il féconde, & celle-ci, tenant tout de la main de son mari, est plus disposée à la fidélité & à l'obéissance" (Mercier 1774, 316; personal translation: "Every man feeds the woman he impregnates, and she, taking everything from her husband's hand, is more disposed to fidelity and obedience"; in the 1772 English translation: "Every man is bound to provide for his wife; and she, depending entirely on her husband, is the better disposed to fidelity and obedience"; Mercier 1774, 152). And Arthur B. Evans to conclude: "Despite its very progressive ideas about many of society's institutions (including marriage), its reactionary vision of women's rights must rank it as among the most anti-feminist utopias ever written" (Evans 2003, 131). Among the most disturbing sentences in this chapter are: "Our women, virtuous by principle, are delighted with domestic pleasures" (Mercier 1772, 158) and

> Nature has destined women to domestic employments, and to cares every where of the same kind. They have much less variety in their characters than have men; almost all women resemble each other; they have but one end, and which they manifest in every country by similar effects (Mercier 1772, 153, footnote b).

Contrary to Mercier's idol Rousseau (1712–1778), French playwright and novelist Marivaux (1688–1763) considers that human beings are not inherently good (Montoneri 2018, 44). Interestingly, in his plays, he raises the issue of the education and emancipation of young girls and women. In his utopian comedy, *La Colonie* (*The Colony*; attacked and censored in 1729; shorter new version in 1750), Marivaux introduces a democratic republic in which women and men are equals and women want to undertake any type of jobs (Montoneri 2018, 43–45 and 49–50); he clearly is more progressive and goes much further than Mercier in *The Year 2440*. One of the claims of the noble Arthénice in *The Colony* is exactly the opposite of what Mercier wrote: "Les dieux et les lois de l'univers avaient prévu que les hommes et les femmes soient égaux. En se révoltant, les femmes restaurent la volonté des dieux," Montoneri 2018, 49; personal translation: "The gods and the laws of the universe intended men and women to be equal. By revolting, women restore the will of the gods").

But Mercier was quite sadly right about the little progress women's rights would experience in the years after the publication of his novel. The 'Déclaration des droits de l'homme et du citoyen de 1789' (Declaration of the Rights of Man and of the Citizen) was drafted by the Marquis de Lafayette, who consulted regularly with Thomas Jefferson (Fremont-Barnes 2007, 190). It states that all human beings are free and equal in rights, but in truth the right to vote was not granted to women. The Constitution of 1791, adopted on September 3 and signed by Louis XVI, despite proclaiming that all citizens are admissible to offices and employments, notes that Monarchy is delegated hereditarily from male to male, to the perpetual exclusion of women. Universal male suffrage is adopted, and France becomes a Republic in 1792. Women are no longer excluded from inheritance rights, but the legal incapacity of married women is confirmed in the Civil Code of 1804 and will not be removed until 1938. Women have to wait until July 1944 to be granted by law the right to vote (first election in 1945).

On Colonialism and Slavery

Slavery and serfdom have been abolished worldwide in 2440, in the Americas as well as serfdom in Russia. All former colonies have become independent nations and countries such as Italy are united. In chapter XXII, the narrator visits a hall of monuments and presents the statue of the man who freed slaves:

> In going from this place, I observed toward the right, on a magnificent pedestal, the figure of a negro; his head was bare, his arm extended, his eye fierce, his attitude noble and commanding; round him were spread the broken relics of twenty sceptres; and at his feet I read these words: To the avenger of the new world (Mercier 1772, 170).

The "figure of a negro" was replaced by "the figure of an American" in the 1797 English translation by Harriot Augusta Freeman (Block 2016, online). Her translation is faithful to the original and quite close to hooper's version. This seems to be the only change Freeman made. In chapter XXII, he is called "the exterminating angel, to whom God resigned his sword of justice" (Mercier 1772, 172). Mercier's dream of a world delivered "from the most outrageous, the most inveterate and atrocious tyranny" (171) came true relativelly quickly: According to Laure Marcellesi, this man is the "Black Spartacus," a hero that will be "incarnated by Toussaint Louverture, leader of the slave uprising in Saint-Domingue in the 1790s" (Marcellesi 2011, 247). Toussaint Louverture (1744–1803), known as "The Father of Haiti," was born as a slave in the French colony of Saint-Domingue. A free man working on a plantation was Toussaint's godfather. He raised and educated him. Toussaint worked on the same plantation as a salaried employee and was freed in 1776. A major slave rebellion began in August 1791 and Toussaint joined the fight. According to Langley (1996, 111), he chose the name Louverture ('l'ouverture': 'opening' in French) as a symbol: he is "the one who opened the way." Slavery was abolished in all French colonies by the Law of February 4, 1794, but the Law of May 20, 1802 passed by Bonaparte reinstated slavery and the slave trade (Blackburn 1988, 248). The Haitian Revolution began in 1791 as a slave uprising (the biggest since Spartacus' unsuccessful revolt in c. 73–71 BC) that ended in 1804 with the founding and independence of the free republic of Haiti (Dubois 2005).

In *The Year 2440*, the narrator and his guide share the same joy that "the most odious servitude" (Mercier 1772, 171) had been abolished. The narrator, in a footnote page 172, also remarks that he is happy the "generous Quakers" freed their slaves and was upset that other Christians didn't. Mercier later deplored the violence of slave rebellions and wished for a peaceful transition; he hoped the French Revolution too would be peaceful and got shocked by the later developments. According to Block (2016), "this vision of the heroism and violence required to overthrow slavery and restore the world to equilibrium may explain why the 1799 Richmond edition of this novel sold so poorly" in America. Freeman's 1797 English translation, by deleting the fact that the hero was Black, was more successful, "as only white American freedom fighters could be celebrated in print" (Block 2016).

During the 19th century, the Slavery Abolition Act of 1833 made the ownership of slaves illegal in most of the British Empire. The French Revolution of 1848 definitively abolished slavery. In Russia, 23 million serfs were freed as the result of Czar Alexander II's 1861 Emancipation Edict. And of course, in 1863, President Abraham Lincoln issued the Emancipation Proclamation freeing millions of slaves in the Confederate states (Chung 2021, online).

*THE YEAR 2440'*S LEGACY AND INFLUENCE

Mercier had quite an influence in Germany during his lifetime (Pusey 1939; Hill 2003); he was popular, notably among Sturm und Drang writers ("storm and stress"). This proto-Romantic movement in German literature began in 1771 and ended in 1778. The period was named after Friedrich Klinger's play performed in 1777. It was a reaction against Neoclassicism and Enlightenment rules and conventions and provided the foundation of Romanticism. According to Mercier, drama should be used to promote political ideas and discuss societal issues. Mercier's *Traité du théâtre ou Nouvel essai sur l'art dramatique* (1773 *On the Theater or New Essay on Dramatic Art*) was translated into German by prominent member of Sturm und Drang Heinrich Léopold Wagner (1747–1779) in 1776. According to Valentin (2013), the German translation made Mercier more famous abroad and influenced early works of Friedrich Schiller (*Die Räuber*; 1781) and Goethe (*Götz de Berlichingen*; 1773 drama). He was also very close to German poet and translator August Wilhelm Schlegel (1767–1845) to whom he dedicated his *Satyres contre Racine et Boileau* (1808; *Satire against Racine and Boileau*).

Mercier's essay later influenced French writers Victor Hugo (1802–1885) and Alfred de Musset (1810–1857).

As to *The Year 2440*, it inspired a large number of authors in France, Holland, Germany, and Russia. Nicolas Restif de la Bretonne (1734–1806) was one of the first French authors to write a utopian anticipation; he met Mercier in 1782 and Beaumarchais in 1786 and published *L'An deux mille* in 1790 ("il n'est point sans avoir été inspiré par le livre de Sébastien Mercier, un ami de Rétif, "L'an 2440" [1770]"; personal translation: "it is not without having been inspired by the book of Sébastien Mercier, a friend of Rétif, "L'an 2440" [1770]"; Gröber 1905, 9). Many European writers inspired by Mercier also began to write futuristic novels. The choice of 2440 in their title leaves little doubt: *Holland in the Year 2440* (1777), attributed to Betje Wolff-Bekker (1738–1804), a Dutch poetess and admirer of Mercier who lived in France for a while. She escaped the guillotine and returned to Holland in 1795. Another Dutch novel inspired by Mercier is *The Coming Year 3000* (1792) by Arend Fokke-Simonsz (Degenaar & Lokhorst 1996), which tells the story of a rustic utopia where people live in self-sufficient farms. In Germany, there were several published books paying tribute to Mercier: K.A. Dyrhn's *Supplement to The Year 2440* (1781), and *Das Jahr 2440* (1783; *The Year 2440*) by H.H. Witzel. German author Julius von Voss (1768–1832) published *Berlin im Jahre 1924* (1824; *Berlin in the Year 1924*). Daniel Gottlieb Gebhard Mehring told the story of a dream of the future by an Arab in *Das Jahr 2500 [i.e. Zweitausendfünfhundert]; oder, Der Traum Alradi's, Aus einer arabischen Handschrift des sechszehnten Jahrhunderts* (*The year 2500 [i.e. two thousand five hundred]; or, Alradi's Dream, From a sixteenth-century Arabic manuscript*) published in Berlin in 1794. As to German poet, fiction writer and prominent member of the Romantic Movement Johann Ludwig Tieck (1773–1853), he wrote *The Future Court: A Vision* in 1800.

In France, Turrault de Rochecorbon published *The Year 2800, or the Dream of a Recluse* (1829), while in America, Mary Griffith (1779–1846) wrote *Three Hundred Years Hence* (1836), and probably the first futuristic utopia written in the US, with a character who falls asleep and dreams of a land where slavery has been abolished and women are emancipated. Griffith was presumably inspired by the 1795 Philadelphia edition of Mercier (1772; Hooper's English translation), which was "the first utopian novel published in North America" (Alkon 1987, 117).

In Russia, influential biographer of Mozart and member of the Decembrist movement (1825) Aleksandr Dmitrievich Ulybyshev (1794–1858) is credited with publishing the first futuristic utopia: *A Dream* (1819), in which St. Petersburg is a republic in 2119 (Raeffs 1966). Imperial philosopher and writer Prince Vladimir Odoyevsky (1803–63), like Mercier, focuses on social reform. *The Year 4338: Petersburg Letters* (1835–40; the fullest version appeared in 1926) describes St. Petersburg of the future, a place that values meritocracy. His novel also describes technological advances (air and space travel, the telephone) and the warming of the Arctic. More shocking, France and Germany don't exist anymore and England is bankrupted. Interestingly, the story is presented in the form of letters from a Chinese student in St. Petersburg to his fellow students (Lukin 2003). The first letter from January 4, 4338 warns that "Halley's Comet is expected to fall to Earth" (online English translation: https://www.feeldothink.org/4338.htm).

Another futuristic time slip novel inspired by Mercier and mentioning warming was written by Russian writer Faddei Bulgarin (1789–1859), who mentions "the famous French writer Mercier" [xxii] in a footnote to his 1824 novel *Plausible Fantasies, or, A Journey in the 29th Century* (Fetzer 1982, 5): the protagonist wakes up in the year 2824 in Siberia, which has become a warm and comfortable place (eutopia).

Many 19th-century French writers also wrote stories about Paris in the future, notably none other than Jules Verne (*Paris in the 20th Century*, written in 1863, published for the first time in 1994). Many other French writers imagined the future: Théophile Gautier's *Future Paris* (1851), Jacque Fabien's *Paris in Dream* (1863), George Pellerin's *The World in 2000 Years* (1878), and Emile Calvet's *In a Thousand Years* (1884). These stories were not very popular. The first really successful futuristic utopia or uchronia of the 19th century was published by New England-born novelist Edward Bellamy (1850–98): *Looking Backward: 2000–1887* published in 1888, quickly became a bestseller. This story of Julian West, a young American, who falls asleep and wakes up 113 years later even got translated in China in 1891; this first publication of a Western science fiction novel was followed by many others, notably paving the way to the success of Jules Verne's adventure novels (Wang 1998, 310). Just like Mercier's uchronia one century earlier, Bellamy's novel and its sequel (*Equality*; 1897, focusing on women's rights and education) inspired numerous writers.

CONCLUSION

Louis-Antoine, Comte de Bougainville (1729–1811), was a French admiral and explorer, famous not only for his participation to the Seven Years' War (1756–1763) and the American Revolutionary War (1775–1783), but for his scientific expedition around the globe in 1763–1769. His book, *Le voyage autour du monde, par la frégate La Boudeuse, et la flûte L'Étoile* (*A Voyage Round The World, on Frigate La Boudeuse and the Store-ship L'Étoile*) was published just before *The Year 2440* in 1771 and marks a turning point: the globe is finite and there are no new lands to discover (famed German historian Koselleck, 2006). According to Michel Lallement,

> À défaut de pouvoir encore tirer pleinement parti des deux infinis (l'atome et l'univers) qui s'ouvrent à la conscience humaine, il fallait, pour conquérir de nouvelles îles d'utopie, inventer un troisième infini. Ce sera le temps" (Lallement, 2010, 11).
>
> Personal translation: For lack of being able to take full advantage of the two infinities (the atom and the universe), which are opening up to human consciousness, it was necessary, to conquer new islands of utopia, to invent a third infinity. It will be time.

Written almost 20 years before the French Revolution, Mercier's uchronia, *The Year 2440* was an underground success, a clandestine novel banned by the Inquisition, which described a secular, egalitarian, and pacifist France. According to Arthur B. Evans, "Mercier's uchronia was not just an exercise in idyllic wish-fulfillment; it was a concrete blueprint for social change based on the ideals of the eighteenth-century *philosophes*" (Evans 2003, 132).

While almost forgotten in France until the second part of the 20th century, Mercier remained quite popular and influential in some European countries, especially in Germany, among notable proponents of the Sturm und Drang movement, such as H. L. Wagner, Goethe and Friedrich Schiller. He was also close to August Wilhelm Schlegel, highly influential within Jena Romanticism (first phase of German Romanticism before 1804). As to *The Year 2440*, it inspired and influenced numerous writers, in France, Germany, Holland, Russia, and America.

REFERENCES

Académie des sciences morales et politiques. 2021. *Listes des membres titulaires et associés étrangers. Liste des correspondants. Textes règlementaires*. La seconde classe de l'Institut national (1795–1803). Retrieved March 5, 2022 from https://academiesciencesmoralesetpolitiques.fr/wp-content/uploads/2021/04/TAT-ASMP-v16032021.pdf.

Aldiss, Brian W. 1973. *Billion Year Spree. The True History of Science Fiction*. New York: Doubleday.

Alkon, Paul. 1987. *Origins of Futuristic Fiction*. Athens: University of Georgia Press.

Béclard, Léon. 1903. *Sébastien Mercier, sa vie, son oeuvre, son temps; d'après des documents inédits avec un port. en héliogravure. Avant la révolution, 1740–1789*. Paris: H. Champion. Retrieved March 6, 2022 from https://ia802708.us.archive.org/8/items/sbastienmercie00bcuoft/sbastienmercie00bcuoft.pdf.

Blackburn, Robin. 1988. *The Overthrow of Colonial Slavery, 1776–1848*. London: Verso.

Block, Kristen. 2016. *Translating Mercier in the Atlantic world: avengers of the future, past, and present*. Age of Revolutions. Posted on February 8, 2016. Retrieved March 5, 2022 from https://ageofrevolutions.com/2016/02/08/translating -mercier-in-the-atlantic-world-avengers-of-the-future-past-and-present.

Bronowski, Jacob (1990) [1973]. *The Ascent of Man*. London: BBC Books.

Breña, Roberto & Puga, Gabriel. 2019. Enlightenment and Counter-Enlightenment in Spanish America. Debating Historiographic Categories. *International Journal for History, Culture and Modernity* 7, no. 1: 344–371. https://doi.org/10.18352/ hcm.562.

Chung, Cynthia. 2021. "Why Russia Saved the United States." Strategic Culture Foundation. Retrieved March 15, 2022 from https://www.strategic-culture.org /news/2021/12/11/huxleys-ultimate-revolution-the-battle-for-your-mind-and-the -relativity-of-madness.

Cloutier, Annie. 2009. Entre préjugé et pratique: Louis-Sébastien Mercier, homme de lettres et journaliste. *Etudes litteraires*, 40(3): 15–28. https://doi.org/10.7202 /039241ar.

Darnton, Robert. 1983. Bohème littéraire et Révolution. Le monde des livres au XVIIIe siècle. Paris: Éditions du Seuil.

——— 1996. *The Forbidden Best-Sellers of Pre-Revolutionary France*. New York: W.W. Norton.

Degenaar, Marjolein & Lokhorst, Gert-jan. 1996. *The Coming Year 3000: the first Dutch uchronia*. In G. Groot, H. Oosterling, & A.W. Prins, eds., From agora to market: Proceedings of the 18th Dutch-Flemish Philosophy Conference, vol. 21 of Rotterdam Philosophical Studies, 299–303. Rotterdam: Erasmus University of Rotterdam.

Delon, Michel. 2017. Utopie et Esprit Critique au Temps des Lumières. *Revue Des Deux Mondes*: 142–48. Retrieved March 12, 2022 from http://www.jstor.org/stable /44436523.

Dubois, Laurent. 2005. *Avengers of the New World: The Story of the Haitian Revolution*. Cambridge, Mass.: Harvard University Press.

Encyclopaedia Britannica. 1998. *Louis-Sébastien Mercier*. The Editors of Encyclopaedia Britannica. Article added to new online database: Jul 20, 1998. Retrieved March 5, 2022 from https://www.britannica.com/biography/Louis -Sebastien-Mercier.

Evans, Arthur B. 2003. "Revisiting Mercier's L'An 2440" [Review of Riikka Forsström's *Possible Worlds: The Idea of Happiness in the Utopian Vision of Louis-Sébastien Mercier*, Helsinki: Suomalaisen Kirjallisuuden, 2002]. *Science Fiction Studies* 30, no. 1: 130–132. Retrieved March 10 from https://core.ac.uk/ download/pdf/214030913.pdf.

Fremont-Barnes, Gregory. 2007. *Encyclopedia of the Age of Political Revolutions and New Ideologies, 1760–1815*. Westport, CT: Greenwood Publishing Group.

Fetzer, Leland. 1982. *Pre-Revolutionary Russian Science Fiction: An Anthology (Seven Utopias and a Dream)*. Ann Arbor, Mich.: Ardis.

Fitzpatrick, Martin. 2000. "Toleration and the Enlightenment Movement" in Grell, Ole Peter, and Roy Porter, eds. *Toleration in Enlightenment Europe*. Cambridge: Cambridge University Press. https://doi.org/10.1017/CBO9780511628269.

Forget, Evelyn L. 2002. *The Social Economics of Jean-Baptiste Say: Markets and Virtue*. Taylor and Francis. London: Routledge.

Gröber, Gustav. 1905. *L'an deux-mille by Restif de La Bretonne, 1734–1806*. Strasbourg: J.H.E. Heitz. Retrieved March 12, 2022 from https://archive.org/details /landeuxmille00restuoft/page/n63/mode/2up

Hastings, Selina. 1994. "The Courageous, Intransigent Antoine de Saint-Exupéry." *The New Yorker*. Retrieved March 15, 2022 from https://www.newyorker.com/ magazine/1994/12/05/lost-in-the-stars.

Hill, David. 2003. *The Literature of the Sturm und Drang*. Vol. 6, Introduction, 1–44. Rochester: Camden House.

Holcroft, Thomas; Hazlitt, William. 1852. *Memoirs of the Late Thomas Holcroft: Written by Himself; and Continued to the Time of His Death*. London: Longman, Brown, Green, and Longmans. Retrieved March 5, 2022 from https://archive.org/ details/memoirslatethom00hazlgoog.

Jefferson, Thomas. 1787. *To James Madison from Thomas Jefferson, 2 August 1787*. National Archives. Founders Online. Retrieved March 3, 2022 from https:// founders.archives.gov/documents/Madison/01-10-02-0080.

———. 1817. *Thomas Jefferson to Abigail Adams, 11 January 1817*. National Archives. Founders Online. Retrieved March 3, 2022 from https://founders .archives.gov/documents/Jefferson/03-10-02-0509.

Koselleck, Reinhart, 2006. "Zur Begriffsgechichte der Zeitutopie," in Reinhart Koselleck, *Begriffsgeschichten*, Frankfurt am Main: Suhrkamp, 252–273.

Lallement, Michel. 2010. Le songe du livrier. *Temporalités* [En ligne], 12. https://doi .org/10.4000/temporalites.1345.

Lambert, Anne-Sophie. 2010. La Bastille ou "l'Enfer des vivants"? Bibliothèque nationale de France. Classes, ressources pédagogiques en ligne. http://classes.bnf .fr/pdf/Bastille1.pdf

Langley, Lester. 1996. *The Americas in the Age of Revolution: 1750–1850*. New Haven: Yale University Press.

Leibniz, Gottfried Wilhelm. 1714. *The Principles of Nature and of Grace, Based on Reason*. In: Loemker, L.E. (eds) Philosophical Papers and Letters. 1989. The New Synthese Historical Library, vol 2. Springer, Dordrecht. https://doi.org/10.1007 /978-94-010-1426-7_67.

Lukin, Alexander. 2003. The Bear Watches the Dragon: Russia's perceptions of China and the evolution of Russian-Chinese relations since the 18th century. New York: Routledge. https://doi.org/10.4324/9781315290539.

Marcellesi, Laure. 2011. Louis-Sébastien Mercier: Prophet, Abolitionist, Colonialist. Studies in Eighteenth-Century Culture, 40, no. 1: 247–273. https://doi.org/doi:10 .1353/sec.2011.0012.

Mercier, Louis-Sébastien. 1771. *L'An Deux Mille Quatre Cent Quarante. Rêve s'il en fut jamais*. London: E. van Harrevelt. PDF retrieved March 15, 2022 from https://ia800304.us.archive.org/25/items/landeuxmillequa01mercgoog/landeuxmillequa01mercgoog.pdf.

_____ 1772. Translated by Hooper, William. *Memoirs of the Year Two Thousand Five Hundred: Volume I, Volume II*. London: G. Robinson. Retrieved March 5, 2022 from https://archive.org/details/memoirsofyeartwo01merc/page/n5/mode/2up (volume 1) and https://archive.org/details/memoirsofyeartwo02merc/page/n7/mode/2up (volume 2).

_____ 1774. *L'An 2440. Rêve s'il en fut jamais*. Nouvelle édition, Revue & corrigée par l'Auteur, qui a jugé à propos de refondre le Chapitre de la Bibliothèque du Roi. Retrieved March 15, 2022 from https://fr.wikisource.org/wiki/L'An_deux_mille_quatre_cent_quarante.

_____ 1979 [1799]. *L'An 2440. Rêve s'il en fut jamais suivi de L'homme de fer, songe*. Genève: Slatkine Reprints (Bibliothèque des voyages aux pays de nulle part, éd. Raymond Trousson).

_____ 1797. *Astraea's Return, or The Halcyon Days of France in the Year 2440: A Dream*. Translated by Harriot Augusta Freeman. London: Hookham and Carpenter.

Mercier, Louis-Sébastien & Desnoiresterres, Gustave. 1853. *Tableau de Paris: précédé de Etude sur la vie et les ouvrages de Mercier* [. . .]. Paris: Pagnerre. Retrieved March 3, 2022 from https://books.google.fr/books?id=KWsOAAAAQAAJ&pg=PA355#v=onepage&q&f=false

Monselet, Charles. 1885. *Oubliés et dédaignés, Linguet, Fréron, Rétif de la Bretonne, Mercier, Cubières*. Paris: Bachelin-Deflorenne.

Montoneri, Bernard. July 2018. Le Mariage de Figaro et La Colonie, deux comédies sur le drame humain. *Fu Jen Studies, Literature & Linguistics*, 51: 23–62. Retrieved March 3, 2022 from https://www.researchgate.net/publication/357299361_Le_Mariage_de_Figaro_et_La_Colonie_deux_comedies_sur_le_drame_humain.

_____ September 2018. *Plagiarism and Ethical Issues: A Literature Review on Academic Misconduct* (Chapter 1: 1–25). In Ethics, Entrepreneurship, and Governance in Higher Education, co-edited by Suja R. Nair and José Manuel Saiz-Alvarez. IGI Global, USA. https://doi.org/10.4018/978-1-5225-5837-8.

Mulryan, Michael. 2016. La Valeur métaphorique de la Bastille chez Louis-Sébastien Mercier (1740–1814): Un Point de mire pour la cité corrompue. *Lingua Romana*, 12, no. 1: 55–65. Retrieved march 15, 2022 from https://linguaromana.byu.edu/archives/volume-12-issue-1-fall-2016.

Nielsen, Wendy C. 2006. A Tragic Farce: Revolutionary Women in Elizabeth Inchbald's The Massacre and European Drama. *European Romantic Review* 17 no. 3: 275–288. https://doi.org/10.1080/10509580600816702.

Pure, Michel de [aka Jacques Guttin]. 2005 [1659]. *Épigone, histoire du siècle futur*. Editors: Lise Leibacher-Ouvrard, Daniel Maher. Québec: Presses Université Laval.

Pusey, William Webb. 1939. *Louis-Sébastien Mercier in Germany: His Vogue and Influence in the Eighteenth Century*. New York: Columbia University Press.

Raeffs, Marc. 1966. *The Decembrist Movement*. Englewood Cliffs, N.J: Prentice-Hall.

Saint Exupéry, Antoine. 1943. *The Little Prince*. Translation by Katherine Woods. New York: Reynal & Hitchcock. Retrieved March 15 from https://blogs.ubc.ca/edcp508/files/2016/02/TheLittlePrince.pdf.

Schiff, Stacy. 2000. "Par avion." *The New York Times*. Retrieved March 15, 2022 from https://archive.nytimes.com/www.nytimes.com/books/00/06/25/bookend/bookend.html.

Trousson, Raymond. 2006. "Sciences et religion en 2440." Cahiers de l'Association internationale des études francaises, 58, no 1: 89–105.

University of Otago. 2010. Heresy, Sedition, Obscenity: The Book Challenged. Exhibition. 30 October 2009 to 29 January 2010. Cabinet 10: Charron, Milton & Mercier. New Zealand: University of Otago. https://www.otago.ac.nz/library/exhibitions/bannedbooks/#10Charron.

Valentin, Jean-Marie. 2013. *Ed. August Wilhem Schlegel. Comparaison entre la Phèdre de Racine et celle d'Euripide (et autres textes). L'accueil en France 1807–1808* (323–462). Arras: Artois Presses Université. Retrieved March 12, 2022 from https://books.openedition.org/apu/16502#bodyftn74

Wang, David D. W. 1998. "Translating Modernity." In: Pollard, David E. (editor). *Translation and Creation: Readings of Western Literature in Early Modern China*, 1840–1918. Amsterdam: John Benjamins Publishing.

Wilkie, Everett C. Jr. 1984. Mercier's L'An 2440: Its publishing history during the author's lifetime, Part I. *Harvard Library Bulletin XXXII*, no. 1 (Winter): 5–35. Retrieved March 3, 2022 from https://dash.harvard.edu/handle/1/37364176.

Chapter Two

Origins of Hard Science Fiction: An Approach

Fernando Darío González Grueso, Tamkang University, Taiwan

The Argentine writer Leopoldo Antonio Lugones Argüello (1874–1938) played an important role in the development of Science Fiction in America; however, I believe that his importance lies in the fact that he could be considered the father of Hard SF, defined as a subgenre or style depending on the academic terminology. As I will show in this chapter, Lugones's approach to this type of literature was not followed closely by most of the Hispanic academics, for his name, as well as his literary trajectory tell, superficially, a different story.

Eduardo Ladislao Holmberg (1852–1937), along with Rubén Darío (1867–1916)—another of the founders of Fantastic literature in Argentina—was also the initiator of Science Fiction (SF) in that country with his book, *El viaje maravilloso del señor Nic-Nac* (1875) (*The Wonderful Journey of Mr. Nic-Nac* (1875). Not surprisingly, Lugones, being involved in this creative environment, a short time later, published his story "El Psychon" on January 31 of 1898, and he became immersed in the composition of works of Science fiction, or *fantaciencia* (fantastic science), as he used to call it.

Robert Scholes and Eric S. Rabkin (1977, 169–173) on the one hand, and Mark R. Hillegas (1979, 2) on the other, defend that SF has very strong ties with Fantastic literature and myth. I believe that, perhaps, this is one of the reasons why several stories written by Lugones have been denied for many years its belonging to this genre; since most of the critics have avoided the subject and have focused on other topics and characteristics, mainly regarding esotericism and the fantastic.

The stories that concern this study have been called "fantaciencia," "cuentos cientifistas de carácter especulativo" (scientist tales with speculative characteristics (Lugones 1996, 51, 61), "relatos de anticipación" (anticipatory stories; Lugones 1987, 33), or "fantástico ambiguo" (ambiguous fantastic; Castro 2003), all these denominations, due to the approach of many of the stories to philosophy, theosophy, esotericism, and the occult (Monet-Viera 2000). I will not be the first to argue that Leopoldo Lugones wrote SF, as it was also stated by Speratti Piñero as early as 1957, and later on by Scari in 1964 and 1975. A few years later, Goorden and Van Vogt (1982, 8), and Barei and Barrenechea (1989, 38–40, 53–56) included some of this works in their Science Fiction anthologies. More recently, in 2005, Riva highlighted this fact that Lugones utilized a story model that applied the argumentative and expository scientific text, based on scientific and/or pseudoscientific bases.

The classification that Speratti Piñero proposed in 1957 still seems perfectly valid for my purposes, despite the fact that other authors have emerged to highlight other poetic factors and various influences. According to his classification, the following stories are scientific fiction, while others, show philosophical traces: "El Psychon"—published for the first time in *Tribuna*, on January 31, 1898; "La metamúsica"—published for the first time as "La Meta Música" in *Tribuna*, on June 29, 1898; "Un fenómeno inexplicable"—first published as "La licantropía" in *Philadelphia*, on September 7, in 1898; "La Fuerza Omega"—published for the first time in *Caras y Caretas*, on January 1, 1899; "Viola acherontia"—published for the first time as "Acherontia atropos" in *Tribuna*, on January 31, 1899, and "Yzur," published in 1906 in a compendium named *Las fuerzas extrañas*.

SCIENCE IN LEOPOLDO LUGONES STORIES

Lugones loved science and stood out in his desire for knowledge. He was interested in Archeology, Botany, Etymology, Mathematics, Philology, and Zoology, sciences on which he wrote various essays and gave lectures. In addition, he translated from several languages: Arabic, English, French, Greek, Italian, Latin, and Portuguese, among others (Lugones 1987, 12–13). As a curious fact, that was pointed out by García Ramos, Lugones maintained a close friendship with Albert Einstein (Lugones 1996, 32).

Against his assimilation to Science Fiction, some studies argued that Lugones' approach to esotericism and the occult distanced him from this genre (Marini Palmieri 1988; Monet-Viera 2000; Perea Siller 2004). Perhaps, that curiosity led him to become a mason and enter the Logia Libertad Rivadavia n° 51, on November 13 of 1899. He also joined the Blavatsky Theosophical Society. However, in his words, certain occult sciences that he defended have made postulates that over time have become to be true. Lugones himself warns us about this issue in the second edition (1926) of *Las fuerzas extrañas*:

> Algunas ocurrencias de este libro, editado veinte años ha, aunque varios de sus capítulos corresponden a una época más atrasada todavía, son corrientes ahora en el campo de la ciencia. Pido, pues, a la bondad del lector, la consideración de dicha circunstancia desventajosa para el interés de las mencionadas narraciones.
>
> Personal translation: Some occurrences of this book, edited twenty years ago—although several of its chapters correspond to a still more backward time—, are now common in the field of science. I ask, therefore, kindness to the reader, and the consideration of said disadvantageous circumstance for the interest of the aforementioned narrations (Lugones 1987, 33).

The interests and knowledge of Lugones on different sciences drove him to make use of them in his short stories. For instance, among the theories and hypothesis that he mentions are—which articulate the discoveries or inventions of his characters:

1. The liquefaction of gases studied by Antoine Lavoisier, Michael Faraday, Charles Cagniard-Latour, and Adrien-Jean-Pierre Thilorier, as well as the advancements on suggestive therapy by Jean-Martin Charcot, Victor Alphonse Amédée Dumontpallier, Hans Heinrich Landolt, and Jules Bernard Luys ("El Psychon");
2. The Hertzian waves, verified by Heinrich Hertz; the discovery of X-Rays by Wilhelm Konrad Roentgen, and the composition of the form of the wave, the Fourier Series, by Jean-Baptiste Joseph Fourier ("La fuerza Omega").
3. The photography of colors using mercury by Gabriel Lippmann, furthermore, the universal harmony of the cosmos imagined by Johannes Kepler ("La metamúsica").
4. The studies of Willliam Crookes on molecular weight of the bodies in the vacuum ("Un fenómeno inexplicable");
5. The relations between the color of animals and environment and physiological evolution in studies by John Gould, Charles Darwin, and the botanical works of Augustin Pyramus de Candolle ("Viola Acherontia");
6. The convolution of Paul Broca, and the Darwinian Evolution ("Yzur").

A clarifying example of what I am supporting—and perhaps his conversations with Einstein were at the origin—is his conception of the music in the story "La metamúsica." According to Pythagoras, the mathematical laws that govern harmony also govern the universe. Similarly, Plato (Platón

1992, 172–174) in his *Timaeus*, and Kepler many years later, defended the same idea. Although Thomas Young demonstrated in 1801 that the relation between music and light, like in "La metamúsica," rests in waves similar to light (Asimov 1975, 360), not light itself, during the nineteenth century, many scientists believed in the most esoteric lines of science regarding this subject. The Theory of Unity affirms that movement is light, heat, sound . . . At this respect, during the week of September 24–30, 2007, the Institute of Astronomy at the University of Cambridge showed an exhibition in which visitors could listen to the sonic performance produced by black matter from a galaxy cluster at one billion light years from Earth. The data for this experiment was extracted from X-ray images produced by the galaxy cluster.

Furthermore, the Doppler Effect postulates that light and sound waves behave in the same manner when faced with moving objects, hence, in the case of light, when an object approaches our eyes, color is produced, and the more speed it takes, the closer it seems to violet. Contrary to that, if the object moves away, the perception of the retina brings it closer to red (Asimov 1975, 48).

Moreover, researchers from LIGO project (Laser Interferometer Gravitational Wave Observatory) announced that gravitational waves, already predicted by Einstein in 1916, had been heard for the first time on September 14, 2015, at 5 o'clock: 51 ET by the two LIGO detectors (Zavla 2016). This fact would confirm what was anticipated by Lugones in his story. Furthermore, I could add that the same approach to music that Lugones employed in his SF can be found in different works of well-known contemporary neuro-musicologists of great prestige, such as Oliver Sacks and Daniel Levitin, as Fraser demonstrated (2008).

According to Robert Scholes and Eric S. Rabkin, faith in science has been promoted, not only by scientists, but by SF writers themselves (1977, 114). One of the most representative advances, if not the most relevant, has been the scientific method. It seems that one cannot speak of a unique method in Science Fiction, because the three basic methods can appear in the same work, depending on the data to be analyzed. Lugones utilizes the inductive and hypothetico-deductive methods in "El Psychon," "La fuerza Omega," "La metamúsica," and "Un fenómeno inexplicable"—more appropriated to the sciences in all his stories, Mathematics, Physics, and Chemistry—with the only exception of "Viola Acherontia" and "Yzur," where he adds the deductive method—and to which he also applies biological content. In his fiction, every *mad scientists* makes mistakes until he finally identifies the solution, which is almost never happy, but always successful.

Some critics have adduced against Lugones inclusion in the genre of Science Fiction his negative determinism regarding the possible projections of science. However, that deterministic materialistic scientific predictions have always been present in many of the works of this genre. Nobody doubts that H. G. Wells is a Science Fiction writer, and both of them, prelude the destructiveness of progress. A few examples regarding this issue of the British writer are *The Island of Dr. Moreau* (1896), *The Invisible Man* (1897) and *The War of the Worlds* (1898). Lugones always voiced his skepticism toward positivism:

> La verdad por la verdad, fundamento de nuestro positivismo, tampoco tiene por objeto el amor de los hombres. Su descubrimiento es una satisfacción de la curiosidad y del orgullo. Los horrores de la vivisección, muchas veces ejecutada *in anima mobile* en nuestros hospitales; la difusión de las más terribles recetas explosivas, de las fórmulas venenosas de los microbios, provienen de ese culto desatentado. Pero la misma verdad es odiosa cuando causa daño y lo causa, cuando, en vez de ser un instrumento del bien, resulta ídolo implacable y helado en la inútil finalidad de sí misma.
>
> Personal translation: The foundation of our positivism, truth for the fact of the truth, and the foundation of our positivism, does not have the love of men as its object. Its discovery is a satisfaction of curiosity and pride. The horrors of vivisection, many times carried out *in anima mobile* in our hospitals; the spread of the most terrible explosive recipes, of the poisonous formulas of microbes; they all come from that neglected cult. However, the very truth is hateful when it causes damage, and causes it, when, instead of being an instrument of good, it is an implacable and frozen idol in the useless purpose of itself (1962, 1006).

Like our author, other famous writers of the genre have fled from the optimism of science, and their ability to explain everything; famous are the cases of Philip K. Dick and his *Do Androids Dream of Elecric Sheep?* (1968), H. P. Lovecraft in all his work, Kurt Vonnegut and his *Galapagos* (1985), almost any cyberpunk work, or the innumerable scientific dystopian works with *Brave New World* (1932), by Aldoux L. Huxley, at the helm. Therefore, this argument is not valid either.

Finally, I would also like to mention that the use of irony, satire and burlesque humor may take place in Science Fiction, contrary to what Scari postulated in 1964 (164), since without these elements, *A Clockwork Orange* (1962), by Anthony Burgess would be discarded.

SCIENCE FICTION AND LUGONES

Darko Suvin stance is recognized as one of the strictest among scholars regarding SF. For instance, he removes Space Opera from the canon of subgenres of Science Fiction and states that everything is possible in a Fairy

Tale, because any Fairy Tale is impossible. He connects his argument with the said Space Opera, and sustains that the literary work that consists in the triangle of hero-princess-monster is committing suicide (1976, 62). Agreeing with him up to some point, and clarifying that Darko Šlesinger did not include the works of authors like Iain M. Banks, his analysis led us to the conclusion that, at least, the Space Opera literature might linger between two different genres: SF and Fantasy.

Later on, Suvin explains in the following manner one of the characteristics about the relationship between the empirical, naturalistic or realistic world, and the fictional, or metaphysical world:

> The Realist literature is based on the fact that man's destiny is his own, while in what the Croatian academic calls non-naturalistic literary genres, or metaphysical genres, the circumstances surrounding heroes are never passive nor neutral. In realistic literature, the human being makes and unmakes during the narrative process of the fictional construction. In other words: Man is the origin, the middle and the end. Conversely, in the metaphysic literature, the influences that context and circumstances have over characters drive them during the action (1976, 64–65).

Suvin affirms that within several of the fantastic genres, the world is oriented toward the triumph of the hero or the failure of him, as in Fantasy and the myth, respectively, but that in Science Fiction, that world is not oriented, a priori, towards any point, neither positively nor negatively. And that is due— he claims—because it shares with our civilization an approach analogous to that of modern science and philosophy. Myth refers to the past, and naturalistic novel to the present. Science Fiction, however, encompasses all three temporal stages: past, present and future (1976, 64–66).

For all these reasons, I have selected this author among many esteem academics, as an example of what SF should be. Suvin offers a very specific definition of the genre:

> SF is, then a literary genre whose necessary and sufficient conditions are the presence and interaction of estrangement and cognition, and whose main formal device is an imaginative framework alternative to the author's empirical environment (1976, 62).

And Suvin clarifies to us the meaning of estrangement: "A representation which estranges is one which allows us to recognize its subject, but at the same time makes it seem unfamiliar" (1976, 62).

In short, he presents variations such as the treatment from the author's empirical point of view, and the purposes toward which the speech is directed. It is due to these two differences that I prefer to adopt this definition as the one to be taken into account for the concept of Science Fiction in this chapter, because all of them are in accordance with the stories of Lugones that I highlighted in the introduction.

Certain criticism emphasizes the differentiation that emerged during the last third of the 19th century and the first third of the 20th, appertained to two styles of Science Fiction that marked their time (Alkon 1994, 6–8, 42–55 and 67–82; Angenot 1979, 18–33; Huntington 1979, 34–50; Martin 1985, 122–160; Muñóz Puelles 1998, 26; Scholes and Rabkin 1977, 8–15). It has been established a classic differentiation between authors who mainly use machines and scientific and/or technological discoveries that already exist to launch scientific hypotheses, and those who invent and create fictitious discoveries. Jules Verne and Aldous Leonard Huxley are a perfect example of the first case of writers. They belong to the group that we are going to call *non-speculative scientific technological fiction*, and where we can highlight the work *Voyage au center de la Terre* (1868), by Jules Verne for its originality. In this novel, Verne echoes the idea in vogue at the time that water existed in the lower layers of the mantle, and even in the outer core. Verne then, makes a quick review of the theories and hypotheses at that moment regarding the existence of the gaseous state of the Earth's core, in addition to a fairly specific exposure of the strata and minerals that an alleged group of explorers would find in its path. On the other hand, we would have the vast majority of Science Fiction writers who invent and create. This is the case of H. G. Wells, Robert A. Heinlein, Isaac Asimov, Theodore Sturgeon, A. E. Van Gogt, Ursula K. Le Guin, to name a few. It is the *speculative Science Fiction*, within which we can highlight the work *The Time Machine* (1895), by H. G. Wells, which shows us a traveler in time, and how he arrives at a time in the future when humanity has been reduced to two physically and culturally degraded species: the eloi and the morlocks. After a stay there, he continues his temporal journey to speculate on the possible future of Planet Earth, from a geological and biological point of view, with a degradation of molecular structures toward gradually simpler organisms, in order to evolve again toward more complex forms of life. This second group of writers could, be divided into two: the first one that substantiates its scientific-technological projections and speculations on the rudiments of the science of the narrative moment, and coherent future possibilities; a place where we would dare to position Lugones. And a second that lets fantasy fly, which sometimes causes lack of verisimilitude, which they hide under the mantle of Fantasy literature, with which they form a perfect hybridization, this is the case of the so-called space operas.

If we return to the first subgroup, I should add that Judith Merril differentiates speculative science fiction from didactic and predicative fiction by arguing that the first type reflects stories whose objective is to extrapolate, discover, and learn, and for that purpose, they utilize analogy, experimenta-tion, extrapolation, and projection, by offering diverse hypothesis in the plot (Merril 1971, 60). Not in vain Lugones' Science Fiction has also been called speculative, since it constantly respects the postulates of science, from which he invents variants, but without ever disregarding them (Scari 1964, 166). Both, types of postulates, of physical nature, like in "El Psychon," "La fuerza Omega," "La metamúsica," and some of more Darwinian motives, namely: "Un fenómeno inexplicable," "Viola Acherontia," and "Yzur."

HARD SCIENCE FICTION AND LUGONES

Hard Science Fiction is a subgenre in which science is the essential element of the plot, and its accuracy reaches its maximum expression, as long as fiction allows it. Essentially, it places all its emphasis on the descriptions of a very advanced technology and/or science, whether it exists at the time of creation of the artistic work or not, and on the milimetric verisimilitude, on multiple occasions, of the scientific and technical descriptions. This style would be what many scholars consider the true Science Fiction, and they would not be short of arguments if we stick to the purity of the genre. Critics have considered Jules Verne as the first author of this style; however, his symbiosis with the adventure novel places him as the predecessor of the sub-genre. When examining his works, he adds scientific elements to the fictional plot, and whose later development is very similar, broadly speaking, to that of any adventure novel, like Victor Hugo, Robert Louis Stevenson, or Dumas's father. However, most of the Hard SF is far removed from the themes, motifs, and types of the adventure novel. Perhaps the two most internationally recog-nized authors of the style could be: Arthur C. Clarke with, for example, *A Fall of Moondust* (1961), and Stanislav Lem and his acclaimed *Solaris* (1961), while great masters of the genre such as Robert A. Heinlein, Isaac Asimov, and Poul Anderson move between various subgenres and styles. In relation with Lem, our Argentinian writer influenced him enormously, as Irigoyen García (1999) meticulously explained.

David Harwell wrote a quite clever article compiled by Cramer in 2003, where he listed the criteria to elucidate whether a text belongs to Hard Science Fiction or to other branches of SF. Although we must be cautious regarding the hybridation noted by Stanislav Lem (1984, 31), these are valu-able criteria, since they would demarcate the limits of this subgenre in its pure state. A summarized version of his characterization would include the following five points:

1. Hard Science Fiction offers the truth; it concerns the emotional experience of describing what is true to science.
2. This subgenre makes the plot in the story feel authentic to the experienced reader, when it is plausible and coherent.
3. In certain parts, the story progresses using expository prose, rather than literary prose. The main objective of the exposition is to describe the nature and the reality.
4. This literature depends and relies on external scientific knowledge. The reader must be aware of some scientific content in order to understand and follow the story.
5. Hard Science Fiction should be didactic. The reader would acquire scientific knowledge without feeling that this content interferes with the movement of the plot (Cramer 2003, 188).

In case of applying these criteria accepted by most of the specialists, we could easily recognize some of Lugones' stories as, perhaps, the first texts of this subgenre. Thus, I am going to give some examples extracted from Lugones' short stories, which will show these correlations:

1. The six short stories written by Leopoldo Antonio Lugones deal with the truth and the emotional experience of describing and facing what is scientifically true, as the narrators and scientists of these fictions in question expressed it. During his stories, the main character, usually a wise man, or an eccentric scientist, starts his appearance by giving a theoretical approach to the facts that the narrator—with the only exception of "Yzur"—discovers at the end, sometimes, surrounded by other witnesses. These theories and hypothesis are the foundation to the inventions and discoveries of each story. Lugones also adds some non-scientific hypothesis when the fiction needs it; however, almost all of them are traced in the history of human exploits, and are not his invention, but commonly accepted at his time. In addition, in the end, the result of the experiment, which is the climax, can be deduced from the theoretical approach given before and during the long explanations.
2. The experienced reader understands the concatenation of the facts presented in the story in a plausible way, and for this he uses real scientific references, altered or not, as a literary mechanism for the introduction of verisimilitude. This is the case in, for example, "La fuerza Omega," where the narrator and the *wise man* commented on studies written by Heinrich Hertz, Wilhelm Konrad Roentgen, César-Mansuète Despretz, and John Tyndall, among others, and whose theories are explained, and serve as part of the argumentative discourse of the *mad scientists*.

3. Lugones uses expository prose at numerous points, if not in almost the entire story, more than literary prose, especially in "El Psychon," "La Fuerza Omega" and "La metamúsica," where he transforms the exposition and the argumentation into the essence of the plot, and the argumentative texts serve as the common thread to the narrative.

4. The emphasis falls on scientific knowledge external to the short story. The prose of Lugones is filled with definitions and expositions of data, hypotheses and theories of his time known and concrete—whether scientific or esoteric—as it occurs in "Un fenómeno inexplicable," where he opposes the Rutter pendulum to that of Hans Reichenbach, and even adds one made by an unknown Dr. Ledger—who does not seem to exist. He also creates other hypothesis and presents them as part of the plot, like when the weird scientist in "La metamúsica" argues that waves in the air cause ethereal vibrations, unaccepted idea, but no so far from the studies of Hendrik Anton Lorenz on alterations in the oscillation of light in a magnetic field.

5. Finally, he gets his characterization through information, and the didacticism is present in all stories, for a non-expert reader on Physics or Astronomy, for instance, may learn and understand the evolution of ideas in text. In this manner, and as an example, he makes us aware of many chemical and medical hypotheses of his time in the search for the *liquid of thought* carried out by the protagonist of "El Psychon."

The factual discourse offered here, not a literary interpretation, leads to understand that Lugones wrote, alongside weird tales and Fantasy, Hard SF, and his works is one of the purest examples any reader can encounter.

CONCLUSION

The work of Scari analyzing the scientific nature of Leopoldo Antonio Lugones Argüello's writings in 1964, stated that some of his short stories are, in fact, Science Fiction. I would like to go in depth over the previous statement, and add that half a dozen of these short stories are Hard Science Fiction as well. For that matter, I employed Suvin's definition of Science Fiction, which best stresses the characteristics and essence of the purest SF genre. I found that other definitions accepted by critics cover a wide range of subgenres and hybridations.

Lugones uses theories and hypothesis of his era showing a remarkable appetite for scientific knowledge—not only esoteric, as most of the studies examine, forgetting, maybe, that we can find two quite different types of short stories in this fiction. He did not only write fantastic literature, but also the subgenre of Hard Science Fiction. It is true that the genius of Jules Verne added sections of scientific exposition to his early scientific romances; however, it is the whole, its aims and objectives, which determines what is a genre or subgenre is its pure state.

The meticulous explanations in these six short stories, the use of the argumentum ad verecundiam, the contrast of various hypotheses and theories, the examples adduced to defend a certain argument, the use of definitions, and the abundant scientific neologisms used by the author, should have been enough to prove my assertion. Nevertheless, here, I have illustrated a few cases of real science of his time as a conductor of the stories, his affiliation to the general distinctive aspects of the subgenre, and I have finalized with the application of the five characteristics of Hard Science Fiction from Harwell. All of it, to prove that some of Lugones' accounts are, possibly, the first pure exercise of Hard Science Fiction globally published.

ACKNOWLEDGEMENTS

I wish to express my gratitude to both of the reviewers of this text and to Dr. Montoneri for their positive comments and their clever assessments.

NOTE

This chapter is a revision, extension, and translation of a paper entitled "Leopoldo Lugones, el padre de la ciencia ficción rigurosa" given at Congreso Internacional liLETRAD 2016, Seville, Spain.

REFERENCES

Alkon, Paul Kent. 1994. *Science Fiction before 1900. Imagination. Discovers. Technology*. New York: Twayne Publishers.

Angenot, Mark. 1979. "Jules Verne: the Last Happy Utopianist." In *Science Fiction. A Critical Guide*, edited by P. Parrinder, 18–32. London/New York: Longman Group Limited.

Asimov, Isaac. [1960] 1975. *Guide to Science. 1 The Physical Sciences*. Harmodnsworth: Pelican Books.

Barei, Silvia, and Barrenechea, Ana María. 1989. *Leopoldo Lugones, cuento, poesía y ensayo: antología*. Buenos Aires: Ediciones Colihue.

Castro, Andrea. 2003. "La ciencia en el fantástico ambiguo: «Un fenómeno inexplicable» de Leopoldo Lugones." *RILCE Revista de Filología Hispánica* 19, no. 2: 193–204.

Cramer, Kathryn. 2003. "Hard Science Fiction." In *The Cambridge Companion to Science Fiction*, edited by E. James and F. Mendlesohn, 186–196. Cambridge: Cambridge University Press.

Fraser, Benjamin. 2008. "Un Neuro-musicólogo antes de su tiempo Discursos actuales del sonido a través de dos cuentos de Leopoldo Lugones." *Hispania* 91, no. 4: 794–804.

Goorden, Bernard and Van Vogt, Alfred Elton. [1980] 1982. *Lo mejor de la ciencia ficción latinoamericana*. Barcelona: Ediciones Martínez Roca, S. A.

Hillegas, Mark Robert. 1979. "The literary background to science fiction." In *Science Fiction. A Critical Guide*, edited by P. Parrinder, 2–17. London/New York: Longman Group Limited.

Huntington, John. 1979. "The Science Fiction of H. G. Wells." In *Science Fiction. A Critical Guide*, edited by P. Parrinder, 34–50. London/New York: Longman Group Limited.

Irigoyen García, Javier. 1999. "La ciencia ficción en Leopoldo Lugones." *Boletín da Asociación Galega de Ciencia Ficción* 5, no. 3. https://doi.org/10.5195/reviberoamer.1964.2157

Lem, Stanislaw. 1984. *Microworlds. Writings on Science Fiction and Fantasy*. San Diego: Harcourt Brace Jovanovich Publishers.

Lugones, Leopoldo. 1962. *Prometeo (un proscrito del sol). Obras en prosa*. México: Aguilar.

———. 1987. *Cuentos fantásticos*, edited by P. Luis Barcia. Madrid: Editorial Castalia.

———. 1996. *Las fuerzas extrañas*, edited by A. García Ramos. Madrid: Cátedra.

Marini Palmieri, Enrique. 1988. "Esoterismo en la obra de Leopoldo Lugones." *Cuadernos hispanoamericanos* 458: 79–96.

Martin, Andrew. 1985. *The Knowledge of Ignorance. From Genesis to Jules Verne*. Cambridge: Cambridge University Press.

Merril, Judith. 1971. "What do you mean: Science Fiction." In *SF: The other side of Realism*, edited by T. D. Clareson, 53–95. Bowling Green: Bowling Green University Popular Press.

Monet-Viera, Molly. 2000. "Occult Realities, Alternate Realisms: Latin American Narrative Genres at the «Fines de Siglo»." PhD diss. Yale University. UMI Microformat 9991196.

Muñóz Puelles, Vicente. 1998. *La ciencia ficción*. Valencia: Editorial La Máscara.

Perea Siller, Francisco Javier. 2004. "Ciencia y ocultismo en el primer Lugones cuatro cuentos." *Alfinge: Revista de filología* 16: 241–252. https://doi.org/10.21071/arf.v16i16.6860.

Platón. 1992. *Diálogos VI. Filebo, Timeo, Critias*. Madrid: Editorial Gredos.

Riva, Reynaldo. 2005. "Yzur, Funes y el Inmortal: Una convergencia metafísica." *Revista chilena de literatura* 66, no. 2: 47–62. http://dx.doi.org/10.4067/S0718-2295200 5000100003.

Scari, Robert M. 1964. "Ciencia y ficción en los cuentos de Leopoldo Lugones." *Revista Iberoamericana* 57, no. 1: 163–187. https://doi.org/10.5195/reviberoamer .1964.2157.

Scholes, Robert E., and Rabkin, Eric S. 1977. *Science Fiction. History. Science. Vision.* Oxford-New York: Oxford University Press.

Speratti Piñero, Emma Susana. 1957. "La expresión de las 'fuerzas extrañas' en Leopoldo Lugones." In *Literatura fantástica en Argentina*, 1–16. México: Imprenta universitaria.

Suvin, Darko. 1976. "On the Poetics of the Science Fiction Genre." In *Science Fiction. A collection of critical essays*, edited by M. Rose, 57–71. Englewood Clifts: Prentice-Hall Inc.

Tatsumi, Takayuki. 2005. "Japanese and Asian Science Fiction." In *A Companion to Science Fiction*, edited by D. Seed, 223–250. Malden/Oxford/Melbourne: Blackwell Publishing Ltd.

Zavía, Matías S. 2006, November 2. "Chirp: éste es el sonido de la primera onda gravitacional jamás escuchada." Retrieved February 21, 2022 from http:// es.gizmodo.com/chirp-este-es-el-sonido-de-la-primera-onda-gravit-aci-1758502467.

Chapter Three

Beyond Utopia

The Dystopian Capitalist Society in Paris in the Twentieth Century (1863)

Murielle El Hajj, Lusail University, Qatar

Jules Verne's novel *Paris in the Twentieth Century* (*The Lost Novel*), translated by Richard Howard and published by Random House New York, goes beyond science fiction and anticipates the capitalist development that generates advances in science and technology. On the one hand, Verne praises the scientific and technological developments. On the other hand, he highlights how these developments are not able to cure societal misery in Paris and how the evolution of science and technology, that resulted from the industrial revolution, had monetized and mechanized twentieth century Parisian society at the hands of bankers and industrialists.

At first sight, the reader thinks that *Paris in the Twentieth Century* depicts a utopian aspect of the Parisian society in the twentieth century. Verne opens the novel with a portion of the Parisian populace heading to the metro stations from where local trains will take them to Champ-de-Mars. It was August 13, 1960: The Prize Day at the Academic Credit Union. The latter and the age's industrial aims were "in perfect harmony" (Verne 1996, 21). However, this ideal state of society, where no distress prevails and where no one is unhappy or hopeless seems to be just an illusion. The reader deduces the declination of society, and even its dehumanization, underlining a dystopian world controlled by tyrannical governments and facing environmental disasters.

The present chapter titled "Beyond utopia: The dystopian capitalist society in *Paris in the Twentieth Century*" sheds light on Verne's dystopian "prophecy" about the New Paris. It aims to underline how the industrial positivism, the *laissez-faire* capitalism, and the accelerated technological growth,

45

emphasized by the author, are at the center of a dystopian society, where arts have disappeared completely or have been conveyed toward utilitarian purposes, where education has been vocationalized and standardized for all, where electricity serves as an efficient tool for capital punishment, and where Parisians themselves have lost their feelings and become machines in a repressive society. This research will address the following questions: In going beyond a utopian science fiction, how does *Paris in the Twentieth Century* depict a dystopian society? From underlining the advantages of technological growth as well as utilitarian and capitalist culture, how and why Verne pointed out their disadvantages? To do so, the discussion will focus on the following axes: The transition from utopia to dystopia in *Paris in the Twentieth Century*, the impact of technological advances on society, the emergent dangers of a utilitarian culture, and the philistine culture of capitalism. I conclude that *Paris in the Twentieth Century* is not only limited to the new Parisian society, but is an anticipation that Verne has made about the world—the capitalist system—in which we currently live.

LITERATURE REVIEW

In his article titled "The 'New' Jules Verne," Arthur B. Evans points out the rejection of the novel by Hetzel and discusses its impact on Verne's career:

> For Verne experts, the sudden and unexpected (re)appearance of *Paris au XXᵉ siècle* will also cause some problems. Indeed, its very existence has already forced some to redefine their understanding of Jules Verne, the man and the writer. And they have begun to call for a complete reappraisal of Verne's life and works. This reaction is somewhat ironic since, for decades, they have fought long and hard against the popular notion of Verne as "The Father of Science Fiction" and the prophet-novelist of things to come (Evans 1995, 38).

In addition, the paper focuses on discussing how *Paris in the Twentieth Century* serves to prove that Verne is a writer of "real" science fiction despite the literary critics that concluded that he never wrote a truly futuristic novel due to the fact that his similar tale titled "In the Year 2889" and many of his works were actually written by his son Michel. Talking about the novel's impact on Verne's career, John L. Brown highlights in his review of *Paris in the Twentieth Century* that the novel has rehabilitated the author's reputation, as "up until the post-World War II period, he was often looked down upon by the official literary establishment as 'a writer of children's books'" (Brown 1995, 321). Showcasing the story of the main character Michel Jérôme Dufrénoy, the article observes how the various aspects of Paris brought by Verne are familiar to all of us: the electric railways, the gaz-cabs that jam streets lighted with electricity, the polluted air by industrial waste, the recorded noisy music, and the domination of machines and money. In addition, Brown mentions the decline of humanities in the business setting, the rise of science to the detriments of arts and literature, the death of old languages such as Greek and Latin, the sharp fall of the French language, and the disappearance of the once-prestigious École Normale Supérieure. He also stresses that "education, like the rest, has been industrialized and capitalized" (Brown 1995, 321). Besides education, he highlights the impact of industry and capitalism on the French society and family, he says:

> But now even the gracious and elegant Parisienne has become "Americanized and businesslike" and can no longer enchant either an artist or a lover. And the family? It is destroying itself in a society where everyone "works" and the itch to make money "tue les sentiments du cœur" (Brown 1995, 321–322).

Another paper titled "Jules Verne's *Paris in the Twentieth Century*" discusses Hetzel's criticism of the novel underlining that the latter "will most disappoint readers because its plot is thin and lacks susbtance" (Taves 1997, 135). The paper also highlights that the story includes loosely related episodes shaped in the form of a "catalog of prophecies about life in the metropolises of the 1960s" (Taves 1997, 135), noting that most of the English translations lack the possible impact of the novel because they comprise only a fraction of the depth or number of the notes appearing in the French edition. However, the paper praises Richard Howard's translation:

> Howard's translation of *Paris in the Twentieth Century* is literal, faithful to the wording and syntax of Verne, to the point of preserving Verne's sometimes convoluted style, which makes *Paris in the Twentieth Century* often flow in an unwieldy manner for modern readers (Taves 1997, 136).

Taves points out that Verne's prophecies of the world to come in this novel "are breathtaking in their extent and nearly unerring accuracy. [. . .] The accuracy of the prophecies cannot be overstated, and I would estimate that nearly 90% have come to pass" (Taves 1997, 134). He accentuates that Verne's most "amusing" error is in anticipating that the government would conduct itself in a businesslike way to show a dividend (Taves 1997, 134). He also indicates that the novel makes allusions to individuals, works, and events of the mid-nineteeth-century France, noting that Verne's irony in this regard is not clear to the contemporary reader, who does not have any specialized background. As an example, he underlines that the tenth chapter of the novel presents literary commentaries on the authors of Verne's era.

From his side, Carter Kaplan emphasizes in his article titled "The Advent of Literaty Dystopia" that Verne coined "the notion of the university-as-industrial-operation" (Kaplan 1999, 206) naming his market-driven university the "Academic Credit Union." Kaplan also highlights that in his description of the university's prospectus, Verne notes that "no scholars or professor's name appeared on the Board of Directors, a matter of some reassurance with regard to the commercial prospects of the enterprise" (Kaplan 1999, 206).

While Maria Kaika and Erik Swyngedouw discuss in their article titled "Fetishizing the Modern City: The Phantasmagoria of Urban Technological Networks" how Verne views the Seine "in his mid-nineteenth century futuristic account of 1960s Paris" (Kaifa and Swyngedouw 2000, 121). In this regard, they emphasize that the author sees the giant waterworks and mesmerizing pumping stations along the banks of the Seine in central Paris as the beating heart that satisfies the thirst of the city (Kaifa and Swyngedouw 2000, 121). Mentioning the Seine in the twentieth century, they underline that:

> [. . .] the symbolic and material shrines of progress started to lose their mobilizing powers and began to disappear from the cityscape. Water towers, dams and plants became mere engineering constructs, often abandoned and dilapidated, while the water flows disappeared underground and in-house. They also disappeared from the urban imagination (Kaifa and Swyngedouw 2000, 121–122).

In his article titled "Jules Verne's Captain Nemo and French Revolutionary Gustave Flourens: A Hidden Character Model?," Leonidas Kallivretakis shows the link between Captain Nemo in *Twenty Thousand Leagues under the Seas* and Gustave Flourens, a freedom fighter, praised in *Paris in the Twentieth Century*. In this regard, the article highlights that the former's life is based partly on the latter:

> Anyhow, in this Vernian "lost novel", there is a scene where the hero, Michel Jérôme Dufrénoy, is "passing in front of the Sorbonne where M. Flourens was still giving his lectures with the greatest success, still keen, still young". This phrase, according to William Butcher's own words, is the "vital clue" that Nemo is based on Gustave Flourens" (Kallivretakis 2005, 218).

The paper also discusses a critical question, which is the following: "when did really Verne write *Paris in the Twentieth Century*?" (Kallivretakis 2005, 219) and for which the author provides the hypothesis that the novel was probably written between the spring of 1860 and the winter of 1860–61. Another question is discussed in the paper. It is related to its main subject: Gustave Flourens and what Verne could have known of him in 1860–1861, or even in mid-1863, in order to mention him in the novel. In this regard, Kallivretakis observes that when Gustave Flourens appeared for the first time in the amphitheaters of the Collège de France in mid-November 1863, it is evident that the manuscript of *Paris in the Twentieth Century* had been already submitted and rejected. Therefore, "it is highly improbable that the mentioned 'M. Flourens, giving his lectures with the greatest success,' is Gustave. What seems most probable, is that Verne refers to Flourens' father" (Kallivretakis 2005, 224).

In the *The History of Science Fiction*, Adam Roberts qualifies *Paris in the Twentieth Century* as a "future-fantasy" (Roberts 2006, 132). He also points out that "inventive and engaging if narratively underpowered, this version of a future France tends towards the dystopian; which is to say, it was part of what was a vigorous nineteenth century tradition of future fictions" (Roberts 2006, 132). While Terry Harpold mentions in the chapter "European Science Fiction in the Nineteenth Century," published in the edited book titled *The Cambridge History of Science Fiction*, that *Paris in the Twentieth Century* mourns the city's overtaking by capitalism, technology, and the "demon" electricity (Harpold 2018, 62). However, no further details about the novel have been provided in both works.

These readings are evidence that the literarure around *Paris in the Twentieth Century* focuses on the impact of the novel on Verne's career and reputation, its rejection by his publisher Hetzel, and its futuristic, minimalist, and dystopian aspect, as it paints a Parisian industralized and capitalized society at all levels. However, and despite their added value to the discussion of Verne's prediction of twentieth-century Paris, the highlighted works did not discuss with depth the degeneration from utopia to dystopia in the novel, neither the negative impact of the technological progress on the human being and society as underlined by Verne, nor the dangers of utilitarianism and capitalism. Therefore, this present chapter aims to discuss all these issues while showing that Verne's prophecy is not limited to the twentieth century, as he also predicted life and society in the twenty-first century. To do so, I will start by providing a brief introduction about Verne's life and work.

JULES VERNE, HIS LIFE AND WORK

Born in 1828 in Nantes, France, Verne attended a boarding school and then traveled to Paris, where he earned his law degree in 1851. However, during his childhood he was interested in stories of nautical adventures and shells shared by his first teacher and the sailors who visited the ports in Nantes. While studying in Paris, he became friends with the son of the renowned novelist Alexandre Dumas. He was able to get his first play, *The Broken Straws*, produced at Dumas's theater in 1850. A year later, he started writing magazine articles combining his interests in history, science, and travel. One of his first stories published in 1851, *A Voyage in a Balloon*, brought together the components that contributed to the success of his later novels. However, writing was not a sufficient profession to earn a living. Thus, Verne accepted a brokerage job arranged by Honorine de Viane Morel's family, whom he fell in love with and then married in 1857. Four years later, the couple had their child Michel.

Verne's literary career took off in the 1860s, when he met the publisher Pierre-Jules Hetzel, a successful businessman who worked with the greatest writers of nineteenth-century France including Victor Hugo, George Sand, and Honoré de Balzac. Hetzel launched the *Magazine of Education and Recreation*, in which Verne's novels were continually published and later released in a book format as part of a collection, *Extraordinary Voyages*. His most famous and lasting novels were written in the 1860s and 1870s, at a time when Europeans were still exploring and exploiting new areas of the globe. His typical novel included a cast of men—often including one with brains and one with strength—who develop a new technology that allows them to travel to exotic places. His publications include over a dozen plays and short stories, numerous essays, and four nonfiction books. However, he earned his notoriety from his novels. The latter take the reader "across continents, under the oceans, through the earth, and even into space" (Grove, 2019). In addition to the fifty-four novels published during his lifetime as part of the *Extraordinary Voyages* collection, his son Michel added eight novels to the collection after his death in 1905.

Known as the "father of science fiction," Verne was one of the most influential science fiction writers. Many of his novels have been adapted into movies, television series, radio shows, animated children's cartoons, computer games, and graphic novels. He inspires contemporary writers of the genre and has a considerable influence on popular culture. Nowadays, Verne's scientific visions are more and more becoming realities:

The first nuclear submarine, the USS Nautilus, was named after Captain Nemo's submarine in *Twenty Thousand Leagues Under the Sea*. Just a few years after the publication of *Around the World in Eighty Days*, two women who were inspired by the novel successfully raced around the world. Nellie Bly would win the race against Elizabeth Bisland, completing the journey in 72 days, 6 hours, and 11 minutes. Today, astronauts in the International Space Station circle the globe in 92 minutes. Verne's *From the Earth to the Moon* presents Florida as the most logical place to launch a vehicle into space, yet this is 85 years before the first rocket would launch from the Kennedy Space Center at Cape Canaveral (Grove, 2019).

Among Verne's most prominent novels are *Five Weeks in a Balloon* (published in 1863), *Journey to the Center of the Earth* (published in 1864), *From the Earth to the Moon* (published in 1865), *Around the Moon* (published in 1870), and *Around the World in Eighty Days* (published in 1873). In *Five Weeks in a Balloon*, Verne tells the story of Dr. Fergusson who develops a device to change the height of his balloon without relying on a ballast so that he can find favorable winds, and who passes through the African continent in his balloon, combating extinct animals, cannibals, and savages. In *Journey to the Center of the Earth*, one of Verne's most popular and sensational works, the characters travel across Europe through a series of underground caverns, lakes, and rivers. The reader is amazed by the subterranean world illuminated by glowing green gases and by the encountered adventures from pterosaurs to a herd of mastodons to a twelve-foot-tall human. In *From the Earth to the Moon*, a group of adventurers build a very large cannon to shoot a bullet-shaped capsule with three occupants to the moon. "Needless to say, the physics of doing this are impossible—the speed of the projectile through the atmosphere would cause it to burn up, and the extreme g-forces would be lethal to its occupants" (Grove, 2019). But, the characters succeed in orbiting the moon and the story continues in the novel's sequel, *Around the Moon*. In *Twenty Thousand Leagues Under the Sea*, Verne imagines the Nautilus, a miraculous submarine capable of circling the globe underwater. The novel also predicts the nuclear submarines of the twentieth century. Last but not least, *Around the World in Eighty Days* presents a feasible race around the globe. "The completion of the First Transcontinental Railroad, the opening of the Suez Canal, and the development of large, iron-hulled steamships made the journey possible" (Grove, 2019). While the novel celebrates existing technologies, it also includes elements of adventure as the travelers save a woman from being slaughtered and are chased by a Scotland Yard detective.

THE NOVEL: *PARIS IN THE TWENTIETH CENTURY*

The discovery of *Paris au XXe Siècle* (*Paris in the Twentieth Century*) and its posthumous publication in France in 1994 were chronicled worldwide. The novel was translated and published in many countries in the following two years, and it has been adapted into a stage play, in The Netherlands. However, according to the preface written by Piero Gondolo della Riva, Verne's publisher, Pierre-Jules Hetzel, refused the manuscript of *Paris in the Twentieth Century* in 1863, shortly after the publication and immediate success of Verne's first novel, *Five Weeks in a Balloon*. In a letter addressed to Verne, Hetzel explained his reasons for rejecting the manuscript, he wrote:

My dear Verne,

I would give almost anything not to have to write you today. You have under-taken an impossible task and, like your predecessors in such matters, you have not been able to pull it off well. It is much below the level of your *Five Weeks in a Balloon*. If you were to reread it one year from now, you would surely agree with me. It is tabloidish, and the topic is ill-chosen.

I was not expecting perfection—to repeat, I knew that you were attempting the impossible—but I was hoping for something better. In this piece, there is not a single issue concerning the real future that is properly resolved, no critique that hasn't already been made and remade before. I am surprised at you . . . [it is] lackluster and lifeless.

I am truly sorry to have to tell you this, but I believe that publishing this would be a disaster for your reputation. [. . .]

You are not yet ready to write a book like this. Wait twenty years, and then try it again [. . .] (Gondolo della Riva 1994, 15–16).

Hetzel also marked numerous editorial comments in the margins of Verne's manuscript as he was reviewing it. He made critical comments such as "avoid using neologisms in the opening scene" (Gondolo della Riva 1994, 14), "these grandiose dialogues are not what you believe them to be; they seem phony, and the circumstances don't warrant them; this procedure is good in the hands of a Dumas, in a book full of adventures; but here, they are tire-some" (Gondolo della Riva 1994, 14), "all these things are not very pleasant" (Gondolo della Riva 1994, 14), and "I really do not find these hypotheses interesting at all" (Gondolo della Riva 1994, 15). At one point, Hetzel offers what is perhaps his most harsh criticism against Verne's futuristic tale, say-ing "My dear Verne, even if you were a prophet, no one today would believe this prophecy [. . .] they simply would not be interested in it" (Gondolo della Riva 1994, 15). The manuscript seems to have been lost after 1911, until Verne found it by chance in 1989 while going through some of his great-grandfather's papers. After verification, it was quickly snatched by Hachette and became a bestseller.

Written in 1863, the story of *Paris in the Twentieth Century* takes place in the 1960s-Paris. It deals with a few months in the unhappy and frustrated life of Michel Jérôme Dufrénoy, a 16-year-old orphan, son of a talented musician and whose ambition is to become a poet. Later, he finds that literature and classics have been forgotten in a futuristic world, where only technology and science are favored. Thus, his book of poetry is impossible to sell. The gov-ernment sponsorship of the arts resulted in an officially sanctioned creativity and in mass-market theater, composed along the lines of the machine-made collaborations of the 1930s Hollywood studio system. However, "Dufrénoy's alienation is, in fact, inspired by Verne's own situation; at the time, to support his family, he was writing in the mornings before spending his days working at the Paris Stock Market, which he loathed" (Taves 1997, 133). Hopeless and broke after being fired from the Le Grand Livre, Dufrénoy spends his last sou to buy flowers for his beloved Lucy. With the bouquet in hand, he makes his way to her grandfather's apartment, only to know that he has been kicked out because he cannot pay the rent. In an extremely overly dramatic climax, the brokenhearted Dufrénoy, deprived of friends and loved ones, wanders and starves in the bitter cold weather of Paris and falls unconscious on the snow. It is noteworthy that the sinister imagery of this peroration to *Paris in the Twentieth Century* may be inspired by Edgar Allan Poe:

> Poe was one of Verne's principal models as a writer, and was also the subject of Verne's only literary essay—written at the time of *Paris in the Twentieth Century*. Poe may have also provided direct impetus for the characterization of Dufrénoy. Like his portrayal of Dufrénoy, Verne believed that Poe's potential creativity had clashed with the uncongenial background of an industrial, material society in America. The strange end of Poe's life, when he wandered for several days, lost, before his death, may even have provided the idea for the bizarre climax of *Paris in the Twentieth Century* and the death of Dufrénoy (Taves 1997, 134).

Besides the story of Dufrénoy, *Paris in the Twentieth Century* portrays the improvements that took place in the 1960s-Paris. These improvements seem to belong to a utopian world: the boulevards lit by the sun, the carriages circulating in the streets, the luxurious stores, the broad avenues, the enormous hotels providing comfortable lodging for thousands of travelers, the elegant galeries, the bridges, and the shiny trains. However, an in-depth reading of *Paris in the Twentieth Century* puts into doubt the utopic aspect of these improvements. Therefore, I will discuss the transition from utopia to dystopia in the novel.

THE TRANSITION FROM UTOPIA TO DYSTOPIA IN *PARIS IN THE TWENTIETH CENTURY*

Discussing "The Academic Credit Union," the first chapter of *Paris in the Twentieth Century* depicts the image of a "new France," a "new Paris," highlighting the thirty years of success achieved by the Union, under the financial leadership of Baron de Vercampin, whose notion is to establish a single vast institution, in which every branch of the three knowledges may flourish, "it being the State's responsibility, moreover, to pollard, prune, and patrol such growth to the best of its ability" (Verne 1996, 22). Among the other wonders that astonished the nineteenth-century Parisian, Verne mentions the mutiplication of university branches, lycées, primary and secondary schools, Christian seminaries, and cramming establishments, as well as the various asylums and orphanages (See Verne 1996, 21). He adds: "at least everyone could read, could even write. There was no ambitious artisan's son, no alienated farm boy, who failed to lay claim to an administrative position [. . .]" (Verne 1996, 21). Capital was abundant and all capitalists were seeking financial enterprises or industrial deals.

However, while listening to the litany of modern discoveries that have been observed in the remarks of the orator at the Academic Credit Union, the reader thinks about a utopic new Paris. The orator even spoke with a benevolent scorn of the tiny Paris of 1860 and the pygmy France of the nineteenth century, he enumerated the following: "the rapid communication between various points of the Capital, locomotives furrowing the asphalt of the boulevards, electric power in every home, carbonic acid now dethroning steam" (Verne 1996, 26). Therefore, it is significant to provide a definition of the term 'utopia.'

The word 'utopia' was coined by Thomas More "from the Greek ou-topos meaning 'no place' or 'nowhere.' It was a pun—the almost identical Greek word eu-topos means 'a good place'" (The British Library). Talking about the minds of Utopians, More says:

> The minds of the Utopians, when fenced with a love for learning, are very ingenious in discovering all such arts as are necessary to carry it to perfection. Two things they owe to us, the manufacture of paper and the art of printing; yet they are not so entirely indebted to us for these discoveries but that a great part of the invention was their own (More 2005, 94).

For Andreas Voigt, 'utopias' are "[. . .] idealistic pictures of other worlds [. . .]" (Voigt 1906, 1), while Joyce Oramel Hertzler defines 'utopia' as "[. . .] More depicted a perfect, and perhaps unrealizable, society, located in nowhere, purged of the shortcomings, the wastes, and the confusion of our own time and living in perfect adjustment, full of happiness and contentment" (Hertzler 1923, 2). Thus, for many authors a utopian society must be unrealizable and perfect, where people live happily ever after. However, according to Lyman Tower Sargent, "people do not 'live happily ever after' even in More's *Utopia*. [. . .] perfection has never been a characteristic of utopian fiction, but the misuse of the word perfect continues" (Sargent 1994, 6). Therefore, if perfection does not exist in any utopian society, we question its existence in the twentieth-century Paris depicted by Verne.

At first glance, it is significant to note the dilemma of Michel Dufrénoy in the second chapter "A Panorama of the Streets of Paris." On the one hand, he felt that he is abandoned on the high seas, requiring the talents of a fish and having the instincts of a bird. He wants to live in space, in the ideal regions no longer visited, in the land of dreams from which one never returns. On the other hand, while following the crowd, his excitement had subsided, he felt alone like an alien, isolated in the void. He feels regret for his labors, school, and professor. Dufrénoy's conflict is an evidence that he does not live in a perfect world. This is later highlighted when he visited his uncle Monsieur Boutardin who offered him a position in the Casmodage and Co. banking house, under the direction of his cousin. However, his uncle after hiring him criticized his artistic talents, saying: "Your father was an artist—a word which says it all. I should like to think that you have not inherited his unfortunate instincts. [. . .] Now, I want no poets in my family, you must realize" (Verne 1996, 40).

While leaving his uncle's office, Dufrénoy's eyes were filled with tears. He was feeling despair and lack of freedom. He consoled himself with the idea of buying books of the great poets and illustrious authors with which these readings would relieve him from the vexations of each day. In fact, Dufrénoy is the prototype of the human being living in the twentieth century Paris, thus, he represents the new Parisian society. Being miserable is a sign that the latter diverges from utopia to become a dystopian society, noting that dystopia or negative utopia is "a non-existent society described in considerable detail and normally located in time and space that the author intended a contemporaneous reader to view as considerably worse than the society in which that reader lived" (Sargent 1994, 9).

In fact, the dystopian society of *Paris in the Twentieth Century* is reflected in Dufrénoy's life. Despite the technical, societal, and infrastructural progress and innovations, his life is filled with "sleepless nights" (Verne 1996, 62) and with "disappointments of this world" (Verne 1996, 62). Besides feeling hopeless, Dufrénoy is also sinking in poverty. His savings are declining to nothing, he has no fire, his room has no heat, and he even reached the point of decreasing his food to the strict minimum. During the season of bread scarcity, he was reduced to eating coal bread until he was down to his last coin. I note here that Dufrénoy's miserable life symbolizes the life of the twentieth century Parisian society, as a whole. Thus, Verne did a transition from the individual to the collective. Having said this, I highlight the following unanswerable questions in chapter XVII: "What became of poor Michel during the rest of that terrible night? [. . .] Did he wander without being able to espace this deadly capital, this accursed Paris?" (Verne 1996, 143). Therefore, it is necessary to point out the mentioned "deadly capital" and "accursed Paris" in the raised questions, noting again Dufrénoy's tragic end in such a society dominated by death. The latter is metaphorically expressed through the "cemetery" and "graves" that seemed like tiny towns, with their streets and squares, their houses and signs, their churches and cathedrals, represented by a more vainglorious grave (Verne 1996, 146).

Referring to the deadly and pessimistic Parisian life, where poorer people live far from the center of the town lost in the accelerated progress—which is a matter of fatigue and not of time—it is significant to stress on the inexistence of perfection and happiness in the presented society. Even if the latter "seems" to be a perfect place where everything is evolving, it is a place where the human being loses his value and emotions. This is expressed in the novel through the decline of music and its related feelings. In fact, Verne did not only paint a society, which is worse than the one where he lives, but he anticipated a society that is not limited to a space (Paris) or a time (the twentieth century). This is a future dystopian totalitarian and capitalist society dominated by technology enterprises. In this regard, it is crucial to emphasize the failure of utopian states in the twentieth century and their tendencies toward totalitarianism. "For even Thomas More's closure of the Island of Utopia from the mainland in the sixteenth century was a critical engagement with the dependence of the utopian imagination upon capitalism, its tendencies toward closure in a dialogic relation with the expansive, assimilative tendencies of capital" (Ryan and Sellars 2009, 7). Hence, Verne's predicted twentieth-century society consists of the challenges and problems that the current human being is facing, such as the negative impact of the technological developments on society in general and the human being in particular, as well as the dangers of utilitarianism and capitalism.

THE IMPACT OF TECHNOLOGICAL ADVANCES ON SOCIETY

While reading *Paris in the Twentieth Century*, we cannot overlook the high-tech futuristic society and its developed infrastructure. Thus, it is significant to shed light on the following aspects: the long viaduct supporting the railway track, the asphalt highways, the electric lights that illuminate entire cities at night, the elegant bridge through which the viaduct crosses the main streets that traverse its path, the gas cabs, the multistory buildings, the elevators, the wind power, the picture-telegraphs, the sophisticated electrically powered mechanical calculators which send information across vast distances (an anticipation of the Internet), the automated security systems, the electric chair, and the Lenoir machine invented in 1859 and applied to locomotion that empowers the countless carriages which clog the boulevards. Verne spoke in detail about this machine, showing its technical breakthrough:

[. . .] this machine had the initial advantage of doing away with boiler, firebox, and fuel; a little lighting gas, mixed with the air introduced under the piston and lit by an electric spark, produced the movement; gas hydrants, set up at the various carriage parking places, supplied the necessary hydrogen (Verne 1996, 34).

Thus, the provided details aim to accentuate the easy use of the Lenoir machine and its role in facilitating the targeted work. Isn't the supposed core objective of machines manufacture and technological and scientific advances to contribute to simplifying life at all levels? The promise of technology and science was to make life more efficient and easy by upgrading the standard of living. Here, I recall the following quote by US President John F. Kennedy: "As we begin to master the potentialities of modern science, we move toward an era in which science can fulfill its creative promise and help bring into existence the happiest society the world has ever known" (Kennedy 1965, 311–19). However, the use of technology and science has changed and this has impacted the society as a whole.

If the Lenoir machine has a number of advantages—mentioned earlier, Verne also spoke about the destructive war machines that fought on behalf of men, which made the impulse to put an end to wars impossible and even "ridiculous." In fact, as said by Uncle Huguenin in chapter XI, "I could still conceive of battle, in the days when you stood man to man, and when you killed your adversary with your own hands" (Verne 1996, 99). According to Dufrénoy, these machines have even "killed bravery, and soldiers have become mechanics" (Verne 1996, 100). Therefore, in addition to their deadful function, machines became a substitution of the human being and the latter has become mechanized, robotized, hence the loss of human emotions. This is not the only technological impact! With urbanization and industrialization, France lost its fresh air and became polluted. With ten thousand factory chimneys, the production of chemical products such as artificial fertilizers, coal smoke, deleterious gases, and industrial miasmas, the Parisian air became equal to the United Kingdom's.

Furthermore, in this Parisian dystopian society, a version of feminism has also risen, with women moving into the workplace and an increase in illegitimate births. When providing his opinion about women in chapter XII, Quinsonnas confirms that there are no women left and that the species has vanished "like pug-dogs megatheriums" (Verne 1996, 104). He also states that family is tending toward self-destruction, underlining the private interest that impels each of the family members into divergent paths, the need to get rich at all costs that destroys the sentiments, and the marriage becoming a heroic futility. He also points out the difference between the past and the present, saying: "[. . .] the husband nowadays lives far from his wife, he sleeps at his club, eats there, dines there, works there, plays there . . . Madame's life is her own affair, in every sense of the word" (Verne 1996, 106).

This described image of the man-woman relationship demonstrates the effects of the progress and innovations on society in general, and on the family in particular. The 24/7 work and the anticipation of making a large amount of money engender a lack of desire and emotions, thus, has a huge impact on human relations and marriage. Quinsonnas continues: "[. . .] it requires a great deal of money to lead an existence-times-two; a girl no longer marries unless she has her weight in gold in the parental coffers [. . .]" (Verne 1996, 107). He also highlights that this issue exists in every class of society. By highlighting the affected and disrupted society, it is noteworthy to underline that each of the technological, the political, and the biological aspects had been sources of stability in the past—for both society and the individual. However, as the present is visibly different from the past, the future opened up as a space of difference and possibility: from the promise of a better life to the threat of a species unrecognizable, from new devices to new governance. In this regard, Verne speculated a new space, structured by the numerous intersections of these three key vectors—the technological, the political, and the biological—not only to anticipate the future, but also to make sense of a present in crisis.

Nevertheless, "the overthrow of dystopia, of course, implies the establishment of a new kind of society, one supposedly better than the generally very confining and often highly mechanized culture that has been overthrown" (Levy 2018, 277). The Vernian disordered society does not only go beyond utopia. It also goes beyond dystopia, as it is the predicted model of the society in the twentieth century onwards. Verne captured the entwining of humanity, society, and machines with lucid and prescient clarity, showcasing how machinism will destroy humanity and societies in the future. His prediction is not limited to fiction, even if it was imaginary when he wrote the novel. It became a fact. I would say the reality of our era, when humankind is committed hopelessly to the machines. Consequently, if "'technological utopianism' refers to the belief that scientific advance and technological development are capable of solving all of mankind's problems" (Kurtz 2018, 203), the Vernian technological dystopianism is a demonstration of the opposite. This is also evidenced through the discussion of the dangers of the utilitarian culture, which is also reflected in *Paris in the Twentieth Century*.

THE EMERGENT DANGERS OF A
UTILITARIAN CULTURE

Through his futuristic narrative in *Paris in the Twentieth Century*, Verne identifies the emergent dangers of a utilitarian culture that sacrifices human values for commercial accountancy. This is confirmed through Quinsonnas's declaration: "Let's do our cog work and get back to the litanies of Holy Accountancy!" (Verne 1996, 62). In her article titled "The History of Utilitarianism," Julia Driver defines the latter to be:

> generally held to be the view that the morally right action is the action that produces the most good. There are many ways to spell out this general claim. One thing to note is that the theory is a form of consequentialism: the right action is understood entirely in terms of consequences produced. What distinguishes utilitarianism from egoism has to do with the scope of the relevant consequences. On the utilitarian view one ought to maximize the overall good—that is, consider the good of others as well as one's own good (Driver 2014).

However, despite its aim to expand the good of others and oneself, utilitarianism represses indirectly one's freedom to fulfill his/her aspirations, as they may not be aligned with the collective good. In addition, utilitarianism is characterized by impartiality and agent-neutrality. Everyone's happiness counts the same. When one maximizes the good, it is the good impartially considered. One's good counts for no more than anyone else's good. Moreover, the reason one has to support the overall good is the same reason anyone else has to support the good. It is not peculiar to anyone (Driver 2014).

By driving a utilitarian culture, the Vernian twentieth century Parisian society promotes sciences to the detriment of arts and humanities. Sciences are divided into six branches: mathematics (subdivized into arithmetic, algebra, and geometry), astronomy, mechanics, chemistry, and applied sciences, with subdivisions of metallurgy, factory construction, mechanics, and chemistry adapted to the arts. Sciences also invaded the realm of poetry. In addition, "introductions to mathematics, textbooks on civil engineering, mechanics, physics, chemistry, astronomy, courses in commerce, finance, industrial arts [. . .] sold by millions of copies" (Verne 1996, 23). This is not the case of dictionaries, manuals, grammars, study guides, and topic notes, as well as classical authors and the entire book trade in *de Viris*, *Quintus-Curtius*, *Sallust*, and *Livy* collapse to dust on the shelves of the old Hachette publishing house (Verne 1996, 23). Each year, quantities of scientific works are printed, and the State itself became a publisher: "the nine hundred volumes bequeathed by Charles V, multiplied a thousand times, would not have equaled the number now registered in the library; the eight hundred thousand volumes possessed in 1860 now reached over two million" (Verne 1996, 45). Moreover, Greek and Latin language are only good in providing a few roots for modern science, and are not understood by students. For French language, it is not in high favor anymore and has lost its special consideration, while English language coined terminologies for various disciplines of sciences and knowledge. Painting and sculpture do not exist anymore, and even in the Louvre, there are no more canvases. Thus, by promoting the overall good, many disciplines, publications, and languages lost their value.

Additionally, literature is dead. The works of authors such as Hugo, Musset, and Lamartine are no longer read. If there is not anything sensational to tell, noone will read. Hence, if poetry is not utilitarian, or if literature does not replace a compressed air or power brakes, they are both useless. "Art is no longer possible unless it produces a tour de force! These days, Hugo would have to recite his *Orientates* straddling two circus horses, and Lamartine would perform his *Harmonies* upside down from a trapeze!" (Verne 1996, 67). Thus, despite its contribution to a good life and society in the utilitarian system, commerce becomes futile when it turns out to be excessive and employed in all domains. If commercialized and monetized, arts and humanities become meaningless, and this is the case in the Vernian depicted society, and as is in our current society. Authors such as Amyot, Ronsard, Rabelais, Montaigne, Mathurin Régnier, Malherbe, Corneille, Racine, Molière, Pascal, and La Fontaine served their time and are now relegated to the rank of archeological specimens. They speak an incomprehensible language in this age.

However, the negative impacts of utilitarian ethics in capitalist culture are not only limited to disciplines of knowledge and arts, as they influenced and even destroyed values and moral codes. Honor does not exist anymore. Personalities who have not killed enough people are forgotten, despite their works and achievements. Democracy lost its core values and principles, elections do not interest anyone: "Député-sons succeed Député-fathers, calmly plying their legislators' trade without making much noise about it, [. . .] what's journalism good for? Nothing!" (Verne 1996, 119). Even diseases are wearing out, and the Faculty of Medicine is inoculating us with new ones so doctors have work to do. While lawyers, they no longer plead, they compromise and a good transaction is more profitable, faster, and preferred to a good trial.

Therefore, in the Vernian twentieth-century society, most forms of art, literature, and music have either disappeared entirely, or have been redirected toward strictly utilitarian purposes. In addition, most professions, such as medicine and law, have diverged from their ethics and standards to satisfy utilitarian goals. Even democracy is suppressed in a society where politics became harshly hereditary and where journalism disseminates fake and propagandist news. The frenzy of newspapers led to the death of journalism, for the indisputable reason that writers outnumbered readers (Verne 1996, 120). Verne has drawn a society in which human happiness and its stability is the defining quality. However, it is a dystopian society—as I mentioned earlier— where the militaristic-mechanistic aspects are not really efficient as they seem to be, and where the utilitarian criterion of the maximization of happiness for the greatest number of people has engendered many dangers. Thus, *Paris in the Twentieth Century* profoundly interrogates the utopian associations of happiness and makes us wonder:

> whether the ideal of happiness towards which we are striving may not turn out to be totally unrealisable, or, if realizable, utterly repellent to humanity? Do people want to be happy? If there were a real prospect of achieving a permanent and unvarying happiness, wouldn't they shrink in horror from the boring consummation? (Huxley 1925, 86).

To answer these questions, it is necessary to shed light on the capitalist aspect of the Vernian society and its philistine culture.

THE PHILISTINE CULTURE OF CAPITALISM

In chapter VII, a discussion between the characters Michel, Quisonnas, and Jacques focuses on commerce and its role in drawing nations closer. They mention the money invested by the British, the Russians, and the Americans in the French commercial enterprises, pointing out that money is the enemy of the bullet and that the cotton bale replaced the cannonball. However, they conclude that "the day a war earns as much as an industrial investment, then there'll be wars" (Verne 1996, 71). In twentieth-century Paris, industrialism has come into its own, its empire, and its triumph is in the present. On the one hand, industry, commerce, and mass consumerism seem to have achieved the extreme limits of the possible not only at the local, but also at the international level. On the other hand, agriculture is affected by the hard weather and the snow. Here, I recall climate change and global warming that threaten our planet and engender many natural disasters. In Provence, the vines and various trees—chestnut, fig, mulberry, and olive—perished and the river had frozen over.

Therefore, the future Vernian Paris demonstrates rampaging capitalism, a world where money transactions, industrialism, and technology are at their peak; where nature is being demolished; where the arts, feelings, and emotions are suppressed. Aren't these facts characteristics of our twenty-first-century society? The Vernian dystopian society emphasizes the effects of the capitalist system, in which happiness has become a fragile word. In fact, we live in a world where work became the site of libidinal and narcissistic investment, spinning a web of despairs and dependencies that abuses rather than represses desire, thus, we become attached to our own unhappiness. The world in which we currently live also serves not only to illustrate the ubiquitous ecological dangers, but also the effects of rampant capitalism on the environment and the emergence of a lifestyle in which all needs are controlled by capital. In addition, this world emphasizes the impact of capitalism on every relationship, especially relations among the family, as previously discussed. In fact, *Paris in the Twentieth Century* shows that:

> capitalism is a natural and unalterable feature not only of the human species but of all possible social relations, on any world, and that anything that interfered with the unfettered operation of the market is thus an "inefficiency" that needed to be eliminated. The disjuncture between these worldviews [. . .] would only intensify in the next major period in SF [science fiction] history, the cyberpunk era, which would foresee a humanity that would be either liberated or destroyed by the emergence of a wholly autonomous economic-industrial sphere, also known as the rise of the machines (Conley 2018, 459).

However, this monetized and mechanized society is a driver of consumerism. The latter is insinuated in *Paris in the Twentieth Century* by the luxury shops at the Rue Impériale constructed on the axis of the Opera down to the Gardens of the Tuileries. These shops "projected far out onto the sidewalks the brilliant patches of their electric light; streetlamps operated by the Way System— sending a positive electric charge through a thread of mercury—spread an incomparable radiance; they were connected by means of underground wires" (Verne 1996, 34) while the old-fashioned shops still use hydrocarburated gas, as "the exploitation of new coal pits permitted its current sale at ten centimes per cubic meter; but the Company made considerable profits" (Verne 1996, 34). This comparison between the old and the new shops highlights how the luxurious new ones attract consumers through their fancy and glowing lights. In fact, consumerism is at the core of capitalist societies, and it is promoted and encouraged through many ways. Furthermore, consumerism

> has then become the active searching for personal gratification through material goods. People in the modern society are absorbed into the vicious circle of consumption, which is to buy products, use them, throw them away and buy them again. They are convinced to believe that by consuming these goods, they can be fulfilled materially and socially. Most often that social need seems to overtake material need in influencing purchaser's decision-making (Harmanci 2017, 62).

Consequently, despite changing life for the better—from reduction of disease to increased food and health—technology has engendered many negative impacts at the social, economic, environmental, and mental levels. Hence, in *Paris in the Twentieth Century* Verne predicted a tech dystopia and a model of an advanced capitalist society which is vulnerable due to specific social stressors (family instability and distortion, job insecurity) and socialization processes (individualism, materialism) that are associated with lower well-being, noting here Dufrénoy's depressed and miserable life, as well as his tragic end.

CONCLUSION

While reading *Paris in the Twentieth Century*, we rethink the technological advances that contributed to our dehumanization and mechanization, and we find a duplication of our dystopian society. The latter is weakened by administrative corruption and physical deterioration, and is exposed to an impending capitalist and economic colonization. While being voiced through his characters in a satiric, grim tone, Verne's predictions depicted a tech-obsessed Paris a century in the future. The author predicted the skyscrapers, elevators, cars, trains, and electric city lights of today with prophetic accuracy. He also envisaged our pessimistic present time underlining the bleakness of a world in which human values and ethics will vanish, and how human feelings will become commercialized in a world dominated by a utilitarian and capitalist logic.

However, if *Paris in the Twentieth Century* was considered before the twentieth century a science fiction, it is nowadays considered a prophecy that details the present world. Verne exposed the various issues that we are currently facing from the decline of arts, humanities, and French language to the prevalence of sciences and technology in all domains of society to the disadvantages of utilitarianism and capitalism. Thus, if the novel was not liked and "lost" at Verne's time as well as first banned from being published, it is surely liked by contemporary readers, who will find it more realistic than fictive.

REFERENCES

Brown John L. 1995. "Comparative Literature: States of the Art." *World Literature Today* 69(2): 321–322. Retrieved March 4, 2022 from https://www.jstor.org/publisher/bruo.

Conley, Greg. 2018. "Stagflation, New Wave, and the Death of the Future." In *The Cambridge History of Science Fiction*, edited by Gerry Canavan and Eric Carl Link, 447–459. UK: Cambridge University Press.

Driver, Julia. 2014. "The History of Utilitarianism," *The Stanford Encyclopedia of Philosophy* (Winter 2014 Edition). Edward N. Zalta (ed.). Retrieved March 4, 2022 from https://plato.stanford.edu/archives/win2014/entries/utilitarianism-history.

Evans, Arthur B. 1995. "The 'New' Jules Verne." *Science-Fiction Studies* 22(1): 35–46. Retrieved March 4, 2022 from http://scholarship.depauw.edu/mlang _facpubs/11.

Gondolo della Riva, Piero. 1994. "Préface." *Paris au XXᵉ siècle*. By Jules Verne. Paris: Hachette. Hartwell, David and Kathryn Cramer, eds. *The Ascent of Wonder: The Evolution of Hard SF*. New York: Tor Books.

Grove, Allen. 2019. "Jules Verne: His Life and Writings." *ThoughtCo.* Retrieved March 4, 2022 from https://www.thoughtco.com/jules-verne-biography-4151934.

Harmanci, Nimet. 2017. "Consumerism is the Core Ideology of the Capitalism." *International Journal of Business, Humanities and Technology* 7(4): 61–66.

Harpold, Terry. 2018. "European Science Fiction in the Nineteenth Century." In *The Cambridge History of Science Fiction*, edited by Gerry Canavan and Eric Carl Link, 50–68. UK: Cambridge University Press.

Hertzler, Joyce Oramel. 1923. *The History of Utopian Thought*. New York: Macmillan.

Huxley, Aldous. 1925. *Those Barren Leaves*. Harmondsworth: Penguin.

Kaifa Maria and Swyngedouw Erik (2000). "Fetishizing the Modern City: The Phantasmagoria of Urban Technological Networks." *International Journal of Urban and Regional Research* 24(1): 120–138.

Kallivretakis, Leonidas. 2005. "Jules Verne's Captain Nemo and French Revolutionary Gustave Flourens: A Hidden Character Model?" *The Historical Review/La Revue Historique* 1: 207–243. https://doi.org/10.12681/hr.177.

Kaplan, Carter. 1999. "The Advent of Literary Dystopia." *Extrapolation* 40(3): 200–212. Retrieved March 4, 2022 from https://www.proquest.com/openview/ec9 e38169340ff8f87935cd0bd35a961/1.

Kennedy, John F. 1965. "A Century of Scientific Conquest." In the National Academy of Science, *The Scientific Endeavor*, 311–19. New York: Rockefeller Institute Press.

Kurtz, Malisa. 2018. "Utopia . . . : Science Fiction in the 1950s and 1960s." In *The Cambridge History of Science Fiction*, edited by Gerry Canavan and Eric Carl Link, 201–217. UK: Cambridge University Press.

Levy, Michael. 2018. "'The Golden Age of Science Fiction Is Twelve': Children's and Young Adult Science Fiction into the 1980s." In *The Cambridge History of Science Fiction*, edited by Gerry Canavan and Eric Carl Link, 265–278. UK: Cambridge University Press.

More, Thomas. 2005. *Utopia*, edited by Henry Morley and by Stephen Duncombe, translated by Gilbert Burnet. London: Cassell & Company Editions.

Roberts, Adam. 2006. *The History of Science Fiction*. UK: Palgrave Macmillan.

Ryan, Matthew and Sellars Simon. 2009. Demanding the Impossible: Utopia, Dystopia and Science-Fiction. *COLLOQUY text theory critique* 17: 1–119. Retrieved March 4, 2022 from www.colloquy.monash.edu.au/issue17.pdf.

Sargent, Lyman Tower. 1994. The Three Faces of Utopianism Revisited. *Utopian Studies* 5(1): 1–37. Retrieved March 4, 2022 from http://www.jstor.org/stable /20719246.

Taves, Brian. 1997. Review of Jules Verne's "Paris in the Twentieth Century," by Jules Verne and Richard Howard. *Science Fiction Studies* 24(1): 133–38. Retrieved March 4, 2022 from http://www.jstor.org/stable/4240581.

The British Library. *Thomas More's Utopia*. Retrieved March 4, 2022 from https://www.bl.uk/learning/timeline/item126618.html#:~:text=Sir%20Thomas%20More%20(1477%20%2D%201535,culture%20and%20way%20of%20life.

Verne, Jules. 1996. *Paris in the Twentieth Century (The Lost Novel)*. Translated by Richard Howard. New York: Random House New York.

Voigt, Andreas. 1906. *Die socialen Utopien*. Leipzig: G.J. Goschen' sche Verlagshandlung.

Chapter Four

With Second Sight and Afro-pessimism

The Im/Possibility of Black Utopia in Martin R. Delany's Blake; or, The Huts of America

Michaela Keck, Carl von Ossietzky
University, Germany

In *Blake; or, The Huts of America* (1859–1862), Martin Robinson Delany envisions the struggle for a future free Black society. Although the novel seems to be incomplete, scholars view it as having significantly shaped the lineage of African American and Afro-diasporic political intellectual thought and literature. Generally cited as the first Black utopian and/or science fiction novel, *Blake* highlights the major predicament of Black utopia, which is the sheer impossibility to escape the dystopian aspects of Black lives and bodies even when devising ways for a better life, whether in nineteenth century America as described in Part I of the novel, or in a dynamic "speculative geography" (Brittan 2019, 81) as envisaged in Part II. Indeed, this study contends that Delany's utopia, which imagines pathways to the im/possible freedom of Black people, does not resolve the tension between a hopeful vision of Black emancipation and a pessimistic sense of continuing racial violence.

While the early scholarship of the 1970s of Delany's *Blake* focused on its Black Nationalist ideas, in the 1980s and 1990s, scholars reconsidered the novel's literary and cultural relations from a constructivist and transnational perspective. Not until the 2010s have scholars begun linking these perspectives with questions of Delany's contribution to African American science fiction, speculative fiction, and utopianism, often stressing the distinctness of these genres. However, Delany's novel, which is commonly mentioned to be the first African American utopia (Sargent 2020, 28; Zamalin 2019, 21; Tabone 2019, 60), tends to blend elements of utopia, science fiction, the fantastical, and speculative fiction.

This chapter aims to contribute to the recent scholarship on Delany's nineteenth century Black utopia based on Ruth Levitas's broad definition of utopia as "the desire for" (Levitas 2011, 9) and "imagination of alternative worlds intended to represent a better way of being for the human beings in them" (Levitas 2011, 207). At the same time, however, Black utopia is understood as being inseparable from the Black dystopia of enslavism, i.e., "enslavement *and* its afterlife" (Broeck 2017, 138). *Blake*, I argue, desires and imagines the Black journey to freedom as a process of expanding the awareness of the racialized condition of African Americans into what W. E. B. Du Bois calls the gift of second sight in order to devise ways of organizing a better world and ways of being Black in this world, ways that grow out of the lived experiences of enslavement. However, alongside *Blake*'s vision of Black self-ownership and self-reliance, as well as the emergence of a distinct future Afro-diasporic society and identity, *Blake* also anticipates the contemporary Afro-pessimist insistence on Black people's enduring social death. In the final part of this chapter, I address the question of the im/possibility of a narrative of Black redemption.

CRITICAL PERSPECTIVES ON DELANY'S
BLAKE AND BLACK UTOPIA

Delany's novel was published in serial installments in the *Anglo-African Magazine* (1859–1860) and the *Weekly Anglo-African* (1861–1862) in two different versions at the same time as, by 1859, Delany had put together "a 600-page manuscript" (Shreve 2017, 453) that was as yet incomplete and open to revisions. The earlier serial print version included twenty-six chapters, the later one the seventy-four chapters that we commonly study and discuss today (McGann 2017, xxxiii). In the following, and for the purpose of this contribution, I use and refer to the latter rendition edited by James McGann with Harvard University Press, a version which Delany heavily revised and expanded from 1861 to 1862 for publication. Originally, the magazine editors and Delany anticipated eighty chapters (McGann 2017, xxxiii), but it remains unclear what happened to the missing six chapters. Some assume that the chapters were lost, whereas others speculate that Delany purposely left the novel incomplete. The latter presumption coincides with Alex Zamalin's observation of the frequently "unfinished" (Zamalin 2019, 12) and "unelaborated" (Zamalin 2019, 14) character of Black utopia despite its aim to provide a hopeful and promising outlook.

Both the *Anglo-African Magazine* as well as the *Weekly Anglo-African* provided important nineteenth-century American platforms for Black self-representation and self-expression by African American and Afro-diasporic writers for a Black readership. Here, Delany's novel was published alongside such well-known writers and intellectuals as the West Indian born Edward Wilmot Blyden, who emigrated to West Africa; the American born Mary Ann Shadd, who settled in Canada where she herself published a weekly newspaper; James McCune Smith, whose academic education in Scotland allowed him to later become one of America's first Black doctors and scientists; or the Black American educator, activist, and author Frances Ellen Watkins Harper. *Blake*'s serialized publications in the *Anglo-African Magazine* and the *Weekly Anglo-African* indubitably helped push the efforts at launching a successful Black press in nineteenth century America and attest to the fact that Black utopia is not only expressed through art but also constitutes a "popular culture phenomenon" (Zamalin 2019, 17). Moreover, Black utopia's characteristic concerns with transformation and "creative conflict" (Zamalin 2019, 14) prefigure the radically oppositional position that Samuel R. Delany ascribed to Afrofuturism more than a century later (qtd. in Dery 1994, 193). Hence, Delany's story about an emerging diasporic movement fueled by African American resistance and revolution would, as Ivy G. Wilson reminds us, "hardly be palatable to antebellum white reading audiences, let alone have gained the initial approval of white editors" (Wilson 2013, 25). Yet, as Damion Kareem Scott claims, *Blake* proved tremendously effective, in that it greatly inspired "'Radical Republicans' and abolitionists" (Scott 2021, 160) in their crusade against slavery.

With the magazines' demise in White-dominated America Delany's novel also disappeared, and we do not know what impact Delany's novel had on Black political and intellectual ideas until *Blake* resurfaced in the 1960s. Now the antecedents of the twentieth century Black freedom struggles were recovered and studied anew in the context of the Civil Rights and Black Power movements, as well as the emerging African American Studies programs. Even though the literary practices of the 1960s and 1970s were still steeped in aesthetic judgment and found *Blake* more of a literary embarrassment than an accomplishment (Zeugner 1971, 98; 105), the scholarly focus on Delany's Black Nationalist ideas brought the novel to general scholarly attention, so much so that *Blake* entered Black literary histories. New historicist practices, as well as the multicultural, postcolonial, and transnational perspectives of the 1980s and 1990s, prompted a critical revaluation of *Blake* "as an exemplary hemispheric text" (Schoolman 2018, 354). Exemplary for this phase of scholarly reappraisal is Paul Gilroy's *The Black Atlantic*, which includes a brief reading of *Blake* that elucidates "the topography of the black Atlantic" (Gilroy 1993, 27) and points to the novel's "utopian move beyond ethnicity and the establishment of a new basis for community, mutuality and reciprocity" (Gilroy 1993, 29). Since then, scholars have routinely examined *Blake* alongside the works of Frederick Douglass, Harriet Beecher Stowe or Herman Melville, explicating the multilayered issues, discourses, and contexts of Delany's novel, while the utopian aspects still await further scrutiny and elaboration.

The 2010s have shown an incipient interest in the utopian, science fiction, and speculative dimensions in *Blake*, mostly by literary and cultural studies scholars. Britt Rusert illuminates the links between the novel's fantastical imaginaries and Delany's own active engagement with the natural sciences, especially with astronomy. The novel, she argues, "draws on astronomy and other speculative sciences" to intervene in the racism in nineteenth-century science discourse, imagining "a truly grandiose vision of fugitivity" that "stretches throughout the globe and cosmos" and ruminates "on the conditions of black existence under slavery" (Rusert 2013, 802). Broaching the overlap of realist and speculative fiction in *Blake*, Jennifer C. Brittan attends to speculations *in* (the investments) as well as speculations *about* (the conjectures) the financial markets of the slave economy, which she reads as "starting points" for a Black futurity that envisions "new geographies of slave mobility and resistance" (Brittan 2019, 82). Political scientist Zamalin, by contrast, concerns himself with the novel's political utopian ideas and their situatedness within the White and Black intellectual currents of the political moment of *Blake*'s publication. Delany's "alternative political theory" (Zamalin 2019, 23), Zamalin contends, reveals race and racism as strategic practices rather than natural sentiments of the White ruling class and imagines Black utopia as an interracial, pluralistic society. However, contrary to the nineteenth-century movement of communal experiments modelled on Charles Fourier's socialist utopianism, *Blake* ultimately falls short of a truly egalitarian vision because the novel sustains a patriarchal capitalist economy under a male ruling class (Zamalin 2019, 21–30). This literature review indicates that Delany's novel blends the utopian desire for and vision of an alternative world with actual changing physical conditions and the protagonist's spatial and temporal travels, which result from an engagement with modern science and extend equally into the realms of the speculative and the fantastical.

In 1994, Mark Dery introduced the conceptual term Afrofuturism which interlinks rather than differentiates these genres. Afrofuturism has since come to categorize a body of works expressive of African American themes and voices that aim to oppose, critique, and intervene in dominant socio-economic, political, and epistemological structures and technological, spatial, and temporal arrangements in order to reimagine and "reinterpret the histories of black subjectivity" (Bennett 2016, 93). Read through such an Afrofuturist lens, Scott showcases the novel's powerful impact on Delany's own contributions to Black emancipation. The author's position during the American Civil War had him—like his protagonist Henry Blake—recruit a large army of Black soldiers for battle, so that Delany's fictional conceptions of the African American freedom struggle indeed came to shape the actual emancipatory process (Scott 2021, 156). Contrary to Rusert, Scott does not register any usage of advanced science or technology in *Blake* and, instead, identifies the novel's Afrofuturism in its "moral persuasion" (Scott 2021, 160) for active resistance.

Zamalin deplores the still underexplored state of Black utopia in the Black literary tradition. He conjectures that the cause for this research gap lies in the fact that "much of black American life has been nothing short of dystopian" (Zamalin 2019, 6). In fact, the paradox of imagining better Black lives by overcoming enslavement while continuing to grapple with the ongoing practices and prejudices that make Black lives worse, characterizes Black utopian imaginaries notwithstanding their hopeful and forward-looking quality. Hence, I propose incorporating the dystopian dimension in the theoretical perspective to the exploration of Black utopian texts as well. To do so, I draw on Broeck's notion of enslavism, which she defines as "that circum-Atlantic modern to postmodern regime which has abjected Black existence from the world of human subjectivity, and sociability" and, furthermore, has "entailed a purposeful absence and denial of interpellation by post-Enlightenment prerogatives of 'freedom,' and 'equality,' which have successfully pre-ordained the status of human-ness for subjects to be able to circulate within conflicting civil and democratic claims at all" (Broeck 2016, par. 10). It is therefore not only the enduring threat of (re)enslavement and (re)colonization which shapes Black utopian dreams, but also the inescapable future deleterious effects—the "afterlife" (Broeck 2017, 138)—of the actual dystopian conditions of Black lives and bodies, regardless of an author's pessimist stance vis-à-vis governmental politics and/or the human condition. The Black utopian imagination in *Blake* is therefore as much entangled with the past and present enslavement of African Americans under the history of slavery in the Americas, as it anticipates the persistent oppression, racial trauma and violence associated with Black lives and bodies that stretches far into the future. This study of Delany's *Blake* aims to expand the examination of its Black utopian dimensions by focusing on the process of individual and collective Black self-formation, which is key to the novel's desired and imagined journey to Black freedom while also taking into account the novel's dystopian tendencies. To do so, I will draw on Du Bois's concept of double consciousness in the context of racialization as well as contemporary Afro-pessimist notions.

THE IM/POSSIBILITY OF BLACK UTOPIA IN
DELANY'S *BLAKE; OR, THE HUTS OF AMERICA*

Although scholarly speculations about the missing final chapters of Delany's *Blake* are plausible when considering that the relevant spring issues of the *Weekly Anglo-African*, in which these last installments would have been published, have not yet been recovered (Levine 2003, 297), it is nevertheless striking that the extant seventy-four chapters can be divided into two equally long parts and indubitably provide an extant "sense of overarching structure" (Shreve 2017, 453). Part I is mostly set in America. Here, the protagonist Henry Blake—also called Carolus Henricus Blacus—first traverses the South to impart his secret mission of a this-worldly as opposed to an otherworldly Christian utopia with an emphasis on the freedom struggle to the enslaved population. Afterwards, he leads other fugitives on one of the standard Underground Railroad routes along the Mississippi Valley through the northern states (Indiana and Michigan) into what today is the province of Ontario (formerly Canada West). In Part II, Blake arrives in Cuba, where he succeeds in liberating and reuniting with his wife Maggie before he departs once more, travelling the route of the Atlantic slave trade to the coast of West Africa and back. Once he returns to Cuba, he witnesses and assists with the founding of an Afro-diasporic nation.

Throughout the novel, powerful cataclysmic metaphors abound, such as Blake's "sowing [the] seeds" (Delany 2017, 74) of White supremacist destruction and Black revolution across the Southern states, or his spreading of a Black revolutionary propaganda "like smallpox" (Delany 2017, 42) among the slaves. While these two metaphors are in keeping with utopian literature as an art that aims to affect, even seduce the audience to the point of dangerously infecting it with what it desires and imagines (Morson 1981, 95–96), Martha Schoolman claims that the reference to the smallpox would have been understood as a reference to "a disease of genocide in the Americas," whose "'viral' quality of unfettered word-of-mouth communication" would make it "a scourge" (Schoolman 2018, 350) directed at the White ruling class. Moreover, the manifold meteorological omens such as sublime sunsets and terrifying thunder, a glorious rainbow after a sinister storm, or promising clear skies replacing threatening clouds, alternately symbolize the characteristic utopian "journey from darkness to light" (Morson 1981, 89), as well as the hopeful prospects and righteous retribution for the oppressed Blacks during the Middle Passage.

The shift in focus to the island of Cuba in Part II seems to suggest that the novel leaves behind Black enslavement in North America so that the desired and imagined utopia is finally established. However, the bloody yet mighty arm of American slavery reaches well beyond the national borders of North America and continues to exert its powers even as the dreamed of Afro-diasporic society gathers in Havana. Indeed, the horrors of slavery consistently intertwine with Blake's travels and efforts to realize a better life and society for his fellow Black brothers and sisters in bondage. Already the opening chapter of *Blake* introduces three White slave traders, whose investments and interests in the slave trade extend across the same geographical regions that Blake traverses in the course of the novel: the South and the North of the United States, as well as Canada in Part I; and Cuba and West Africa in Part II. What both parts of the novel and its geographical relations share is the enormous challenge to unite a scattered Black population.

Both parts of *Blake*, then, dwell on the enslavement of Black people, with Cuba offering a version of slavery that is slightly less restrictive; and both parts show Blake committed to bringing about a full-scale uprising against continued White enslavement. Even though both parts of the novel are permeated by an atmosphere of an imminent Black uprising, higher forces perpetually delay the liberating strike against White supremacy. Given *Blake*'s presently existent seventy-four instead of eighty chapters, the Black revolution remains forever desirable and imaginary. Hence, we have to look somewhere else for Delany's Black utopia, namely Black identity formation—individual and collective—as the key element of an alternative and better way of being Black in the world.

BLACK SELF-FORMATION AND THE GIFT OF SECOND SIGHT IN THE FACE OF SOCIAL DEATH

With the character of Blake, Delany constructs a remarkable Black protagonist. Most immediately obvious is perhaps the resonance of the name Blake and Black with a capital B. Blake is a free, educated Cuban, who was "decoyed away [from his family and home country] when young" (Delany 2017, 18). The beginning of the novel finds him living with his enslaved wife, Maggie, their son, and Maggie's parents in Natchez, Mississippi, on the plantation of Colonel Franks. Despite his status as a free man, it is the separation from his family through the sale of his wife, Maggie, as well as Franks's threat to sell him, which makes Blake acutely aware of his racialized condition. The incident powerfully impresses on him that, based on "race," the White world justifies his and other Blacks' treatment as objects to be exploited and sold at will rather than recognizing and respecting them as self-determined and free persons. Blake's awareness of being racialized, dehumanized, and denied recognition by White American society constitutes what Du Bois calls "two-ness" (Du Bois 2007, 8), an integral element of his concept of double consciousness, a notion which Du Bois expounds not only in his well-known study of *The Souls of Black Folk* (1903), but also in such later works as *Dusk of Dawn* (1940).

The constituent elements and metaphors of Du Bois's theory are the veil, twoness, and second sight. The veil, according to Du Bois, separates Blacks and Whites. Without recognizing Black people nor communicating with them on equal terms, the dominant White society projects its racializing views of Blackness onto the veil. For Blacks, these dominant White projections of Black selfhood result in a sense of twoness, which Du Bois so famously defines in *The Souls of Black Folk*: "an American, a Negro; two souls, two thoughts, two unreconciled strivings; two warring ideals in one dark body" (Du Bois 2007, 8). While Du Bois describes twoness as a burden and source of inner pain that is not to be trivialized, he insists that twoness also harbors the possibility of gaining "second-sight" (Du Bois 2007, 8), that is, Black self-recognition apart from White prejudices and projections. This positive self-recognition involves, as José Itzigsohn and Karida Brown explain, the realization that there exists "a rich cultural and social world behind the veil" (Itzigsohn and Brown 2015, 239). Moreover, twoness enables second sight, which not only makes apparent to Blacks their social invisibility and abject status, but importantly, also presents a "gift" with "the potential ability" to "see other possibilities for organizing the world" (Itzigsohn and Brown 2015, 240). To Du Bois, Itzigsohn and Brown elucidate, there are varying "degrees of awakening" (Itzigsohn and Brown 2015, 241) to second sight, including the possibility that some individuals may not awaken to it at all, but instead fully assimilate into and adopt White society's views, values, and ideology. Those who do attain second sight, however, become acutely and painfully aware of the oppressive strictures and practices that confine them. Yet despite the pain involved in their awareness, Du Bois underscores the importance of second sight for opening up a broadened vision and knowledge of the world as fundamental qualities for resisting the veil and devising ways to counter its pernicious ontological, psychological, and social effects.

Importantly, Delany's protagonist Blake learns about and witnesses the varying conditions of enslavement, as well as the vibrant slave culture behind the veil. An outstanding character among his fellow sisters and brothers in bondage from the very beginning, Blake is repeatedly introduced as "intelligent" and "educated" (Delany 2017, 18), which makes him acutely and painfully aware of the dehumanizing practices of America's White slaveholding society. Thus equipped to advocate for Black self-awareness, self-reliance, and liberation from oppression, and rather than escaping to the North on his own, Delany has Blake take flight from Franks's plantation on a mission to the southern states instead. As Blake explains: "I have laid a scheme, and matured a plan for a general insurrection of the slaves in every state, and the successful overthrow of slavery!" (Delany 2017, 40). The specifics of his scheme remain a well-kept secret throughout the novel. Indeed, Blake and his fellow oppressed sisters and brothers agitate in clandestine "seclusions" (Delany 2017, 75; 84; 104; 121; 123; 250; 251; 253; 256; 257; 293; 311), hidden from the view and knowledge of the White slaveholding powers, who cannot penetrate the veil of their own racializing projections. However, holding these secret meetings is no mean feat in light of the militarized state of the Southern states, which the novel underscores by the tight surveillance and policing of the slave population by the Whites. Even so, the slaves' lives behind the veil testify to their resourceful practices of resistance and provide even the educated Blake with vital knowledge, for example, of how to "charm" (Delany 2017, 91) the hounds of the slave patrols for his survival when entering into such heavily patrolled territories as Arkansas. Hence, despite Blake's characterization as "scholar" (Delany 2017, 70) and activist, who imparts to his fellow sisters and brothers in bondage the secret of this-worldly deliverance and freedom behind the veil, his accelerated travels across the slaveholding states prove to be educational for him and, by implication, the readers, as well. Ultimately, it is Blake's experience of the slaves' culture, collective wisdom, and survival skills which transform his sense of twoness into the gift of second sight, thus providing the first glimpses of a future Black utopia.

The unfolding of Blake's second sight is powerfully illuminated in the stark contrast between the haunting death dance of eleven-year-old Reuben and Blake's many encounters with survivors in and of slavery. The episode of Reuben's death dance, which interrupts the focus on Blake and his movement away from the plantation and into the Southern states, epitomizes Black "humanity quail[ing] in dejected supplication" (Delany 2017, 68). Announced as "some rare sport" (Delany 2017, 67) by Colonel Franks to his guests, among them Judge Ballard (who is a potential future slave owner) from the North, the incident escalates as Franks relentlessly beats Reuben into an unrecognizable mass of blood and "gore" (Delany 2017, 69) despite the child's appeals for mercy. This novel's juxtaposition between Reuben's powerlessness and violent death under the slaveholder's whip and Blake's experience of the remarkable resilience of Black individuals and communities poignantly elucidates the intertwined social dystopia and utopia in the lives of the enslaved African Americans.

In his comparative study of slavery, Orlando Patterson points out two distinct features that define American slavery in particular: firstly, the slave owners' absolute authority over the slaves' bodies and, secondly, the exceeding brutality that brought about and maintained the institutionalized master-slave relationship (Patterson 1982, 2). Indeed, whipping, Patterson argues by quoting the historian George Philip Rawick, "was a device to impress upon the slaves that they were slaves" and, therefore, "a crucial form of social control" (qtd. in Patterson 1982, 3). Reuben's lonely dance under the whip and the eyes of present and future White slave masters symbolizes what Patterson calls the slaves' social death, meaning the enforced severance of all formal and legal socio-cultural ties to ancestors, family, community, or places. As a result, slaves become "disposable" (Patterson 1982, 7) bodies of flesh at the whim and will of their masters. In contrast, Blake's journey across the southern states demonstrates that, behind the veil, the enslaved Blacks manage to sustain life-affirming social bonds through families and communities, at times even a sense of place. They develop and preserve cultural practices of their own, be it their food culture and agricultural knowledge, their labor skills and religious practices. Moreover, the Blacks are knowledgeable in the taming of the bloodhounds and other ways of resistance and possess a deep communal spirit and respect for their elders. Blake's first journey into the American South, therefore, not only confirms his sense of twoness, but also provides him with the gift of second sight, in that his experiences provide an impressive testimony of the dignity, intelligence, and irrepressible spirit of Black lives, among whom there is a remarkable number of those who, in contrast to Reuben, have grown old against the odds.

Among the interpersonal, communal, spatial, and cultural attachments formed by the slave population, one community in particular stands out regarding its utopian promise: the maroon society in the Dismal Swamp. Here, Blake finds a wholly "different atmosphere" and "ample scope for undisturbed action" (Delany 2017, 113) to agitate against enslavement without having to resort to the usual "seclusions" due to the maroons' separation from White society. Even though White America does not officially recognize the maroon community as an independently existing African American society, it still offers a desirable community, in that it recognizes its members as independent selves in relation with each other, their distinct culture, and even the geographical space they occupy. Sean Gerrity, who reads Delany's novel through the lens of marronage and Blake as a maroon figure, likewise underscores the "networks of affective, material, and familial support" (Gerrity 2018, 5) fostered by marronage. Gerrity furthermore reminds us that, contrary to the often-cited Underground Railroad with its South-to-North axis to freedom in American literature and culture, many fugitives actually remained in the South. In fact, as John Hope Franklin and Loren Schweninger's research has shown, many of the runaway slaves stayed "in the vicinity of their owner's residence" (Franklin and Schweninger 1999, 122), which may have been due to their desire to stay close to their family, but also due to their familiarity with the spatial surroundings. In addition, by combining the African art of conjure with the American tradition of revolutionary battle in the historical figures of Gamby Gholar and Maudy Gharnus, two legendary "patriots in the

American Revolution" (Delany 2017, 114), Delany's imagined maroon society features a distinct hybrid culture and history that provides its members with valuable ancestral roots and a memorable past.

But Blake's sojourn with the maroons also displays that Delany's utopian vision adopts some of Euro-American expansionist and millennial spirit of the nineteenth century belief in the inevitable progress of civilization, specifically when Blake views the maroons' "order of High Conjurers" and their "time-honored superstition" (Delany 2017, 115) with mild amusement, even condescension, as "innocent" and "harmless" (Delany 2017, 113). The maroons' lack of modern technological and scientific knowledge, the novel thus seems to imply, hampers their communal autonomy and social emancipation. In fact, many of the maroons "are still long-suffering, hard-laboring slaves on the plantations" (Delany 2017, 113) and, therefore, in an acute state of enslavism. Considering the maroons' "religious material practices" from a purely metaphysical perspective, Rusert argues that Henry "finally assents that conjuring and Christianity are good insofar as their metaphysical pretensions can be used for the ultimate aims of freedom" (Rusert 2013, 818). However, the idea of progress also informs Blake's later meeting with the Native Americans who, as he remarks, have not only "permitted a subjugation of their country" but are also "fast passing away" (Delany 2017, 88).

A hitherto underrated utopian momentum of the maroon society, however, lies in their economic self-reliance which, in turn, is premised on the understanding of their self-ownership as opposed to being the property of White masters. The extradiegetic narrator elucidates that the High Conjurers, who act as the "ambassadors from the Swamp," enact their charms and spells among the adjacent slave population so that "[t]hrough this means the revenue is obtained for keeping up an organized existence in this much-dreaded morass—the Dismal Swamp" (Delany 2017, 115). The maroons' pecuniary self-reliance is among the few instances in *Blake* that provide details about the income sources of African Americans. For those who are still enslaved, however, and who are legally "chattel," two ways of accumulating the necessary monetary means for the escape from slavery and the actualization of self-ownership outside of the maroon community are mentioned: savings from the sale of agricultural foodstuffs and meats, as well as the assertion to one's right to the fruits of one's labor by retaining, as Blake does it, money from "the earnings due [to him] for more than eighteen years' service" (Delany 2017, 32–33) for his master. Yet money, Blake insists, is necessary to end slavery:

> Keep this studiously in mind and impress it as an important part of the scheme of organization, that they [the Black people] must have money, if they want to get free. Money will obtain them every thing [sic] necessary by which to obtain

their liberty. The money is within all their reach if they only knew it was right to take it. . . . You must teach them to take all the money they can get from their masters, to enable them to make the strike without a failure. . . . Bear this in mind; it is your certain passport through the white gap, as I term it (Delany 2017, 44).

What Blake calls the "White Gap to freedom" (Delany 2017, 86) refers to bribing Whites who are reluctant to assist in the slaves' journey to freedom. Upon returning from his missionary as well as educational tour across the South, Blake puts this idea into practice and leads a group of fugitives to Canada. The "out-stretched wings of the eagle" on the dollar bills never fail to convince any white individual to oppose the law of the land and accept the money as "evidence of [the fugitives'] right to pass" (Delany 2017, 143–44). Money also funds Blake's mission in the Southern states as well as other Blacks' pathway to freedom; and upon his arrival in Canada, Blake uses it for "the purchase of fifty acres of land" and "the schooling of the children" (Delany 2017, 156). Although Blake and his family own property in their refuge in Canada, contrary to the maroon society, their settlement in Canada does not possess any noteworthy utopian dimensions and remains the "temporary asylum" (Delany 1883, 362) as which Delany had recommended it in an earlier address at the "National Emigration Convention of Colored People" in Cleveland, Ohio. In fact, the extradiegetic narrator in *Blake* harshly indicts the exclusion of Black people from participating in political and civic life, as Canada bars them "from the enjoyment and practical exercise of every right, except mere suffrage-voting" as well as privileges "common to the slave in every Southern state" of America such as "the right of going into the gallery of a public building" (Delany 2017, 154).

Scholarly perspectives regarding Delany's economic vision in *Blake* are divided. Zamalin, who reads the novel's alternative political theory alongside Delany's other writings—specifically his earlier *The Condition, Elevation, Emigration, and Destiny of the Colored People of the United States* (1852)—identifies him as an ardent admirer of American capitalism and, therefore, sees the novel's utopian vision mired in the dominant capitalist system of exploitation as well (Zamalin 2019, 22–23). Gerrity's reading of Blake as a maroon figure, however, complicates such a clear-cut assessment. He argues that maroons typically inhabit liminal spaces which escape the "regulatory mechanisms of control and domination" (Gerrity 2018, 6), including those of capitalism. Citing Stephanie LeMenager, Gerrity posits that marronage "defie[s] all usages associated with property value in the antebellum United States" (qtd. in Gerrity 2018, 11). Jeffory A. Clymer likewise goes so far as to argue that by redefining Black lives and bodies as human rather than "chattel" in the unfolding Afro-diasporic society and nation in Part II, Delany rejects the central legal and economic fictions of "black property and white human-ity" (Clymer 2003, 717), fictions that were as much bound up with America's domestic economy as with international commerce as the example of the forced separation of Blake and his family illuminates.

Blake's use of money as a means to an end—here reaching a country that formally acknowledges Black people's right over their own minds and bod-ies—certainly appears to show him less as a utopian prophet than a "prag-matist" who "recognize[s] that money is far more effective than conjure in aiding escape from slavery" (Sundquist 1993, 195). Even so, the maroon's self-organized and self-sufficient community still presents a Black utopia of sorts, even though it does not eradicate the logics of nineteenth century Western capitalism according to the radical or socialist ideas of such nine-teenth century American utopianists as Charles Lane, John Humphrey Noyes, or Robert Owen. Despite its capitalist orientation, however, Delany's imag-ined Black swamp society aims at mutual support, the pooling of resources, as well as economic security, much like the relatively few extant Black com-munities organized by White reformers in antebellum America and, more suc-cessfully, in Canada (Pease and Pease 1963, 16–19). In this way, the maroon community prefigures a future alternative, economically self-sufficient society which eschews the dominant system's dehumanizing inequalities and whose members possess ownership over their minds and bodies.

ENTER AFRO-PESSIMISM

On his journey through the American South, Blake also meets with the lead-ers of the Choctaw Nation on their reservation in Arkansas. The encounter is represented in the form of the novel's many dialogues, the didacticism of which is characteristic for utopian fiction (Morson 1981, 94–96), but also represents Blake's expanding horizon and second sight. This time, the con-versation between Blake and the leaders of the Choctaw Nation enlightens about past and future alliances among Blacks and Native Americans against White oppression. In this exchange, Delany takes great pains to set the Indian slaveholders apart from the White slaveholders, in that he includes a White American called Donald (the name choice is highly ironic given the antagonistic relationship between former American president Donald Trump and the Black Lives Matter movement). In *Blake*, Donald, who has married into the tribe for purely personal gain, considers himself ontologically supe-rior to all Blacks, whereas the tribal leader assures Blake that the Choctaw live "side by side with [the] black man, eat with him, drink with him, rest with him" (Delany 2017, 87). Furthermore, Native Americans and Blacks intermarry and fight together against White supremacy. Notably, Bake insists on a distinctly Black condition relative to that of the Indian Nations. Upon the elder Chief's greeting, Blake exclaims: "You are slaveholders, I see, Mr. Culver!" (Delany 2017, 87), and the extradiegetic narrator concludes the dialogue between Blake and the Chief with the ironic observation that this was "the only instance in which [Blake's] seclusions were held with the master instead of the slave" (Delany 2017, 89). The exchange between Blake as the representative of the African American slave population and the Choctaw Nation as standing in for the Native American tribes is thus framed by the idea of the slave status of Blacks as opposed to the master status of the Native Americans, an idea which anticipates a core axiom of current Afro-pessimist thought.

Afro-pessimism defines Blackness by its unique social invisibility and civic exclusion and further considers Blackness as the foundation on which all other kinds of intersectional discriminatory practices rest. Sebastian Weier explains that "Afro-pessimism does not intend to deny or delegitimize the . . . importance of non-black contestations to white hegemony" (Weier 2014, 426), yet leading thinkers like Jared Sexton or Frank B. Wilderson III argue that Native Americans, Latinos, Asians, and other marginalized social groups profit from their non-Blackness as "allies" and "junior partners" (Wilderson 2020, 15; 94) in a White civil society, whose exertion of violence on Blacks asserts their status as human subjects. In short, being racialized as Black means to be a slave.

What Delany's novel and Afro-pessimist thought share despite the vastly different historical contexts and political moments, then, is their insistence on the exceptionalism of Black enslavement as a singular experience which must not be compared to the exploitation and dehumanization of other marginalized groups, including non-Black people of color. Delany thus anticipates the contemporary Afro-pessimist notion of a collective Black identity in which "race" is foregrounded and Blackness becomes an ontological social condition that always already excludes the possibility of being recognized as human, a condition which continually places Blacks at the bottom, even outside of, a hierarchy of racial and ethnic groups, all of which are subordinated to White people. At the same time, Delany and Afro-pessimists would agree that "race" is produced through structures of domination. Indeed, one of the central ideas in *Blake* is the imperative of tearing down the institution of slavery, the violence of which also pervades the characteristic utopian insular setting of Part II, the island of Cuba, on which Blake and other fugitives organize their Afro-diasporic society.

Tommy J. Curry asserts Delany's "pessimism" by pointing out that "the legal and political concept of race was so deeply intertwined in [the] cultural geography" (Curry 2009, 14) of nineteenth century America, that Delany concluded over and over again that for African Americans, equality became an impossible goal within it. Even the island of Cuba remains exposed to the violent structures of slavery. Curry also reminds us that Delany considered "race" an essential component of the identity of a person and collective (Curry 2009, 16). While Curry partly targets what he considers White scholars' cooptation of Delany's work into their own negotiation of "the racist legacy of American liberalism and European philosophy with conciliatory theories of diversity and racial compassion" (Curry 2009, 14), my interest lies not in dis/qualifying Delany and/or Afro-pessimists in order to prove them right or wrong. Rather, my concern lies with how Delany's anticipation of Afro-pessimist thought represents and shapes the Black utopian imaginary in *Blake*. How and what, one might ask, do such tendencies contribute to the African American utopian journey to freedom?

On the one hand, then, in Part II of the novel the nascent Afro-diaspora with its vibrant headquarters on the island of Cuba begins to unfold into a formidable community and coalition against the structures of Black subjugation. After Blake's kindling of the slaves' awareness of their own racialized condition as well as the slave traders' realization of their own part in the racializing process, which is personified in the figure of the wealthy Portuguese slave trader Ludo Draco, the ties of the Afro-diasporic community stretch as far as the US South and the coastal regions of West Africa. Its coalition against White supremacy incorporates the maroons, has valuable allies in the Native Americans, the Cuban mestizas, "Indians and even Chinamen" (Delany 2017, 247), as well as the mixed-race mulattoes of Cuba. Moreover, it unites intellectuals, the merchant and the servant classes. Rebecca Skidmore Biggio therefore argues that for the White slaveholding society, "the threat of black community" is greater "than the threat of black violence," because "both locally and on a national scale, [it] fundamentally undermine[s] the system of slavery by creating a place, albeit unsteady, where slaves [can] see themselves as something more than 'socially dead'" (Biggio 2008, 440). On the other hand, instances of mutilated and broken individuals on Cuba's slave plantations, an African collective traumatized by the horrors of the Middle Passage, as well as renewed anti-Black violence at the end of the novel, still weigh heavily on the promise of the solidifying Afro-diasporic union throughout Part II and continue the narrative of Black social death and abjection that already pervades Part I.

Among those Black persons upon whom their owners exert excessive and brute force, is Blake's wife, Maggie. The violence and torture that she suffers from the hands of her most recent owner not only almost kills her physically, it also damages her psychologically to the point that she herself "can't remember hardly anything" (Delany 2017, 170). As a result, neither she nor Blake recognize each other as husband and wife anymore. Eventually, and with Blake's support, Maggie reclaims herself as a human being and successfully purchases her freedom according to the Cuban law of *coartación*, a practice which by the 1850s increasingly occupied Cuban slave owners, lawyers, judges, and local authorities regarding the rights granted to the slaves against their owners (de la Fuente 2007, 661). Still, slavery inscribes itself upon Maggie's body and mind, in that "the sunken sockets and gray smitten hairs still remained" (Delany 2017, 193) and, contrary to her determined husband, she rather acquiesces to the status quo than agitate for the liberation of all Blacks (Delany 2017, 194).

Despite the fact that Maggie and Blake's happy reunion augurs well for the forthcoming Afro-diaspora, Delany has Blake depart on his last journey on the *Vulture*, the American slaver introduced at the very beginning of the novel, fitted out for the slave trade by businessmen from the US North and South. However, instead of taking over the *Vulture* on its return from the African West coast to free the enslaved Africans, Blake is first and foremost a "witness" (Delany 2017, 225) of the atrocities and trauma of the Middle Passage. Significantly, and rather than indicating failure or disempowerment, Blake's watchful reserve represents the ideal of the "restrained" and "judicious" Black revolutionary of the time, which Black intellectuals and activists like Delany, Theodore Holly, Harriet Jacobs, or Frederick Douglass saw as "the best proof of African Americans' capacity for self-rule" (Schoolman 2018, 352).

Delany's representation of the Middle Passage emphasizes as well as deconstructs the abject condition of the kidnapped Africans. Whipped and branded before they are "pack[ed]" (Delany 2017, 217) into the slaver's hold, they are systematically deracinated, stigmatized, and tortured into submitting to their enslavement. On board, they are "ventilated" (Delany 2017, 234) and given water and food only once a day. Under these inhumane and unhygienic conditions, they are exposed to thirst, malnutrition, suffocation, disease, and uncleanliness "like brutes wallowing in revolting mire" (Delany 2017, 225). Subjected to these dehumanizing conditions without protection, the Blacks are subsequently loathed and devalued as if the effluvia and disease produced by the very conditions of their enslavement were congenital to the prisoners themselves: "The hatches [of the *Vulture*'s hold] being open, those standing nearest fell back from the stench, escaping as if repulsed by an explosion of gas" (Delany 2017, 223). The process of the violent abjection of the African captives culminates in a moment of crisis when, chased by a British vessel policing the sea against America's illicit slave trafficking, the American mate George Royer commands to "[b]ring out the dead, dying and damaged" (Delany 2017, 231) and "heave them overboard" (Delany 2017, 230):

> Then came a scene the most terrible. Men, women and children raging with
> thirst, famished, nauseated with sea sickness, stifled for want of pure air, defiled

and covered with loathsomeness, one by one were brought out, till the number of six hundred were thrown into the mighty deep, and sunk to rise no more till summoned by the trump of heaven in the morning of the General Resurrection of all the dead . . . (Delany 2017, 231).

I want to suggest that Delany's inclusion of the Middle Passage in Part II— the part in which Blake and his family attain their freedom and a spirited Afro-diasporic society and nation arises—points to a continuing pattern of abjection and social death that characterizes the afterlife of slavery for Black lives in the Western hemisphere. The absolute domination experienced by the Black "cargo" in *Blake*, which renders the African slaves ultimately disposable, repugnant flesh to their owners and most of the Euro-American crew on board of the *Vulture*, links the horrors of the Middle Passage seamlessly to Reuben's haunting death dance on the American slave plantation in Part I, as well as all other instances of the social exclusion of Blacks. What all these instances share is what Wilderson calls the phenomenon of "gratuitous violence" (Wilderson 2017, 18) against Blacks. This means that violence is not applied as the consequence of some wrongdoing or to end an economic or political conflict, but as an act that is pleasurable, gratifying, and psychologically reassuring to those who have the authority to wield violence as it confirms and upholds their own humanness. In short, "[v]iolence against the slave sustains a kind of psychic stability for all others who are not slaves" (Wilderson 2017, 19). On the *Vulture*, these master-slave dynamics play out between the American mate, Royer, who epitomizes the White American ruling class and the African captives, whereas Blake functions as a witness of the "heart rending scenes of the living Potter's Field" (Delany 2017, 226) on the slaver. In contrast to Royer, Blake recognizes the Black captives as "grief-stricken" yet nevertheless "impressive" (Delany 2017, 225) and dignified human beings.

Importantly, one of the central claims of Afro-pessimism is that "whereas Slaveness can be separated from Blackness, Blackness cannot exist as other than Slaveness" (Wilderson 2020, 42). With this admittedly controversial position, Afro-pessimists insist that the gratuitous violence and discriminatory practices directed at Blacks as individuals and as a collective do in no way cease with the end of slavery but, on the contrary, persist so that the social exclusion of Blacks is perpetuated on an everyday basis unknown to other marginalized groups. Delany's *Blake* similarly intertwines 'Blackness' and 'Slaveness' in several ways. Firstly, by inserting the trauma of the Middle Passage in between Maggie's manumission and the making of the Afro-diasporic society on the island of Cuba, the novel joins enslavement and emancipation in the hip and, thus, carries forward this thematic nexus from Part I even as it transcends the national focus on America. Secondly, it foregrounds racial identity as central to the socio-political self-formation of the emerging Afro-diaspora. In fact, Blake's racial identity—Delany characterizes him at the beginning of the novel as "a pure negro" (Delany 2017, 18)—is emblematic of the centrality of Blackness in the desired and imagined self-determined community on the island. While this emphasis on Blackness and its "purity" does by no means prohibit diasporic alliances with other oppressed racial groups such as the American maroons, the Cuban mestizas, or the Chinese on the island of Cuba, Delany's Black utopia nevertheless desires and imagines an Afro-diasporic society that is above all defined by its racial identity, namely a Blackness that is "saturated through and through with Africa" (Curry 2009, 16), an idea which the Middle Passage underscores. Placido, one of the mulatto Cuban founders of the Afro-diasporic union, explains the primacy of Blackness for their common identity to Madame Cordera, one of the founding mothers and herself a mulatta, who is suspicious of new racialist hierarchies, as follows:

> The whites assert the natural inferiority of the African as a race: upon this they premise their objections, not only to the blacks, but all who have any affinity with them. You see this position taken by the High Court of America, which declares that persons having African blood in their veins have no rights that white men are bound to respect. Now how are the mixed bloods ever to rise? The thing is plain; . . . The instant an equality of the blacks with the whites is admitted, we being the descendants of the two, must be acknowledged the equals of both. Is not this clear? (Delany 2017, 262).

By placing Blackness at the center of the emerging utopian society, Delany's *Blake* in fact seeks to counter the prevalent nineteenth century belief in racializing hierarchies, according to which specifically people with a mixed Euro-American and African ancestry were considered superior in intellect and potentialities (Ogunleye 1998, 628).

Delany's Afro-diasporic utopia is therefore not, as Zamalin claims, defined by an identity that is "made through choices" or by "interracial intimacy" (Zamalin 2019, 30), but on the contrary marked and distinguished by its racial affinity with Africa. As Placido further elucidates to Madame Cordera, it is on "the African race" (Delany 2017, 161), its material, commercial, and civilizatory potential, on which the prospects of their organized union rests. Here Delany has Placido reclaim the past greatness of Ethiopia's civilization, an idea that significantly shapes later black literary utopian settings from Pauline Hopkins's mythical Tessalar in *Of One Blood: Or, The Hidden Self* (1902–1903) to the 2018 pop cultural Kingdom of Wakanda in Marvel Studio's film *Black Panther* as well.

Among the various allies of the rising Afro-diaspora on the island of Cuba, one group that is noticeably absent in *Blake* is that of the White women's rights movement. Responding to Harriet Beecher Stowe's successful serialized anti-slavery novel *Uncle Tom's Cabin* (1851–1852), Delany's novel is conspicuously silent about Stowe's frequently invoked solidarity among White women and the Black male and female slaves. Although *Blake* shows White women like Cornelia Seeley to be supportive to the plight of Blake and his family, the novel flatly rejects the White matriarchal utopia envisioned by Stowe, in which racial equality can only be achieved in the afterlife through a redemptive death (by Tom or Eva), or by sending the emancipated Blacks and mixed races off to Liberia. Instead, Delany's utopian society distinguishes itself by an emphatic racial solidarity among the men and women that constitute the Afro-diasporic community. While the women are clearly subordinated to the men, in that they are not assigned any of the official posts of the "provisional organization" (Delany 2017, 258), they are nevertheless shown as active socio-political participants, whose concerns and voices have as much weight as those of the men in the decision-making process (Delany 2017, 264). Tolagbe Ogunleye, who points to Delany's advocacy of Black women's cultural, economic, and political education and participation, including their occupation of public positions, even calls him an "Africana womanist" (Ogunleye 1998, 628). But although *Blake* clearly counters the domestic politics of Stowe's *Uncle Tom's Cabin*, the fledgling Afro-diasporic utopia still shows a gendered hierarchy.

BLACK UTOPIA AND THE IM/POSSIBILITY OF NARRATIVE REDEMPTION

If *Blake* rejects Stowe's utopian desire and vision of redemption through, as Elizabeth Ammons has proposed, a Christian maternal savior as epitomized in the figure of Uncle Tom (Ammons 1986, 164), and given the pessimist tendencies as well as the consistent intertwining of dystopian and utopian aspects, what alternative narrative/s of redemption does Delany's novel offer? In view of the Afro-pessimist insistence that Blacks are "bar[red] from the narrative of redemption" (Wilderson 2020, 16) because of the ongoing gratuitous violence that rests on their social death, this question and, indeed, the question whether *Blake* offers any narrative/s of redemption at all, is of particular relevance. It is, however, severely complicated, if not rendered impossible, by the fact that the ending is missing. Hence, any foreseeable triumphant overthrow of White supremacy remains forever suspended. Instead, the novel concludes with the resurgence of a White regime of terror that deliberately stokes up fears against a Black uprising, to which Gofer

Gondolier, the elected Quarter Master General of the Afro-diasporic community, responds with the final outcry: "Woe be unto those devils of whites, I say!" (Delany 2017, 313).

Scholarly perspectives, therefore, diverge between more optimistic readings by, for instance, Robert S. Levine, who predicts that a "regenerated" (Levine 1997, 216) Afro-diasporic society will ultimately rise at the end of the novel without too much bloodshed, a renewal brought about by emigration; whereas scholars of Black Nationalism generally underline the importance of Black separation and "a black Christianity embodying activism" (Khan 1984, 422). Grant Shreve, by contrast, doubts that a "utopian light" can be "found amidst the pervasive suffering" (Shreve 2017, 467) of the extant final chapters. Levine and Shreve to some extent represent the two major scholarly positions regarding Delany's *Blake*, which are offered, at times, as wholly distinct and, at times, as interrelated yet differently accentuated narratives of redemption: one that focuses on the secular political act of liberation, reading Blake's role as that of a Black Moses in the sense of an emigrationist (or nationalist) leader; and one that foregrounds the religious narrative of redemption without, however, losing sight of its political dimensions. Indeed, Shreve convincingly demonstrates that Blake's leadership in Part I represents a theological crisis rather than an alternative theology of a Black exodus, since God at no point bestows divine affirmation on Blake and his scheme. According to Shreve, this part features rather as a "pedagogical project" (Shreve 2017, 459) that teaches the slaves to demand their freedom; whereas it is in Part II that Delany installs one "common religion back into [the] public life" of the Afro-diasporic society, thus "issuing a liberationist call to collective 'redemption' and making the dignity of black people an article of faith" (Shreve 2017, 466).

While I concur with Shreve's claim that the novel also expounds an educational program, I consider the process of Black self-formation that lies at the heart of Part I central to the novel, since without the development of the gift of second sight in a racializing context the emergence of the Black racial identity of the Afro-diasporic society in Part II is inconceivable. What emerges, then, is not a linear, uninterrupted narrative of redemption, but several narrative strands of redemption—whether self-formative, socio-political, nationalist, emigrationist, or religious. These narrative strands of redemption are, time and again, overwhelmed by racial violence and, thus, forever delayed; sometimes they are also, as Shreve shows, aborted. By taking into account Delany's anticipation of Afro-pessimism regarding the ongoing social death and enslavism of Black lives, then, it becomes apparent that *Blake* reveals the possibility of Black redemption itself as brittle, highly precarious, even questionable.

REFERENCES

Ammons, Elizabeth. 1986. "Stowe's Dream of the Mother-Savior: *Uncle Tom's Cabin* and American Women Writers before the 1920s." In *New Essays on Uncle Tom's Cabin*, edited by Eric J. Sundquist, 155–95. Cambridge: Cambridge University Press.

Brittan, Jennifer C. 2019. "Martin R. Delany's Speculative Fiction and the Nineteenth-Century Economy of Slave Conspiracy." *Studies in American Fiction* 46, no. 1 (Spring): 79–102. https://doi.org/10.1353/saf.2019.0003.

Bennett, Michael. 2016. "Afrofuturism." *Computer* 49, no. 4 (April): 92–93.

Biggio, Rebecca Skidmore. 2008. "The Specter of Conspiracy in Martin Delany's *Blake*." *African American Review* 42, no. 3/4 (Fall–Winter): 439–54.

Broeck, Sabine. 2016. "Inequality and (Social) Death." *Rhizomes: Cultural Studies in Emerging Knowledge* 29, no. 1. https://doi.org/10.20415/rhiz/029.e11.

Broeck, Sabine. 2017. "'It is always now' (*Beloved*): Notes on the Urgency of Enslavism Theory, and Studies." *Zeitschrift für Anglistik und Amerikanistik ZAA* 65, no. 2 (June): 137–43. https://doi.org/10.1515/zaa-2017-0016.

Clymer, Jeffory A. 2003. "Martin Delany's *Blake* and the Transnational Politics of Property." *American Literary History* 15, no. 4 (Winter): 709–31.

Curry, Tommy J. 2009. "Doing the Right Thing: An Essay Expressing Concerns toward Tommie Shelby's Reading of Martin R. Delany as a Pragmatic Nationalist in *We Who Are Dark*." *APA Newsletter* 9, no. 1 (Fall): 13–22.

De la Fuente, Alejandro. 2007. "Slaves and the Creation of Legal Rights in Cuba: *Coartación* and *Papel*." *Hispanic American Historical Review* 87, no. 4 (November): 659–92. https://doi.org/10.1215/00182168-2007-039.

Delany, Martin Robinson. 2017. *Blake; or, The Huts of America*. Cambridge: Harvard University Press.

Delany, Martin Robinson. 1883. "Political Destiny of the Colored Race on the American Continent." In *Life and Public Services of Martin R. Delany*, edited by Frank A. Rollin, 327–67. Boston: Lee and Shepard.

Dery, Mark. 1994. "Black to the Future: Interviews with Samuel R. Delany, Greg Tate, and Tricia Rose." In *Flame Wars: The Discourse of Cyberculture*, edited by Mark Dery, 179–222. Durham, NC: Duke University Press.

Du Bois, W. E. B. 2007. *The Souls of Black Folk*. Oxford: Oxford University Press.

Franklin, John Hope, and Loren Schweninger. 1999. *Runaway Slaves: Rebels on the Plantation*. Oxford: Oxford University Press.

Gerrity, Sean. 2018. "Freedom on the Move: Marronage in Martin Delany's *Blake; or, The Huts of America*." *MELUS* 43, no. 3 (Fall): 1–18. https://doi.org/10.1093/melus/mly024.

Gilroy, Paul. 1993. *The Black Atlantic: Modernity and Double Consciousness*. London: Verso.

Itzigsohn, José and Karida Brown. 2015. "Sociology and the Theory of Double Consciousness: W. E. B. Du Bois's Phenomenology of Racialized Subjectivity." *Du Bois Review* 12, no. 2 (Fall): 231–48. https://doi.org/10.1017/S1742058X15000107.

Khan, Robert M. 1984. "The Political Ideology of Martin Delany." *Journal of Black Studies* 14, no. 4 (June): 415–40.

Levine, Robert S. 1997. *Martin Delany, Frederick Douglass, and the Politics of Representative Identity*. Chapel Hill: University of North Carolina Press.

Levine, Robert S., ed. 2003. *Martin R. Delany: A Documentary Reader*. Chapel Hill: University of North Carolina Press.

Levitas, Ruth. 2011. *The Concept of Utopia*. Peter Lang.

McGann, Jerome. 2017. Editor's Note to *Blake; or, The Huts of America*, by Martin R. Delany, xxii-xxxviii. Cambridge: Harvard University Press.

Morson, Gary Saul. 1981. *The Boundaries of Genre: Dostoevsky's Diary of a Writer and the Traditions of Literary Utopia*. Evanston, IL: Northwestern University Press.

Ogunleye, Tolagbe. 1998. "Dr. Martin Robison Delany, 19th-Century Africana Womanist: Reflections on His Avant-Garde Politics Concerning Gender, Colorism, and Nation Building." *Journal of Black Studies* 28, no. 5 (May): 628–49.

Patterson, Orlando. 1982. *Slavery and Social Death: A Comparative Study*. Cambrdige: Harvard University Press.

Pease, William H., and Jane Pease. 1963. *Black Utopia: Negro Communal Experiments in America*. Madison: The State Historical Society of Wisconsin.

Rusert, Britt. 2013. "Delany's Comet: Fugitive Science and the Speculative Imaginary of Emancipation." *American Quarterly* 65, no. 4 (December): 799–829.

Sargent, Lyman Tower. 2020. "African Americans and Utopia: Visions of a Better Life." *Utopian Studies* 31, no. 1 (Spring): 25–96. https://doi.org/10.5325/utopianstudies.31.1.0025.

Scott, Damion Kareem. 2021. "Afrofuturism and Black Futurism: Some Ontological and Semantic Considerations." In *Critical Black Futures: Speculative Theories and Explorations*, edited by Philip Butler, 139–63. Singapore: Palgrave Macmillan. https://doi.org/10.1007/978-981-15-7880-9_8.

Schoolman, Martha. 2018. "Martin Delany, *Blake; or, The Huts of America* (1859–1862)." In *The Handbook of the American Novel of the Nineteenth Century*, edited by Christine Gerhardt, 338–57. Berlin: De Gruyter. https://doi.org/10.1515/9783110481327-019.

Shreve, Grant. 2017. "The Exodus of Martin Delany." *American Literary History* 29, no. 3 (Fall): 449–73. https://doi.org/10.1093/alh/ajx019.

Sundquist, Eric J. 1993. *To Wake the Nations: Race in the Making of American Literature*. Cambridge: Harvard University Press.

Tabone, Mark A. 2019. "Black Power Utopia: African American Utopianism and Revolutionary Prophesy in Black Power-Era Science Fiction." In *Race and Utopian Desire in American Literature and Society*, edited by Patricia Ventura and Edward K. Chan, 59–78. Cham: Palgrave Macmillan. https://doi.org/10.1007/978-3-030-19470-3.

Weier, Sebastian. 2014. "Consider Afro-pessimism." *Amerikastudien / American Studies* 59, no. 3 (Fall): 419–33.

Wilderson III, Frank B. 2017. "Blacks and the Master/Slave Relation." In *Afro-pessimism: An Introduction*, edited by Frank B. Wilderson III, Saidya

Hartmann, Steve Martinot, Jared Sexton, and Hortense J. Spillers, 15–30. Minneapolis: Racked & Dispatched.

Wilderson III, Frank B. 2020. *Afropessmism*. New York: W. W. Norton.

Wilson, Ivy G. 2013. "The Brief Wondrous Life of the *Anglo-African Magazine*; or Antebellum African American Editorial Practice and Its Afterlives." In *Publishing Blackness: Textual Constructions of Race since 1850*, edited by George Hutchinson and John K. Young, 18–38. Ann Arbor: The University of Michigan Press. https://doi.org/10.2307/j.ctv3znzrx.5.

Zamalin, Alex. 2019. *Black Utopia: The History of an Idea from Black Nationalism to Afrofuturism*. New York: Columbia University Press.

Zeugner, John. 1971. "A Note on Martin Delany's *Blake*, and Black Militancy." *Phylon* 32, no. 1 (Spring): 98–105.

Chapter Five

The Phenomenon of Human-Animal Hybridization in Russian Science Fiction of the 20th Century

Anna Toom, Touro University, USA

The author studies two Russian science fiction works: the novel *The Amphibian Man* by Alexander Belyaev and the story *Heart of a Dog* by Mikhail Bulgakov. These works appeared in the 1920s as a response to similar life-events. The young Soviet society, overwhelmed by the idea of revolutionary transformations, developed a tendency to transform everything: from social processes and hierarchies to human nature. Like the few real-life researchers-pioneers in the field of genetic engineering of that time, the main characters of these literary works, prominent scientists and practicing surgeons, experimentally created human-animal hybrids. Belyaev's Doctor Salvator turned a human being into an ichthyander capable of living on land and in the ocean, and Bulgakov's Professor Preobrazhensky managed to humanize a dog.

The present chapter is dedicated to the analysis of life, personality, and tragedy of these outstanding human-animal hybrids of Russian literature. The author also considers the cultural and historical context of these literary works' appearance, conducts their comparative—content as well as genre analysis—and examines their contribution into the world scientific thought.

ON THE HISTORY OF CREATING M. BULGAKOV'S
AND A. BELYAEV'S LITERARY WORKS

Bulgakov's story *Heart of a Dog* was written in 1925, and Belyaev's novel *The Amphibian Man*—in 1927. The appearance of these works, almost simultaneous, was facilitated by the historical situation that had developed in Russia by the mid-1920s.

After the revolution that took place in Russia in 1917, the power of the tsarist monarchy was forcibly replaced by the power of the proletariat. A deep social and ideological split arose in society, which provoked a civil war between the emerging Soviet power ("Red Movement") and its opponents, an economically and socially more advanced class of society ("White Movement"). The five-year bloody war ended with the victory of the Red Army. The country finally entered the path of totalitarian leadership. Devastation and famine reigned in the country.

The ensuing crisis in all spheres of the country's life inevitably manifested itself in the mutual rejection of representatives of different classes: the former bourgeoisie, the intelligentsia, and the clergy suffered oppression from the proletarians, who felt themselves to be the rulers of the country. It was in such an atmosphere that A. Belyaev and M. Bulgakov, both coming from the clergy, created their unique works. To complete the picture, let's add one more stroke from their biography: Belyaev himself was a graduate of a spiritual lyceum, and Bulgakov was a former officer of the White Army.

Meanwhile, the new Soviet government formulated the scientific tasks of paramount importance: the invention of a remedy for aging and the creation of a "new man." The invention of a remedy for aging became so urgent because of the early death of Vladimir Lenin (1870–1924), the head of the Russian Communist Party, the leader of the Soviet government. He was a little over fifty years old, but, according to doctors, his body and brain were completely drained by revolutionary activities. This message caused great concern among other leaders of the state, who also had a long record of revolutionary struggle. They became preoccupied with the idea to find a remedy for premature aging.

It should be noted that at the end of the 19th century—at the beginning of the 20th century, the scientific search for a remedy for premature aging became very fashionable all over the world. The present data is only on the most sensational experiments. In 1889, at the College de France, Charles-Edouard Brown-Sequard (1817–1894), a French physiologist and neurologist, reported that he had rejuvenated himself by injections of an extract prepared from the testicles of guinea pigs and dogs (Britannica, n.d.). His colleague Professor Sergei A. Voronoff (1866–1951), a French endocrinologist and surgeon of

Russian origin, moved from injections to transplantation of the testes from anthropomorphic apes to humans. His experiments happened to be successful and brought their author world fame. Millionaires from leading Western countries were queuing up for the rejuvenation surgeries of Professor Voronoff (Sharifov 2020). In the beginning of the 1920s, Voronoff had performed a few dozen grafting surgeries (Shishkin 2003, 72). The results, while impressive, were not long lasting. After a few years, the effect of "rejuvenation" subsided, giving way to natural aging processes. This caused a general disappointment in the famous surgeon's competence. To this day, the attitude towards him is rather ironic. Only from the position of contemporary medicine it has become obvious that experiments of this kind at the beginning of the 20th century were doomed. It became possible to explain the failure with the incoming of genetics and the discovery of DNA.

Inspired by the successful experiments of S. Voronov, Moscow began preparing for the same operations. In 1925, the first experiments to eliminate premature aging began at the Moscow Institute of Experimental Endocrinology (MIEE). A document has been preserved in the State Archives of the Russian Federation indicating that at the end of December the MIEE placed an order for the purchase of fifty large anthropomorphic apes to transplant their endocrine glands in humans (Shishkin 2003, 75). There is every reason to believe that some high-ranking representatives of the Soviet state underwent rejuvenation surgery. In today's Russian mass media, it is even possible to find the names of those statesmen, but there is no assurance in the reliability of that information. In the Soviet Union, information concerning the life and health of members of the first government and other representatives of the party elite was guarded as vigilantly as the secret of the atomic bomb was guarded later.

The task of creating a "new man" was dictated by the critical situation in the country. After all the cataclysms that occurred involving the deaths of millions of people, mass free labor was needed to raise cities, industry, and agriculture from the ruins. The "new man" was imagined to be extremely physically hardy and obedient—such people were to be used in the most difficult jobs in industry, production, and the army. An urgent need was embodied in an actual social order.

At that time, in Russia there was a scientist whose research plans coincided with the goals of the country's leadership. Ilya Ivanovich Ivanov (1879–1932), Russian zootechnician, developed methods for artificial insemination of animals and was engaged in their intraspecific and interspecific hybridization. In 1910, at the international congress of zoologists in Austria, he announced that his technologies could also be used for crossing Homo sapiens with primates (Rossiianov 2002, 7). Remarkably, such experiments were considered only theoretically in pre-revolutionary Russia; they were banned by the tsarist government for religious and ethical reasons (Shishkin 2003, 93). However, the new times brought new customs and embraced new research endeavors.

The Soviet leaders favorably accepted Ivanov's ideas. His research interested them for its anti-religious nature, so the government funded this project. In an impoverished country, huge amounts of foreign currency were expunged from the Russian economy to fund expeditions to Africa, the purchase of apes, and the building of special nurseries. Experiments on the creation of human-nonhuman hybrids began (Sharifov 2021). All these works were immediately taken under the control of the Russian United State Political Department (OGPU).

It is noteworthy that studies on rejuvenation and the creation of a "new man" were not shrouded in absolute mystery, as it may be customary to think. From time to time, the government shared the scientific achievements with its nation: it was necessary to justify in people's eyes those monstrous losses that Russian culture suffered because of the Bolshevik struggle for power. The discoveries in the field of medicine were discussed at meetings of scientists, published in scientific journals and, sometimes, in the public mass media. Below are just a few examples. They are most directly related to the appearance in the country's cultural life of two literary pieces, to which this work is devoted.

In the early 1920s, a solution was invented that made it possible to revive separate organs of a dead body and keep them alive for a long time (Shishkin 2003, 249–251). In 1924, in Moscow, the book by S. Voronov "Forty-three vaccinations from apes to the man" was published in Russian. (He called his surgeries for transplanting testes "vaccinations" [Shishkin 2003, 111]). In 1926, an article appeared in the collection "Proceedings of the Laboratory of Experimental Biology in the Moscow Zoo" on the transplantation of genital organs in chickens and roosters and the breeding of a special kind of trans-vestite birds (Shishkin 2003, 267). In 1927, the popular scientific journal "Smena" published an article by anthropologist M. Gremyatsky *An extraordinary experience: Is it possible to get offspring from an ape and a human?* (Shishkin 2020, 299). It should be noted that the article was written in beautiful, clear language making scientific ideas intelligible for non-professionals.

The government also informed the public about the most sensational progress in western science. Thus, in January 1928, the "Red Newspaper" reported on the success of the medical clinic of the University of Genoa, where entire groups of endocrine glands, including the pituitary gland, were transplanted to patients, and the insufficiency of which was observed in their bodies (Shishkin 2003, 246–247).

The broad proletarian masses, whose level of interests, spiritual needs, and knowledge were very low, may have not noticed these articles. However, the publications could hardly escape the attention of readers who were intellectually advanced and interested in world events, to which both Mikhail Bulgakov, a physician and writer, and Alexander Belyaev, a lawyer and writer, belonged. According to the memoirs of A. Belyaev's daughter, it was a newspaper article dedicated to the scandal in Argentina with the transplant surgeon Doctor Salvator that stimulated her father to write the novel *The Amphibian Man* (Anatolyev 2019).

As for M. Bulgakov, an important additional source of information for him was his uncle, Professor N. M. Pokrovsky, a well-known practicing gynecologist in Moscow in those years. According to Russian literary critics, he became the prototype of Professor Preobrazhensky in his nephew's story *Heart of a Dog*. Like Belyaev, Bulgakov wrote his story "in hot pursuit" of events in scientific life. When the story was finished, he showed it to friends and colleagues and presented it at literary conferences. The story was well accepted. A contract was signed for its publication. However, M. Bulgakov's story was a satire on Soviet reality, and detractors reported the writer to the OGPU. A hunt took place for the manuscript; it was confiscated, and for several years it ended up in the archives of the Soviet secret services (Bulgakov 1997, 140–44; Chudakova 1988, 843–524). *Heart of a Dog* was published in Russia sixty-two years after it was written and half a century after the death of its author—in the years of *perestroika* and *glasnost* in the former Soviet Union. *Perestroika* is a political rebuilding of the state, and *glastnost* is freedom of speech.

The fate of A. Belyaev's novel *The Amphibian Man* turned out differently. For several years, Belyaev was bedridden with an incurable spinal disease, but in the mid-1920s the illness receded, and he moved from provincial Russia to Petersburg, one of the country's central cities, where he found more opportunities for publishing his works. His novel *The Amphibian Man* was published immediately after its completion in 1928. Moreover, it was produced in three different publishing houses at the same time, and it immediately received the highest readers' recognition. It was reprinted many times and became the first Soviet science fiction bestseller (Kravklis and Levitin 2009, 10; Kharitonov 2018).

M. BULGAKOV'S AND A. BELYAEV'S LITERARY WORKS IN CULTURAL CONTEXT

Varieties of human-nonhuman hybrids are characters in myths and legends of many nations inhabiting our planet. They can be seen in the inscriptions of the pyramids, sculptural images, and cave drawings. One of the most revered gods in Ancient Sumerian mythology and later in West-European mythology of Pre-Christian era was the god Dagan, a half man–half fish (Pott 1997,

194; Stone 2013). The six of the ten most popular characters in Egyptian mythology, were six gods, who were hybrids: with the heads of a crocodile, ibis, jackal and other birds and animals that towered on their human bodies (Pinch 2002). Another famous mythological figure was the Assyrian winged bull-man that adorned palaces and temples of The Mesopotamian Pantheon (Mark 2001). The Great Sphinx of Giza, the most famous hybrid of Ancient Egypt, started a rich tradition: the idea of sphinx was borrowed by Ancient Greeks and Romans (YouTube 2015).

The frequent characters not only of the ancient arts, but also of the Renaissance outstanding painters were Centaurs, human-horse hybrids. In Slavic mythology, centaurs are called polkans, and their images can be still viewed in Russian folk art. Hybrids (sometimes called chimeras, which from a scientific point of view is not quite accurate) adorn the medieval Catholic Cathedral of Our Lady of Paris in France. For millennia, these and many other zoomorphic mythical creatures have been one of the most common narrative themes (Kozhevnikova 2017).

In modern times, the tradition of creating characters that are human-animal hybrids was continued by the English science fiction writer Herbert Wells (1866–1946) in his world-famous novel *The Island of Doctor Moro* in which Dr. Moro, a famous physiologist, who then becomes a disgraced university professor because he makes prohibited vivisections producing hybrid-mutants (Wells 1996). The works of Belyaev and Bulgakov are a continuation of this tradition in Russian cultural thought (Rydel 1978). The main characters of their literary works, prominent scientists and practicing surgeons, experimentally create human-nonhuman hybrids. Belyaev's Doctor Salvator turns a human being into an ichthyander capable of living on land and in the ocean, and Bulgakov's professor Preobrazhensky manages to humanize a dog.

A. Belyaev's novel *The Amphibian Man* had two literary predecessors: the French novel *A man who can live in water* by Jean de la Ire, published in the Parisian newspaper "Le Matin," and the Russian novel *The fish-man* by an anonymous author, published in Petersburg newspaper "Zemshchina" (Zolotonosov 2021). Both novels were published in 1909. Both predecessors of Belyaev's novel about Homo aquaticus were distinguished by extreme politicization. Their main characters, overwhelmed by the idea of world domination, organize an operation to transplant shark gills to a child, and then inspire him with hatred for people. He grows up and becomes a naval saboteur, destroying entire squadrons of ships. In these works, the unique characteristics of fish-people are used by their mentors to consolidate personal power over the world and destabilize the general order—to the detriment of humanity. Both works were soon forgotten by the public. They did not receive a response from readers comparable to that which Belyaev's novel, full of romanticism and lyricism, aroused: first in Russia, and then beyond its borders (Belyaev 1976; Belyaev 2013).

Bulgakov's story *Heart of a Dog* had no literal predecessors. Its plot is in some way unique (Bulgakov 1968; 2004, 217–330). However, the theme of error, oversight, and accident in scientific activity and possible, often fantastic, social consequences of this is presented in Bulgakov's work more than once—he began developing this theme already in the story *Fateful Eggs* written a year earlier (Bulgakov 2004, 127–216). These Bulgakov's works are multifaceted in genre: fantasy, dystopia, and satire on the Russian revolution and the Soviet reality that reigned after it, and on the entire absurd social and everyday order that has developed in the country (Burgin 1978; Doyle 1978). The works are distinguished by such accusatory power, which was not found in any other literary work in Russia of those years.

OUTSTANDING MUTANTS IN THE RUSSIAN SCIENCE FICTION

Sea Monster

He often appeared in the Argentinean Bay of La Plata. He flew over the waves riding a dolphin and blew his horn plunging the coastal population into fear and sending fishermen into a panic. The pearl divers going out to sea on their schooners heard his unfamiliar, unusual voice far from the shore and were horrified. "It's him, the sea devil!" they whispered to each other. "To meet him is more dangerous than meet a shark," they said and left the sea.

Soon the fishermen stopped going out to sea, fearing to meet the "devil." Fishing was reduced and the inhabitants of coastal cities no longer had enough food. The police officers handled the case. They looked for the "devil" for a long time in La Plata Bay and, finding nothing, simply began to arrest the Indians "for spreading false rumors." In the meantime, the "sea devil" had become a favorite topic of newspaper reports in Buenos Aires.

Talk about the appearance of a "sea monster" off the coast of the Atlantic Ocean stirred up the scientific world. An expedition was set up. Scientists failed to meet him, but they closely studied the traces left by him on land and in the sea. The conclusions they came to only exacerbated the mystery: on the ground he moves like a man, but in the water, he swims with the speed of a big fish.

Everything about him was strange and contradictory. He cut the fishermen's nets, preventing them from catching fish, but, at the same time, he put large fish into their boats. Sometimes, he scared people, and other times he saved them from sharks. The crew of the schooner "Jellyfish" once noticed a "sea monster" playing nearby with a group of dolphins. It had a human body and a head with huge eyes like glass balls, silver skin like fish flakes, and hands like frog legs—with long fingers and webs between them. However, the most shocking thing was that it laughed human laughter and screamed in Spanish, in the purest Castilian dialect! Pedro Zurita, captain of the schooner "Jellyfish," made an unexpected discovery: the "sea monster" is endowed with a human mind.

In the meantime, the worries among the people grew. Pearl seekers, hired workers, suffered the most. Their fishing was difficult and dangerous, and the threat of meeting the "sea devil" had been added to all the difficulties now. They could easily lose their jobs for refusing to dive. The ocean had become a curse for them. The "devil" didn't just frighten them—he, they believed, teased them with his independence.

Yet he, cheerful and perky, saddling his sea friend and rushing along the waves, did not understand what horror he instilled in people. He simply felt completely free in the water element, because for him the ocean was a home where he was happy, where his friend the dolphin Leading lived. However, he also had a house on land. This house stood far from the settlements, on a mountain, next to a rock which ended off into the ocean. It was located on a vast territory surrounded by a dense high wall and looked like an impregnable fortress. In this fortress, the "Sea Devil" lived with Doctor Salvator and a dozen black servants.

His name is Ichthyander. He is half human, half fish. The professor calls him "his pride" and "his best work." The professor saved him, a terminally ill baby who was unable to breathe, by implanting in him the gills of a young shark. The surgery was successful, and the professor adopted Ichthyander. He became attached to this unusual boy and loved him like a son. Ichthyander answered to his love and called him "father." Their lives in the professor's house flowed calmly and orderly for many years until one day Ichthyander rescued a drowning girl in the ocean. Love for that earthly girl irreversibly changed his whole life.

Polygraph Polygraphovich Sharikov

Winter. A blizzard howls in the gateway, and a dog's howl echoes it. This is a homeless dog crying from cold and pain. The cook from the public cafeteria splashed boiling water at him and scalded his left side. The dog howls—complains about his unhappy life. Injured, he clung to the cold wall and small bitter dog tears poured from his eyes. He is so terrified that he decided to die in the gateway in the frosty cold.

Suddenly, a gentleman in a luxurious fur coat leaned over him and held out a piece of sausage: "Take it, Sharik, take it." (Sharik means Little Ball and is a popular name for outbred dogs in Russia.) Then he checked if there was a collar on the dog and with the words "you are exactly what I need" took the dog away. A new life began for Sharik.

The gentleman, the well-known professor of medicine in Moscow, Philipp Philippovich Preobrazhensky, led the dog to a magnificent building. The porter opened the door for them. The street dog was invited to a luxurious apartment, treated, and fed. All the following days, Sharik was present at the professor's dinners, each time receiving a piece from the master's table. During the meal, Philipp Philippovich Preobrazhensky liked to talk with his assistant Dr. Bormenthal about how people used to live, about today's Russia, about politics, about art, and Sharik looked at the host with admiration and thought, "This is an outstanding personality, a sage, and a deity." Now, only tears of gratitude rolled from the dog's eyes.

A week later, after Sharik continued to eat well, he fattened up and became strong. Then, the professor fulfilled his scientific dream, for the sake of which he tamed a homeless dog. Together with Dr. Bormental they transplanted human pituitary gland and testes in Sharik. The donor organs belonged to a criminal who was killed in a fight (whose corpse was not claimed by anyone). And the unexpected, simply incredible happened—the dog turned into a humanoid creature. Now, Sharik became a short, ugly man, with a low forehead hanging over his eyebrows and an unpleasant voice. Every day new features and habits appeared; moreover, one trait was more unpleasant than the other.

This man is impolite and disrespectful. He spits on the floor, throws cigarette butts everywhere, swears. He likes vulgar, unaesthetic clothes; at the table, he does not use cutlery, ignoring etiquette. He lies in wait for the housemaid with clearly *abusive* intentions. He also came up with a grandiloquent and ridiculous name for himself—Polygraph Poligrafovich Sharikov (from the Greek *polygraphy* which means the industry engaged in the manufacture of printed products).

From the date of his birth, Polygraph Poligrafovich Sharikov has felt himself unwanted in the professor's home, but he surprisingly quickly found a common language with the proletarians (from the Latin *proletarius* which means *have-nots*). He borrows bad manners, aggressive attitudes, and destructive ideas from them with ease and pleasure. His relations with the residents of the professor's apartment have become more conflictual and his relationships with the proletarians and their leader Shvonder become friendlier. With Shvonder's recommendation, Sharikov gets a job; he becomes a Moscow city department director for elimination of stray cats.

After that day, Sharikov became uncontrollable at home. He lies, steals, abuses alcohol, and when they try to reason with him, he threatens them with a revolver. In the end, he writes a political denunciation on

Professor Preobrazhensky: "He makes counter-revolutionary speeches and even ordered his social servant Zinaida Prokofievna Bunina to throw Engels into the stove . . . " (Bulgakov 1968, 115; Friedrich Engels, 1820–1895—one of the founders of Marxism, a friend and co-author of Carl Marx). A typical consequence of such a letter to OGPU would be a person's arrest. Philipp Philippovich Preobrazhensky avoided any punishment only due to his connection to a powerful member of OGPU, his patient, who *had* received Sharikov's letter and did not open a case. However, Professor's patience came to an end, and as soon as their next clash with Sharikov started, he and Dr. Bormental seized the hooligan, took him to the operating room, and subjected him to another—reversal—surgery.

Shortly after, winter is over. Looking into the professor's office, now you can see Philip Philippovich Preobrazhensky and the faithful dog Sharik sitting peacefully nearby. In the morning, because of the March fog, Sharik suffers from headaches—just where the seam is. But in the warmth of the room in the evening the pain disappears. And then the grateful dog thinks how incredibly lucky it is that the "gray-haired wizard" is keeping him in this luxurious apartment.

GREAT DISCOVERIES OF THE TWO GREAT MASTERS

Doctor Salvator and His Unique Experiments

The name Doctor Salvator was well known to the global scientific community at the beginning of the last century. He was a brilliant surgeon. During the Second World War, he worked in front-line hospitals in France, where he performed complex operations on the brains of the wounded. In America, he dealt with hopeless patients who were abandoned by other surgeons. Thousands of people owe him their salvation. Then he returned to his homeland, Argentina, and took up scientific work in his laboratory. He only healed the indigenous population. They came to him from all the Indian settlements of South America: from Tierra del Fuego and the Amazon, from the desert of Atacama and Asuncion. He enjoyed their accolades as being the glorious wonderworker.

He was a tall and broad-shouldered man with a hooked nose and eagle eyes, incredulous and suspicious. "Every time he looks into my eyes, it's like he is stabbing me with a knife," says Christo, his new servant. All other servants in his household, deprived of the right to speak, lived silently for years obeying the will of the master. His cold gaze instilled fear in people. But not in those whom he helped - they bowed before him. When he examined the sick children brought to him, it was impossible not to admire him. He had unusually mobile and flexible fingers. With these gutta-percha-like fingers and hitherto unseen instruments, Doctor Salvator performed real miracles in his operating room.

Doctor Salvator studied the possibility of transplanting tissues and organs in animals. He was analyzing viability of organs inside or outside the body. As the observation ended, the animals from the laboratory were released into a vast territory within his fortress walls surrounding his laboratory. Hence many unusual creatures lived in the professor's garden: a one-eyed sparrow with a parrot's head, dogs with cat's heads, geese with peacock tails, horned boars, and rams with a puma's body. The most unthinkable and surprising from a scientific point of view were the results of tissue transplantation from fish to mammals.

Doctor Salvator was a reasonable and caring nurturer. In his house, he created for Ichthyander, a unique creature, all the conditions for normal maturation and development. He taught Ichthyander self-discipline, the ability to organize his activities, the regime of staying in water and on land, which is a necessary condition for the life of the latter.

Doctor Salvator also took care of his adopted son's education. Ichthiander received at his disposal a large library, he mastered English and Spanish, mastered the geography of the Earth, astronomy, navigation, and physics. He knew about the races that inhabited the earth, was well versed in botany and zoology, especially in underwater environments, and this allowed Ichthyander to help Doctor Salvator in his scientific research.

One of the daily duties of Ichthyander was to bring to the professor samples of rare plants and metals from the bottom of the sea. The professor taught his son to store knowledge about the ocean, prepared him for collaboration with great scientists and the creation of a work on oceanography which would constitute an epoch in the development of science. He dreamed that Ichthyander would serve all humankind. Doctor Salvator was one of those great scientists and educators who knew how to turn shortcomings into worth, was capable in seeing an interesting and talented child in a problem child—metaphorically speaking, to grow a beautiful flower in infertile soil.

Professor Preobrazhensky and his Advanced Medical Practice

The world-famous Russian surgeon Philipp Philippovich Preobrazhensky lived and worked in post-revolutionary Russia. He did not emigrate to the West, like many of his colleagues, he was still in Moscow in difficult conditions of devastation and hunger. But Philip Philippovich Preobrazhensky had a special status, and therefore, he continued to engage in science and medical practice.

He lived in a privileged house, built before the revolution, in a seven-room apartment, part of which was reserved for an office and an operating room. His servant Zina and the cook Daria Petrovna lived with him. His assistant doctor Bormenthal worked with him. If there were many patients or a situation was critical—in the post-war years, there were frequent interruptions with Moscow transportation—Bormenthal temporarily moved in with his teacher.

The apartment was furnished with antique furniture, the floor was covered with expensive Persian carpets. There was a telephone on the wall in the office. In the half-destroyed Moscow, this was a rarity. The telephone directly connected the professor with his patron, a high-ranking Communist party bureaucrat, an employee of the OGPU, who quickly solved any problem. The life and work of the professor were so unusual that he could not survive without a patron. And that, in turn, led to the required services of such a unique specialist as Philip Philippovich Preobrazhensky.

The professor had a successful surgical practice. He conducted fashionable rejuvenation operations: he transplanted the reproductive organs of large primates to people. From morning until late at night, his waiting room was full of clients interested in his services. This was a creditworthy public. The New Economic Policy (NEP), a short-term reform (1921–1928) based on capitalist principles of economic management, including private trade and the accumulation of private capital, allowed the most enterprising citizens to get rich.

The professor characterizes his activities as eugenics—the improvement of human race. Creative scientists needed new experiments and new results that excited their thought. In the evenings, if Verdi's opera "Aida" was not being performed at the Bolshoi Theater and the Russian Surgical Society did not hold meetings, Philip Philippovich Preobrazhensky stayed home and worked with human brains: he took them out of glass containers, cut and explored them. He was preparing to conduct an experiment, which had no analogue in European science. In a few days, he would have to transplant the man's hypophysis and testes with appendages and spermatic cords to the dog Sharik to determine viability of the hypophysis and its effect on rejuvenation.

It should be noted that the operation was new and unusual, moreover, it took place in the absence of the necessary equipment and medicines, which was natural during the years of devastation in Russia. The professor independently made saline solutions for storing organs and used improvised instruments for craniotomy. The success of the operation was due to his enthusiasm.

Sharik had little chance to survive, but professor Preobrazhensky fought for the dog's life. A fatal outcome was also expected in the first days after the surgery, but the professor continued fighting—he used rare drugs of high demands for renewing blood, revitalizing muscles, and stimulating the experimental patient's heart. Suddenly, his newly created hybrid began to lose hair—the professor invited the leading specialists of the city: a veterinarian and a specialist in skin diseases. Both concluded that the case was unknown in the history of medicine.

Further metamorphosis was swift: the hybrid's body became bald, the tail fell off, barking turned into speech, however, very primitive, the bones of the hind legs lengthened. On the tenth day after the surgery, standing firmly on his feet and grinning, the hybrid swore obscenely at his creator. The professor went into a deep faint.

From this moment on, the product of the experiment evoked only negative feelings in the experimenter. Everything about him was disgusting to the professor: mannerisms, expressions, intentions. Sharikov was not capable of learning anything positive. From the very first days of its existence, he demonstrated a style of behavior and communication characterizing the lowest stratum of society. "Experience!" the Philip Philippovich Preobrazhensky finally exclaimed meaningfully, referring to the street past of the dog Sharik and the life of the social degenerate Chugunkin, the direct ancestors of Sharikov.

The professor's life had become hell. He could not work, was unable to admit patients—he had spent all his time on conflicts with Sharikov. But most importantly, he realized that the scientific rationale for his experiment was wrong. Change of hypophysis did not lead to rejuvenation. Only a great scientist has the courage to acknowledge that he made a mistake unforgivable even to students and not only admit it, but also correct it, no matter what the consequences may have been.

GREAT MISTAKES OF GREAT SCIENCE FICTION CHARACTERS

Utopia of Doctor Salvator

Doctor Salvator kept his experiments secret realizing that the state in which he lived was not yet ready to accept and evaluate them as a unique scientific discovery and knowing that his activity was unacceptable for ordinary consciousness. However, one can't keep such secrets forever. It was a delusion to think that it was possible to hide the results of unimaginable surgeries along with the growth of the experimental animals behind an impenetrable wall, and that all the servants would be silent after taking an oath. For a long time, he succeeded—until he hired an unvetted individual. He let this stranger into the house, and although he was usually incredulous and suspicious, this time he made a mistake and was deceived. A spy entered his house and helped his ill-wishers to uncover his secret.

Misfortune never comes alone. The old Indian Balthazar learned that Ichthyander was his son, whom he considered dead in infancy, and now the Indian was determined to take back Ichthyander. He went to court. At the same time, Zurita, the owner of the schooner "Jellyfish," guessed that Ichthyander was the "sea devil" and developed a plan to capture the "sea toad" capable of making him, Zurita, fabulously rich. It took to eliminate Doctor Salvator. Having collected facts about Salvator's forbidden experimental practice, Zurita also went to court.

At the trial, Doctor Salvator speaks with inspiration about Ichthyander as his beloved son and his best experiment, a unique creation and the first Homo aquaticus on the globe. However, Ichthyander is still imperfect: he cannot descend into the ocean to great depths and does not swim very long distances. In the underwater world, as in any community, there are many inhabitants that have their own hierarchy and their own forms of relationships which are still unknown to Ichthyander, a half-man.

Doctor Salvator underestimated the strength of Ichthyander's human nature—his need for love and affection. Age came, the "biological clock" rang, and Ichthyander fell in love. He began to go ashore more often and was looking for Gutierre on the streets of Buenos Aires. Knowing little about people and their relationships, he behaved somewhat unusually and attracted the attention of others. He often got into unpleasant situations, and Salvator had to save him. Finally, he ended up in prison and managed to get out of there only with his father's help who had grateful patients everywhere, even among employees of the prison.

Doctor Salvator's colleagues, acting as experts at the trial, called him a genius. Indeed, dealing with transplantation and xenotransplantation of organs, he was many decades ahead of his contemporaries. If his professional goal was a utopian one (and in those years when Belyaev wrote his novel, it was utopian), then Salvator was close to achieving it. This is the case when a fairy tale becomes a reality.

Doctor Salvator's creative thought goes far beyond medicine. He reflects on the world's scientific, technical, and ecological problems and ways to solve them. He dreams of exploration of the world ocean. In his speech at the trial, he talks about the water element, as an environment more perfect than dry land. He makes grandiose plans for the reorganization of human society. He is convinced that people, given the opportunity to move to the ocean, would begin to live differently, not like they live on earth. This is, perhaps, Doctor Salvator' biggest utopia. After all, if people have not built an ideal society for many thousands of years of their life on land, then how can they succeed in doing it in a different habitat?

Doctor Salvator is a romantic. He is also a utopian socialist. He is sure that there will be neither poor nor rich in the underwater world—everyone will be equal and, thus, happy. (This description is reminiscent of how some uto-pians of the past imagined communism.) The utopian idea of a happy society of equal people was refuted by reality itself. The historical experience of the USSR has convincingly shown the failure of such a philosophical concept. Perhaps, the Russian cultural and historical roots were not entirely favorable. Maybe the flaw is in the very nature of man. One way or another, several gen-erations of Soviet people, our contemporaries, experienced the impossibility of building communism, more precisely, "communism with a human face."

Delusions of Professor Preobrazhensky

Professor Preobrazhensky went even further in his delusions. He was so self-confident that he allowed himself an adventurous experiment. When transplanting the apes' organs into humans, he received the effects of reju-venation and improvement of people's sexual functioning. But what could be expected by transplanting human glands into a dog? In any case, not that the hybrid would reproduce the features of the transplanted glands' carrier: a recidivist criminal, a drunkard, a brawler, and a deeply asocial being. The professor is shocked and traumatized. The product of his work disgusts him. Due to his disastrous mistake, he has become short-tempered and irritable, and often raises his voice. Patients noticed that he became hunched and turned gray. Therefore, he is punished for his frivolity. How could he, a physi-cian, not know that in cases of animal-human hybridization, one could hardly foresee all the consequences!

Contriving the experiment, Professor Preobrazhensky could not even imagine that the hybrid he reproduced would want to be a member of society and have all human rights. First, to be someone's child, to have, like every-one else, a parent. However, the professor forbade Sharikov to address him as "dad." Soon, the newly born hybrid claimed that he needed a name, then a residence permit, a passport, a job, a living space, and its own family—every-thing that was comparative to people. The professor was extremely dissatis-fied with all this. Finally, Sharikov had a need for comrades with whom there would be a similarity of interests for joint pastime. And he found companions for himself—three street alcoholics, whom the professor immediately kicked out of the door. In addition, as a mentor and adviser, Sharikov chose the Bolshevik ideologist Shvonder, who was very interested in confiscating a part of the professor's apartment and other property for redistributing his wealth in favor of the poor.

Philip Philippovich Preobrazhensky, thanks to his connections with the country's leadership, managed to reduce Shvonder and other insolent prole-tarians down to size. One call to OGPU, and the issue was resolved. Professor Preobrazhensky was needed by political leaders and the Communist party bureaucrats: he prolonged their youth, while they ensured his immunity. But for how long? Once they lost interest in his work—a possibility that could never be ruled out—they would get rid of him. This did not happen in the story, however, the experience of life in the totalitarian Soviet Union allows us to predict such an end of a famous scientist in the 1930s, the Great Terror's era.

Philip Philippovich Preobrazhensky, due to his position and connections, was living quite comfortably even in a half-ruined and hungry Moscow. He dreamt of returning the past with its traditions, customs, and relationships, but he knew that this was no longer possible. He expected to remain in his special status in a country whose order he dissatisfied, and among people who were antipathetic to him. Yet, he believed that it was possible to live in society and be independent from it. This is his biggest misconception.

COMPARATIVE ANALYSIS OF A. BELYAEV'S AND M. BULGAKOV'S LITERARY WORKS

Ichthyander vs. Sharikov

They are diametrically opposed in every way. Ichthyander is tall, athletic, handsome, while Sharikov is small, awkward, and ugly. Unlike Ichthyander with his refined, highly developed, and cultured perception of the environment, Sharikov perceives the world in a primitive and cynical way. Ichthyander is kind, tactful, and empathetic, but Sharikov, on the contrary, is vicious, arrogant, and insensitive. The pupil of Doctor Salvator is open to friendly communication, and his relationships with the household are polite and respectful, while the creation of Professor Preobrazhensky is full of hatred for everyone who differs from him and, especially, for his creator.

Ichthyander is polite to strangers. He observes the norms of behavior even when he is being threatened. In critical situations, he does not lose his self-control. For Sharikov, it is natural to violate the rules of communication—he behaves like an asocial psychopath. Ichthyander is honest even with dangerous people, and gradually learns to be cautious. Sharikov is deceitful and lies even to those who have nurtured him from birth; he has no conscience.

Ichthyander has a romantic attitude towards a woman. He fell in love with Guttiere, an earthly girl. For her, he risks his life and almost dies. Sharikov, on the contrary, does not know the feeling of love. He is guided exclusively by primal instincts. And if the smart cook Darya Petrovna had not intervened in time, he would have raped Zina, the young maid.

The negative actions of Ichthyander are dictated more by naivety than by evil intentions. He cuts the fishermen's nets not to hurt people, but out of a desire to save the fish. He does not understand that people need "more fish than they can eat" not out of greed, but to provide food for the population of the city. Ichthyander poorly understands life outside his home—the concepts of buying and selling are unknown to him. In Sharikov, even at first glance, positive actions are associated only with negative attitudes. He strums the balalaika all day long, not considering that loud sounds interfere with the professor's work, not thinking that all the people around him need rest. The interests and desires of others, even those to whom he depends, are of no concern to him.

Ichthyander saves both people drowning in the ocean and fish thrown ashore by a storm. He treated and fed a young dolphin that hurt its fin, and they became best friends. Ichthyander has a "kind heart." Sharikov's heart is a "dog's heart": even turned into a human, he instinctively attacks birds and cats.

So, gifted and capable of improvement Ichthyander, on the one hand, and primitive, guided by base instincts and uncontrollable malice of Sharikov, on the other. One is pleasant, the other is disgusting. One is decent, the other is obscene. One is virtuous, the other is vicious. This list is endless. It is difficult to find characters more dissimilar to each other. But for all their differences, there is something that they have in common. They are human-nonhuman hybrids, and this dual nature is the cause of their deep discomfort. This creates an insurmountable barrier between them and their environments: in Ichthyander with the whole community of people outside his home, in Sharikov with all the inhabitants inside his household.

Doctor Salvator vs. Professor Preobrazhensky

They are innovators. They even have "speaking" names: Salvator is a word of Latin origin and means "rescuer," and Preobrazhensky in Russian means "transformer." But like their creations, the creators are not at all like each other. The only thing they have in common is that they are both creators of their own destiny.

Professor Preobrazhensky has a high position in the society due to his very successful scientific career and engagement in surgical practice back in pre-revolutionary times which brought him a large income. This explains his way of life: in a privileged house, with excellent living conditions, rich furnishings, home operating room, and a few servants. As for Doctor Salvator, he secured his high position in society by engaging in surgical practice and selling land. His wealth, well-equipped estate with a hospital and a rehabilitation center, a swimming pool, a zoo, and a dozen servants are the fruits of his hard labor.

Doctor Salvator treats only Indians—representatives of the exterminated population of the Americas, that is, those who were unjustly expelled from their lands. He helps people who are on the lowest rung of the social ladder, humiliated, and offended. He does not receive any benefits from his activities, except for the improvement of his skills and the satisfaction of a sense of justice. In contrast to him, Professor Preobrazhensky treats wealthy businessmen and party bureaucrats, i.e., those who after the revolution of 1917 found themselves on the highest rung of the social ladder. They pay well for treatment and protect the vulnerable professor from the proletarians. Professor Preobrazhensky, performing fashionable rejuvenation operations, not only maintains his scientific status, but also receives considerable materialistic benefits.

Doctor Salvator has been charged with illegal activities, but he does not consider his research reprehensible. He sees that society and nature are imperfect and knows how to change them. His bold experiments with animals and Ichthyander are an attempt to correct the mistakes of nature. He always feels confident, even in the courtroom, under the threat of punishment. Meanwhile, no one has charged Professor Preobrazhensky. He is admired. Moscow is full of rumors about a skillful surgeon. Citizens crowd around the building where he lives, hoping to see a "talking little dog." He passes his own judgement—calls himself an old donkey whose discovery is not worth a penny. He confesses to his assistant, Bormental, that he feels hopelessness.

With all these dissimilarities one thing is invariable—the stories' tragic ends. The creators of the hybrids are punished for what they did in one way or another, and their creations forever leave the human world, in which they are not destined to get along.

These creators separate with their creations in different ways. Doctor Salvator loves Ichthyander and feels responsible for his life. In a world ruled by power and money, defenseless Ichthyander, a half-human, is threatened by slavery in business or in the army. Salvator lets his son go into the ocean to provide him with a better future. In contrast to Salvator, Professor Preobrazhensky is horrified by the creature that he brought into the world, and he feels responsible rather for the life of the society in which Sharikov will live. In a country full of aggressive and ignorant proletarians, Sharikov will undoubtedly get along and only increase evil. Professor Preobrazhensky gets rid of Sharikov—turns him back into a dog to protect himself, all in his household, and the future of the country from this moral freak.

Belyaev's Utopia vs. Bulgakov's Dystopia

Belyaev's novel *The Amphibian Man* is a classic example of utopian fiction. The character Doctor Salvator knows how to change an imperfect world, making it bright and fair. He with his unique knowledge and skills are already on the way to this future. And he created a man of the future: Ichthyander is the first inhabitant of the Underwater Republic. The Doctor's ideas about this Republic are very positive: it is a world where the inhabitants will not harm each other, where goodness will reign, and everyone will be happy.

Belyaev's novel is inspirational and encouraging. The author tells about the best features of human nature: the ability to love and sacrifice. Ichthyander sacrificed himself to confess his love to Gutierre. Doctor Salvator, a loving father, sacrificed himself to save Ichthyander's life. In the conflict between good and evil, goodness eventually wins. Doctor Salvator, after serving his sentence, returned home, and intended to soon reunite with his son on the distant islands of the Pacific Ocean.

Bulgakov's story *Heart of a Dog* is an example of dystopian fiction. The character, Professor Preobrazhensky, has an extremely negative attitude towards the society in which he lives. He is antipathetic to the lack of culture of the "new people" that appeared with the revolution: their inability to work, unwillingness to maintain established traditions, including cleanliness and order in the building, and their absolute disrespect for others' private property. The professor warns of the possible negative consequences that ignorant and insolent people endowed with power can lead to. He opposes the proletarians, yet, unwittingly, he creates with his own hands an immoral being. His positive intention led to a terrifying consequence, and this, too, is an attribute of a dystopian work.

The ideas of Professor Preobrazhensky about the future of the country are gloomy and hopeless. It is not in his power to abolish the order that has developed in the country, but he can eliminate the fruit of his labor. The optimistic end of the story dissonates with its general pessimistic orientation, but the contradiction is inherent in Bulgakov as an author, this does not change the general spirit of the work.

The plot of *The Amphibian Man* is built in realistic traditions. Alexander Belyaev's text is a "clear text"—the reality he describes is perceived literally and does not require the ability to read "between the lines." Another thing is the story *Heart of a Dog*. Bulgakov's text is replete with hints, has a double content that must be deciphered to adequately understand what is happening. Being a medical doctor himself, Bulgakov, of course, knew that the transplantation of human hypophysis into a dog could not lead to a dog's transformation into a human. This unrealistic effect is used by him for the pointed meaning of the plot. Bulgakov is a master of satirical dystopia based on allegories.

Professor Preobrazhensky sings some opera verses all the time, yet at the same time he is annoyed by the choral singing of the proletarians. That's because the choral singing in Bulgakov's work is an allegory of a new political system, which the professor hates.

Sharikov, having become a Soviet bureaucrat, fanatically exterminates stray cats in the capital. And these city-cleansing operations that he organizes are an allegory for a sinister trend that has been brewing. In less than ten years, mass arrests and the destruction of dissidents will begin in the country of victorious socialism.

Science fiction writers are visionaries. In their works, Belyaev and Bulgakov could foresee the future of mankind and society. Belyaev focused on the psychological image of Homo aquaticus. Ichthyander has abilities unusual for ordinary people. The writer described them with ingenuity, with detail, and with color. His character has auditory and tactile hypersensitivity—being at a depth, he senses the approach of a shark by the vibrations of the water with his back. He has an especially developed sense of time, and it is coordinated with the speed of his movement in the water: he sleeps, carried by the undercurrent, but wakes up unmistakably when it is necessary to change the direction of movement. This is a description of Ichthyander's extrasensory perception.

In Russia, the scientific study of this phenomenon began half a century after *The Amphibian Man* publication. Officially, its existence has not been recognized, but in investigative practice, specialists often and quite successfully use the help of individuals with extrasensory perception (Britannica, n.d.) Scientists do research, doubt, and argue till now (Rhine 1935; Hansel 1980, 86–122; Targ 2012). Perhaps, Alexander Belyaev with his great intuition of a science fiction writer anticipated the evolutionary direction of the human psyche's development for centuries ahead.

Bulgakov's story has an allegorical plot, in which the social transformation of the 20th-century's Russia is guessed. The violent surgery to create a human-animal hybrid is a symbol of the revolution that forcibly led to a change in political power in the country. The medical error of Professor Preobrazhensky almost ended tragically for him and others in his household, but he put an end to his unsuccessful experiment in time. But the mistake of Russian political leaders in real life led to a social catastrophe for the whole 70 years. In his story *Heart of a Dog*, Mikhail Bulgakov predicted the direction of Soviet society's development as well as the fate of the totalitarian system in general. This was his warning, which, unfortunately, saw the light of day already at sunset of the Soviet regime.

In the works of Belyaev and Bulgakov that were devoted to the creation of human-animal hybrids, issues of the experimentation with animals and people are raised. Doctor Salvator is charged for an illegal surgery made to a child with the purpose of changing his body's structure. The prosecutor and the bishop in collaboration issued a sentence to him—ten years in prison. Professor Preobrazhensky was not charged for the unlawful use of the animal for scientific purposes because in a country where chaos and permissiveness reigned, no one cared about experimental ethics. But constant quarrels with his creation led Philip Philippovich Preobrazhensky to become aware of the moral aspect of his action. In their works written in the 1920s, science fiction writers have touched on many aspects of medical ethics that were comprehended and legalized by the Russian scientific community only by the end of the century.

ETHICS OF CREATING HYBRIDS IN 20TH CENTURY'S RUSSIAN SCIENCE FICTION

Although the ethical principles of experimental surgery on animals and humans had not yet been formulated in the early 1920s, both surgeons intuitively followed these principles in their work. Philip Philippovich Preobrazhensky, having brought a street dog into the house, first sent it to the examination room and treated its scalded side. And then he fattened the dog for two weeks, despite the reproaches of the servants, "He eats a lot!," "I'm surprised it doesn't pop!" (Bulgakov 2004, 255). The actions of Professor Preobrazhensky are consistent with *the principle of responsibility* for experimental animals, which will appear in world medical practice only in the second half of the 20th century (American Psychological Association, n.d.)

The dog underwent surgery under chloroform anesthesia. This is far from the best means of anesthesia, but apparently there were no alternatives in those years in the country. To prevent the dog from dying during the operation, it received two injections of adrenaline into the heart. Anesthetization and resuscitation of the heart comply with *the principle of exclusion of suffering*. The professor from a science fiction story was thirty-five years ahead of the scientists Russell and Burch who formulated this rule in their book *The Principles of Humane Experimental Technique* (Johns Hopkins University, n.d.)

Philip Philippovich Preobrazhensky also took care of the hybrid, providing him with the necessary treatment, shelter, food, and clothing. He tried to instill good manners in the hybrid, but to no avail. From the first days, the hybrid behaved uncontrollably, and he became more and more dangerous every day after. He simply left his creator no other choice—so the professor turned him back into a dog. But even after that, following *the principle of responsibility*, the professor did not drive Sharik away, he kept the animal to live with him.

Doctor Salvator also did not rid of the experimental animals. He settled them in a large garden surrounding his house. Salvator created excellent living conditions for Ichthyander as well. He treated him like a son and never forgot that his son was a special being. He helped whenever Ichthyander was in trouble. He came into a conflict with Zurita, the owner of a pearling business, who was hunting Ichthyander. In the end, he saved Ichthyander's life at the cost of his own freedom. Only one person could escape from the prison where they were both placed, and Doctor Salvator yielded this opportunity to his son.

This was not without the intrigues of enemies who dreamed of getting rid of Salvator to enslave Ichthyander. Salvator was summoned to appear before the court. The accusation was largely false. The doctor did not kidnap the baby—the baby was brought to him and given as an orphan. Transplantation proved to be the only way to save the life of the dying newborn. After that, special care and a mode of life were needed, which poor and uneducated people could not provide to a hybrid-boy. Doctor Salvator was the only one able to raise him, and he resolutely coped with such a task.

In his defendant's statement, Salvator told of Ichthyander as his exceptional scientific success. It's not just the biology and body structure of the hybrid, which happened to be flawless, but also, Ichthyander, being Homo aquaticus, had a human psychology. This unique case was not appreciated even by medical experts invited to the court. The surgical technologies of Doctor Salvator were many decades ahead of the knowledge of his contemporaries. The ethical aspects of xenotransplantology, which he was guided by, will be developed in world medicine only by the third millennium.

Today, as organ transplantation has become a common practice and xeno-transplantation technology has been mastered, experts are raising questions about the admissibility and limits of redesigning the human body (Fan 2019). The concern is that human identity and body integrity may be violated after animal biomaterial transplants (Ushakov 2017). Ichthyander was exceptional in that he did not lose his human integrity and identity. However, this is not so easy to achieve in real experiments.

Also, scientists predict an ethical paradox that the production of human-like hybrids can cause in society. Their appearance will inevitably lead to a social disorder because, to exist, they will claim all human rights (Hubner 2018). An ideal illustration of such an ethical conflict is Polygraph Polygraphovich Sharikov whose problems were impossible to resolve even in the science fiction story.

Another important ethical aspect of the creation of hybrids is the rejection of demi-humans by society, the denial of their social rights because of their, from the point of view of society, inferiority. In Belyaev's novel, people just destroyed the human component in Ichthyander, forcing him to spend a long time in the ocean, collecting pearls for them, and he forever lost the ability to breathe with his lungs.

The character of the story *The Heart of a Dog*, Professor Preobrazhensky, picked up a stray dog for the experiment, used the donor material of a dead homeless person, and, having completely protected himself from possible legal claims, performed the operation. But its outcome, although biologically successful, turned out to be socially disastrous—the cute dog turned into a bandit. Unable to withstand the shock, the professor performed a reversal surgery.

True, in that three-week period, while the dog was a man, he made an accusation against his creator, "Did I ask you for the operation? Maybe I gave you no permission to operate? . . . and likewise, my relatives. I have the right to sue you, maybe" (Bulgakov 1968, 70). Such a claim looks absurd (who asks permission from stray dogs!), but in principle, it is not meaningless. And the threat to sue Philip Philippovich Preobrazhensky which is also inadequate may have become justified under other circumstances.

Sharikov is a demagogue, and there is no logic in his demands. However, the conflict between the characters is indicative—it touches upon an important aspect of the surgeon's research work with human subjects. Only a quarter of a century after Bulgakov wrote the story, *the principle of voluntary and informed consent* to participate in an experiment came into use (World Medical Association 2013).

Sometime after the reversal surgery, the criminal police came to the professor's apartment with a search warrant and intention to accuse all the inhabitants of the household of the murder of Polygraph Poligrafovich Sharikov. The professor showed them a still-walking creature, but already overgrown with fur and barking like a dog. The confused authorities left with nothing.

CONCLUSION

In science fiction literature, the theme of human-animal hybridization is not widespread. Its founder was the great English writer Herbert Wells, author of *Moreau's Island* (1896). More than a quarter of the century later, in the early 1920s, Alexander Belyaev's *The Amphibian Man* and Mikhail Bulgakov's *Heart of a Dog* appeared in post-war and half-destroyed Russia. They have been considered outstanding works of Russian science fiction. There was no significant continuation in world literature.

The novel *The Amphibian Man* belongs to the genre of romantic utopia; the story *Heart of a Dog* is a satirical dystopia. Despite all the differences between them, they pursue the same humanistic goal. Their heroes, the brilliant surgeons Dr. Salvator and Professor Preobrazhensky, mastered the unique operations of interspecies organ transplantation long before xeno-transplantology was recognized as a science and legalized medical practice. Writers A. Belyaev and M. Bulgakov foresaw social, psychological, and moral problems on the way of experimental improvement of Homo sapience.

It is noteworthy that world medicine has not followed the path of human-animal hybridization in its initial form. The advent of genetics and the discovery of DNA in the mid-20th century offered more effective ways to improve human nature. Ichthyander and especially Sharikov have remained in the realm of fantasy. Despite this, the works of Belyaev and Bulgakov are among the greatest examples of literature, as well as philosophical and ethical thought.

Bulgakov, having used Polygraph Poligrafovich Sharikov as allegory of an ugly political society born by revolution, for several decades ahead anticipated a collapse of Soviet power. Belyaev, having created the image of Ichthyander, a representative of the next evolutionary stage, for centuries ahead predicted a possible direction of development of the human psyche. These works touched upon the ethical issues of experimentation with humans and animals long before the advent of the science of bioethics. Both writers foresaw the existential problems that may threaten the world community due to the appearance of a new race of human-animal hybrids in it.

Ichthyander (*The Amphibian Man*) and Polygraph Poligrafovich Sharikov (*Heart of a Dog*) are outstanding human-animal hybrids of Russian science fiction. It is difficult to imagine creatures more dissimilar to each other than these "products of scientific experiments." One is the embodiment of virtue; the other is the personification of vice. However, with all the differences, one thing remains invariable—the tragic end of their stories. The creators of these hybrids are punished in one or the other way—according to the law of the court or conscience—and their creations forever leave the human world in which they are not destined to survive.

REFERENCES

American Psychological Association. n.d. "Guidelines for Ethical Conduct in the Care and Use of Nonhuman Animals in Research." Retrieved February 25, 2022 from https://www.apa.org/science/leadership/care/care-animal-guidelines.pdf.

Anatolyev, Alexei. 2019. "Naprasnaya Zhertva" ("Wasted Sacrifice"). *Premier* 11, no.1112. Last modified March 19, 2019. Retrieved February 25, 2022 from https://premier.region35.ru/article/naprasnaya-zhertva.

Belyaev, Alexander. 1976. "Chelovek-Amphibiya" ("The Amphibian Man"). In *Science Fiction.* Leningrad: Lenizdat.

Belyaev, Alexander. 2013. *The Amphibian Man.* Translated by Maria Kuroshchepova. TSK Group LLC.

Britannica. n.d. "Brown-Sequard." Retrieved February 25, 2022 from https://www.britannica.com/biography/Charles-"Edouard-Brown-Sequard.

Britannica. n.d. "Extrasensory Perception." Retrieved February 25, 2022 from https://www.britannica.com/topic/extrasensory-perception.

Bulgakov, Mikhail. 1968. *Heart of a Dog.* Translated by Mirra Ginsburg. New York: Grove Press.

Bulgakov, Mikhail. 2004. "Sobach'e Serdtse" ("Heart of a Dog"). In *Collection of Works*, 3. Sanct-Petersburg: Azbuka-Classica.

Bulgakov, Mikhail. 1997. *Dnevnik. Pis'ma. 1914–1940. (Diary. Letters. 1914–1940).* Moscow: Contemporary Writer.

Burgin, Diana. 1978. "Bulgakov's Early Tragedy of the Scientist-Creator: An Interpretation of *Heart of a Dog*." *Slavic and East European Journal* 22, n.o.4: 494–508. Retrieved February 25, 2022 from http://m-bulgakov.ru/publikacii/nasledie-mihaila-bulgakova-v-sovremennih-tolkovaniyah/p9.

Chudakova, Marietta. 1988. "About Memoirs and Memoirists. (Instead of Preface)." In *Memories of Mikhail Bulgakov*, edited by M.Ya. Malkhazova and O.V. Timofeeva. Moscow: Soviet Writer.

Doyle, Peter. 1978. "Bulgakov's Satirical View on Revolution in *Fateful Eggs* and *Heart of a Dog*." *Canadian Slavonic Papers* 20 (4): 467–482.

Fan, Shelly. 2019. "Wait, What? The First Human-Monkey Hybrid Embryo Was Just Created in China." SyngularityHub. Retrieved February 25, 2022 from https://singularityhub.com/2019/08/13/wait-what-the-first-human-monkey-hybrid-embryo-was-just-created-in-china.

Hansel, Charles. 1980. *ESP and parapsychology: a critical reevaluation.* Buffalo, N.Y.: Prometheus Books.

Hubner, Dietmar. 2018. "Human-Animal Chimeras and Hybrids: An Ethical Paradox behind Moral Confusion?" *The Journal of Medicine and Philosophy* 43, no. 2 (April): 187–210. https://doi:doi:10.1093/jmp/jhx036.

Johns Hopkins University. n.d. "The Principles of Humane Experimental Technique." Retrieved January 25, 2022 from https://caat.jhsph.edu/principles/the-principles-of-humane-experimental-technique.

Kravklis, Nelli, and Michael Levitin. 2009. "Tri zhizni pisatelya (A.R. Belyaev)" ("Three lives of a writer—A.R. Belyaev"). *Science and Life* 10–11. Last modified March 3, 2022. Retrieved February 25, 2022 from https://www.nkj.ru/archive/articles/16565.

Kharitonov, Yevgeniy. 2018. "Pervyi Sovetskii Bestseller, ili Ihtiandru—90!" (The first Soviet bestseller, or Ichthyander turns to 90!). *Territory,* May 2, 2018. Retrieved February 25, 2022 from https://gazetargub.ru/?p=7743.

Kozhevnikova, M. 2017. *Hybrids and chimaeras of human and animal: from mythology to biotechnology.* Moscow: IFRAN.

Mark, Joshua. 2001. The Mesopotamian Pantheon. *World History Encyclopedia, February 25, 2011.* Retrieved February 25, 2022 from https://www.worldhistory.org/article/221/the-mesopotamian-pantheon.

Pinch, Geraldine. 2002. *Egyptian Mythology: A guide to the Goods, Goddesses, and Traditions of Ancient Egypt.* London: Oxford University Press.

Pott, D. T. (1997). *Mesopotamian Civilization. The Material Foundations.* London: The Athlone Press.

Rhine, Joseph. 1935. *Extra-sensory Perception.* London: Farber and Farber.

Rydel, Christine. 1978. Bulgakov and H.G. Wells. *Russian Literature Triquarterly* 15: 293–311. Retrieved February 25, 2022 from http://m-bulgakov.ru/publikacii/nasledie-mihaila-bulgakova-v-sovremennih-tolkovaniyah/p9.

Rossiianov, Kirill. 2002. "Beyond Species: Ilya Ivanov and His Experiments on Crossbreeding Humans with Anthropoid Apes." *Science in Context* 15 (2): 277–316. https://doi:10.1017/S0269889702000455.

Sharifov, Arthur. 2020. "Kak borolis' so stareniem" (How they were fighting aging). Video, 24:30. Project Home Science. Retrieved February 25, 2022 from https://www.youtube.com/watch?v=no8JxJ-4UGE.

Sharifov, Arthur. 2021. "On oplodotvoryal obez'yan. Neetichnye eksperimenty, no. 4. (He impregnated monkeys. Unethical experiments № 4). Video, 29:50. Retrieved February 25, 2022 from https://www.youtube.com/watch?v=KpVf3kyHapY.

Shishkin, Oleg. 2003. *Krasnyi Frankenshtein: Sekretnye Eksperimenty Kremlya.* (*Red Frankenstein: Secret Experiments of the Kremlin.*) Moscow: Ultra. Culture.

Stone, Adam. 2013. "Dagan (God)." *Ancient Mesopotamian Gods and Goddesses.* London: Oracc and the UK Higher Education Academy. Retrieved February 25, 2022 from http://oracc.museum.upenn.edu/amgg/listofdeities/dagan.

Targ, Russell. 2012. The Reality of ESP: A Physicist's Proof of Psychic Abilities. Wheaton, IL: Quest Books.

Ushakov, Evgeniy B. 2017. "Ksenotransplantazia" (Xenotransplantation). In *Bioethics.* Studme.org. Retrieved February 20, 2022 from https://studme.org/97757/etika_i_estetika/bioetika#google_vignette.

Wells, Herbert. 1996. *The Island of Doctor Moreau.* New York: Dover Publications.

World Medical Association. 2013. "WMA Declaration of Helsinki: Ethical Principles for Medical Research Involving Human Subjects." JAMA. Last modified July 9, 2018. Retrieved February 25, 2022 from https://www.wma.net/policies-post/wma-declaration-of-helsinki-ethical-principles-for-medical-research-involving-human-subjects.

YouTube, n.d. "Great Sphinx of Giza, Egypt." Video, 2:17. Retrieved February 26, 2022 from https://www.youtube.com/watch?v=e4jJpQsrxXw.

Zolotonosov, Mikhail. 2021. "Ihtiandr Navsegda. Otkuda Alexandr Belyaev Vzyal Cheloveka-Amfibiyu" (Ichthyander forever. Where did Alexander Belyaev Get the Amphibian Man from). *City 812.* Retrieved February 25, 2022 from https://gorod -812.ru/ihtiandr-navsegda-otkuda-aleksandr-belyaev-vzyal-cheloveka-amfibiyu.

Chapter Six

Barjavel, *Ravage*

roman extraordinaire (1943)

Bernard Montoneri, Independent
Researcher, Taiwan
Murielle El Hajj, Lusail University, Qatar

This chapter introduces René Barjavel (1911–1985), a French author and
journalist more famous in the French-speaking world than in Anglo-Saxon
countries, despite the fact that he is was one of the pioneers of science fiction
and time travel (the grandfather paradox in *Future Times Three*; French: *Le
Voyageur imprudent*, 1944). *Ashes, Ashes* (French: Ravage, 1943) is a science fiction novel set in 2052 France. The protagonist, 22-year-old François
Deschamps leads a small group of survivors after the sudden disappearance of electricity that causes chaos and destruction in France. This chapter
presents Barjavel, his life and work, the author's motivation and sources of
inspiration, a detailed summary of the novel, the main characters, the influence of absurdism and examples of irony. It then analyzes several themes,
such as Paris in 2052 before the apocalypse (technology/society), censorship
and control, presents a comparison with *Fahrenheit 451*, the technocratic
hubris and the collapse, highlights the creation of a patriarchal society in
New Provence, tribal war and the infernal machine, the issues of racism and
sexism, and durability of love. Barjavel explained later how he came to write
Ravage, insisting on the fact, decades later, that the issues of energy and
blackouts are still very relevant and pose a real threat:

> Mon premier roman c'était *Ravage*. Je l'ai écrit en 42, il est paru en 43. C'était
> l'histoire d'une civilisation qui s'écroule parce qu'elle manque d'énergie. Les

garçons et les filles qui le découvrent aujourd'hui, qui ont seize ans ou dix-huit
ans, s'imaginent que je l'ai écrit avant-hier (Durand 2020, 12).

   Translation of the authors: My first novel was *Ravage*. I wrote it in 42, it
appeared in 43. It was the story of a civilization that is collapsing because it
lacks energy. Boys and girls who discover it today, who are sixteen or eighteen,
imagine that I wrote it the day before yesterday.

BARJAVEL, HIS LIFE AND WORK

René Gustave Henri Barjavel, a French author, critic and journalist, was
born on January 24, 1911 in Nyons, a small commune in the Drôme department, approximately 120 km from Marseille. His father, Aimé Henri Joseph
Barjavel (1886–1962), was a baker. Marie Lydie Barjavel (née Paget; 1880–
1922) was married to her first husband, Émile Achard, a baker from Nyons;
they had two children, Paul (born in 1899) and Émile (born in 1902), but her
husband suddenly died in 1903. Later, Marie met Henri Barjavel and they
married in 1909. René, their only child, was born in 1911. When Henri went
to military service during World War I three years later, Marie ran the bakery.
René spent part of his childhood without the presence of his father, and when
Henri came back from the war, Marie got sick (sleep fever). She died on 29
May 1922 (Geneanet 2022). In his romanticized and emotional autobiography titled *La charette bleue* (*The Blue Cart*; Barjavel 1980), René tells the
story of his parents before his birth, their bakery, his childhood in Provence,
his life without his father during World War I, the sickness of his mother,
and his first years at school. He was awarded the 'prix Saint-Simon' in 1980
(literary prize created in 1975 for the three-hundredth anniversary of the birth
of renowned memoirist Louis de Rouvroy, duc de Saint-Simon; 1675–1755).
In *La charette bleue*, René shared his thoughts, as a child, regarding religion
and the surprisingly harmonious relations between his Catholic father and his
Protestant mother:

   Le nouveau cimetière s'étendait derrière la gare, à Chante-Merle. Dans sa moitié
   droite on enterrait les catholiques, dans sa moitié gauche les protestants. Je me
   demandais si le paradis était aussi divisé en deux. À la réflexion, certainement
   pas: les catholiques pensaient qu'aucun protestant n'entrait au paradis, et les
   protestants pensaient la même chose des catholiques. Le paradis devait être
   vide . . . Mon père était catholique, ma mère protestante. Leur union constituait
   un des cas, encore rares, de mariages mixtes (Barjavel 1980, 19–20).

      Translation of the authors: The new cemetery stretched out behind the station
   at Chante-Merle. Catholics were buried in its right half, Protestants in its left
   half. I wondered if Heaven was also split in two. On the second thought, certainly not: Catholics thought that no Protestant entered Heaven, and Protestants

thought the same of Catholics. Heaven had to be empty . . . My father was a Catholic, my mother a Protestant. Their union was one of the still rare cases of mixed marriages.

The year his mother died, Barjavel entered the collège of Nyons (secondary education) where his principal, Abel Boisselier, took him under his wing. Boisselier then transferred to the Collège of Cusset and René became a boarder there.

Barjavel obtained his 'Baccalauréat' (qualification obtained at the completion of students' secondary education), but for the lack of money, could not continue his studies. He then became a college pawn, a real estate agent and a bank employee before being hired at 18 as a journalist for the *Progrès de l'Allier* (*Progress Allier*) in Moulins. Barjavel notably wrote about cultural events and covered two conferences on famous French author and woman of letters Colette (1873–1954; a biographical drama film was released in 2018, with Keira Knightley playing Colette in her twenties), in February 1934 in Vichy and in March in Moulins. René wrote his first essay, *Colette à la recherche de l'amour* (*Colette in Search of Love*), in May of the same year. 1935 was a turning point in the life of Barjavel: he met his publisher Robert Denoël during a conference organized in Vichy. Éditions Denoël is a French publishing house founded in 1930 by the Belgian Robert Denoël and the American Bernard Steele who became quickly very successful in 1932 with the publication of Céline's *Voyage au bout de la nuit* (*Journey to the End of the Night*, Prix Renaudot 1932).

In September 1935, Barjavel went to Paris to work for Denoël. René and met Madeleine de Wattripont (1915–2005), a Parisian of Belgian origin who was working for a small company called *L'Anthologie Sonore* (*The Sound Anthology*). They married in 1936 and had two children, Renée in 1937 and Jean in 1938. Barjavel and French dramatist Jean Anouilh (1910–1987) founded the literary review *La Nouvelle Saison* (*The New Season*) in 1936. Barjavel also worked for Denoël during the second part of the 1930s, first as a storekeeper, then as a packer, a reader, a foreman, and ended up as a literary director before the beginning of the war. While working for Denoël, he was also in charge of the cinema section for the weekly *Le Merle Blanc* (*The White Blackbird*).

Barjavel was mobilized as a supply corporal in a regiment of Zouaves in September 1939. The Zouaves were light infantry regiments of the French Army (1830–1962) linked to North Africa. They notably participated to the Battle of France (1940) and to the liberation (1944). When Barjavel got demobilized in June 1940, the family went to the Pyrenees and then to Palavas-les-Flots (seaside resort, six km south of Montpellier). As Denoël got mobilized in the Belgian army and closed his company in Paris, Barjavel was jobless. In Montpellier, he met Mr. Causse, the editor of *La Journée vinicole* (*Wine Day*), the only newspaper dedicated to wine at that time. He also founded *L'Écho des étudiants* (*The Student Echo*) before going back to Paris to work for Denoël after the editor got demobilized and reopened his publishing house in October of 1940. In 1942, when he became literary director of *La Fleur de France* (*The Flower of France*), a collection to the glory of the heroes of France, Barjavel wrote his second work: *Roland, le chevalier plus fort que le lion* (*Roland, the Knight More Proud than the Lion*; 1942). Frankish military leader under Charlemagne during the 8th century. *La Chanson de Roland* (*The Song of Roland*; 11th century) is an epic poem based on the Battle of Roncevaux Pass in 778 where Roland died (See http://barjaweb.free.fr/SITE/ecrits/Roland/Roland.html).

The next year, Barjavel published his first great novel and one of his most famous works, *Ravage* (English translation: *Ashes, Ashes*; Barjavel 1967) and then in 1944, a pessimistic time-travel story, *Le voyageur imprudent* (English translation: *Future Times Three*; Barjavel 1971). *Ravage* was published in short series in *Je suis partout* (*I am everywhere*), a French newspaper founded by Jean Fayard in 1930. Anti-Semitic *Je suis partout* got banned in 1940; publication resumed from 1941 to 1944 and was clearly collaboration-ist. Pierre-Antoine Cousteau, brother of Jacques Cousteau, aligned *Je suis partout* with the Nazi leadership in 1943. In the issue of March 12, 1943, the newspaper, then run by Robert Brasillach, published a laudatory article about Barjavel and *Ravage*, seen as the portrait of an ideal society (Durand 2020, 16). The novel was successful and made Barjavel famous. He did not use the term 'science fiction' because it was not known in France yet. He decided to subtitle his work *Roman extraordinaire* (*Extraordinary Novel*). He later explained why:

> Je n'avais pas employé le mot, à l'époque, ne fut-ce que parce qu'il était inconnu du public français. J'avais baptisé mon livre « roman extraordinaire », en hommage à Jules Verne qui avait baptisé les siens « voyages extraordinaires ». En fait, le mot qui était alors en vogue était celui d'anticipation (See quote in French at http://barjaweb.free.fr/SITE/biographie/bio_detail.html).
>
> Translation of the authors: I did not use the term at the time, because it was unknown to the French public. I named my book "extraordinary novel," in hom-age to Jules Verne who had baptized his "extraordinary journeys." In fact, the word that was in vogue then was that of anticipation.

Like *Ravage*, his next novel *Le voyageur imprudent* was serialized in *Je suis partout* from September 1943 to January 1944 and was awarded Le Prix des Dix (Prize of the Ten; awarded by ten humorists, all friends and colleagues of Barjavel). With the Liberation and Denoël being accused of publishing collaborationist authors, Barjavel took care of his publishing house for some months. Denoël was killed in December 1945, days before his trial. Denoël's mistress sold the company to his main competitor Gallimard. Ironically, *The Little Prince*, published in the US by Reynal & Hitchcock in 1943 (the year of the publication of *Ravage* by Denoël), was posthumously published in France by Gallimard because Saint-Exupéry's works were banned by the Vichy Regime (1940–1944). Barjavel was also publicly denounced as a collaborator by the Comité national des écrivains (National Writers' Committee), notably because of his close relationship with Denoël and the publication of his two novels in *Je suis partout*. He quickly got cleared of these charges due to the interference of several friends who vouched in his favor.

Then began a difficult period for Barjavel: the publication of *Le diable l'emporte* (1948; *The Devil Wins*) was a failure, he ran out of money and his health deteriorated (tuberculosis). He decided to leave novel-writing for the cinema and worked as a scriptwriter in the 1950s-1960s. Barjavel's most famous works are *The Little World of Don Camillo* (adaptation and dialogue by Barjavel, 1952) and *Les Misérables* (1958; adaptation of Victor Hugo's novel by Michel Audiard and René Barjavel). He also wrote a few novels, including *Tarendol* (Barjavel 1946; English translation: *The Tragic Innocents*; Barjavel 1948) and *Journal d'un homme simple* (1951; *Diary of a Simple Man*). In the 1960s, science fiction was more popular in France and Barjavel got more involved with the genre, first with *Colomb de la Lune* (1962; *Columbus of the Moon*) and of course with *La Nuit des temps* (1968; *The Ice People*), probably his most famous novel; it quickly became very successful and popular, and won the Prix des libraires (Booksellers' Prize). Barjavel then published several novels, including *Les Chemins de Katmandou* (*The Roads to Kathmandu*; 1969), *Le Grand secret* (*The Immortals*; 1973), and *Les Dames à la licorne* (*The ladies with the Unicorn*; 1974; with Irish astrologer Olenka de Veer). During this period, he also continued to focus on film studies, wrote scripts and took environmentalist positions. In 1972, he notably participated to the foundation of the prix Apollo (Prix Apollo Award; 1972–1990) and promoted the best works of science fiction as one of the eleven members of the panel (for example *Hellstrom's Hive* by Frank Herbert in 1978).

First published in 1981, *Une rose au paradis* (*A Rose in Heaven*) is a science-fiction novel about a family and their twins Jim and Jill who live in an automated shelter buried beneath Paris, after the destruction of the world by bombs. In 1982, Barjavel published *La Tempête* (*The Tempest*), a story based on the Biblical story of Judith and Holofernes (deuterocanonical *Book of Judith*). In 1984, Barjavel published an adaptations of Arthurian legend titled *L'Enchanteur* (*The Wizard*). He died on November 24, 1985, in Paris (heart attack). He was buried with his ancestors in Bellecombe-Tarendol (commune in the Drôme department) cemetery. His novel *Tarendol*, narrating the love story between two teenagers during World War II, Jean Tarendol and Marie Margherite, was named after this commune.

THE NOVEL

Motivations and sources of inspiration

Barjavel was of course deeply shocked by the French defeat in 1940; when he returned to Paris at the end of 1942, the gloomy atmosphere of the capital under the German occupation had a clear influence on *Ravage*, even though he began to write the manuscript in 1939. At that time, René showed his work to Denoël who did not like the title, *Colère de Dieu* (*Wrath of God*), and proposed *Ravage* instead. Barjavel recalls:

> Deux ans avant la guerre, j'avais fait partie des groupes Gurdjieff [philosophe, écrivain, qui unissait dans une même recherche de soi, la pensée, le sentiment et le corps]. Cela avait orienté ma pensée vers une critique fondamentale de notre société moderne. Quand je suis rentré de la guerre, j'ai continué mon activité avec ces groupes. Je me suis aperçu, à un moment donné, à quel point cette société si développée, si puissante, capable de faire des guerres formidables, était vulnérable. Pourquoi? Parce qu'elle dépend entièrement de l'énergie. J'ai donc écrit une histoire, au début de l'Occupation, dans laquelle une civilisation connaît soudain une privation totale de ses sources d'énergie (Durand, 2020, p. 7).
>
>   Translation of the authors: Two years before the war, I had been part of the Gurdjieff groups [philosopher, writer, who united in the same search for the self, thought, feeling and the body]. This had directed my thoughts towards a fundamental critique of our modern society. When I came back from the war, I continued my activity with these groups. I realized, at a given moment, how vulnerable this society, so developed, so powerful, capable of waging formidable wars, was. Why? Because it depends entirely on energy. So, I wrote a story, at the beginning of the Occupation, in which a civilization suddenly experiences a total deprivation of its energy sources.

In *Les années de l'homme* (*The Years of Man*; 1976), Barjavel explained how he came up with the main theme of *Ravage*:

> J'ai vite commencé un roman qui m'a été en partie inspiré par le fait que l'on vivait à Paris à ce moment-là une période de ténèbres. Nous étions dans une ville qui, à partir de quatre heures du soir, était noire. Plus aucune lumière, le black-out total . . . et c'est cet environnement ténébreux qui m'a sans doute inspiré l'idée de la disparition totale de l'électricité qui est le thème à la base de « Ravage » (Durand 2020, 8).

Translation of the authors: I quickly started a novel which was partly inspired by the fact that we were living in Paris at that time in a period of darkness. We were in a city which, from four o'clock in the evening, was dark. No more light, the total blackout . . . and it is this dark environment which undoubtedly inspired me the idea of the total disappearance of electricity which is the theme at the base of "Ravage."

The title of the English translation, *Ashes, Ashes* (Barjavel 1967) makes sense, not only because part III of the novel is titled *Le chemin de cendres* (*The road of ashes*), but also because of *Ring-around-the-rosy*, a children's game, a nursery rhyme and a dance with the following lyrics:

Ring Around the Rosie [circular red rashes on the skin of the victims of the Black Death]
   Pockets Full of Posies [flowers to protect from the bad smells]
   Ashes, Ashes [burning of the dead bodies; variant with A-tishoo, A-tishoo as violent sneezing]
   We All Fall Down [people dying; reference to the Black Death in 1347–1351 or to the Great Plague of London in 1665?]

This is at least the theory of James Leasor in his famous book *The Plague and the Fire* (Leasor 1961), in which he chronicles the suffering of the people of London in 1665. The plague was followed by a fire that reduced parts of the city to ashes. Barjavel was certainly familiar with this tragedy and part II of *Ravage* feels like reading on this event, but set in the future. Nakayama (2022) discusses the Great Plague of 1665 and Leasor's book:

Most burials were done at night. Shouting, "Bring out your dead!" otherwise unemployable toughs collected corpses in carts. They dumped the stacks of bodies into plague pits to overflowing. New ones were dug, invariably too shallow and inadequate because of the haste in which they were needed. The pits became hellish scenes of decaying bodies (Nakayama 2022, 166).

According to Durand (2020), Barjavel was influenced by several authors and intellectuals when writing *Ravage*. Among the most important are H. G. Wells's 1898 science fiction novel The War of the Worlds, especially the death and destruction, and then the exodus of the population of London, and *La fin d'Illa* by José Moselli (1930; *The End of Illa*), a novel about the destruction of the advanced civilization of Illa caused by scientific progress. Barjavel was also influence by two thinkers: René Guénon (1886–1951), a French intellectual, and Lanza del Vasto (1901–1981), an Italian philosopher and non-violent activist who spent six months with Gandhi in India and was in Paris during World War II; he notably published a very influential book:

Return to the Source, which was edited by Denoël in 1943 (*Le Pèlerinage aux Sources*). It seems that Lanza del Vasto inspired the character of François Deschamps (Durand 2020, 7).

Concerning the date, 2052, it appears to be a reference to *Nostradamus*. The quote can be found in *Le voyageur imprudent* (*Future Times Three*):

> L'an que Vénus près de Mars étendue / A le verseau son robinet fermu / La grand'maison dans la flamme aura chu / le coq mourant restera l'homme nu. «L'an que Vénus près de Mars étendue » désigne astrologiquement, d'une façon incontestable, l'an 2052, reprit le savant. Les autres vers nous font craindre des événements terribles. Le coq désigne, ici, la France, ou peut-être l'humanité. «Restera l'homme nu . . . L'homme nu! Vous entendez! que pourra-t-il arriver à notre malheureux petit-fils pour qu'il reste nu?» (Barjavel 1944, 101).
>
> Translation of the authors: The year that Venus is lying near Mars / To Aquarius its tap closed / The big house in flames will fall / The dying rooster the naked man will remain. "The year that Venus is lying near Mars" designates astrologically, in an indisputable way, the year 2052, continued the scientist. The other verses make us fear terrible events. The rooster here, designates, France, or perhaps humanity. "The naked man will remain . . . The naked man! You hear that! what can happen to our unfortunate grandson that he will remain naked?"

Barjavel titled the first draft of his novel *The Wrath of God*, but his editor Denoël convinced him to go with *Ravage* instead. While some critics believe that *Ravage* is a "Pétainist Utopia" (Sobanet 2007), it is undoubtly inspired by religion more than by politics. The first section seems to be a futuristic utopia, but, according to Barjavel who quotes *The Bible* (*Revelation* 16:19) in the epigraph of section 2, *The fall of the cities*, Paris has become the new Babylon and as a result is about to be destroyed: " . . . and the cities of the nations fell: and great Babylon came in remembrance before God, to give unto her the cup of the wine of the fierceness of his wrath" (Barjavel 1967, 47). Follows the declaration of war by the Black Emperor Robinson, the disappearance of electricity, disease, famine and death, and then of course the exodus of a small group of survivors who live Paris to go back to the promised land, that is, what Barjavel considers to be a new Eden, in Provence.

Absurdism, Irony, and Humor in *Ravage*

Ravage "depicts a rather fantastical future—closer to the satirical absurdism of Albert Robida or Boris Vian than to the extrapolative engineering of Jules Verne—in which electricity suddenly ceases to work" (Aradau, 2016, 47).

Albert Robida (1848–1926) was French illustrator, caricaturist, and novelist. According to the *Encyclopedia of Science Fiction* (Stableford, 2021), "he was the most important and popular nineteenth-century figure in this nascent field." Robida was incredibly prolific and published more than 60,000 illustrations. There are many similarities with Barjavel. Robida notably published in 1879 a satirical homage to Jules Verne's *Voyages extraordinaires* titled *Voyages très extraordinaires de Saturnin Farandoul* (*The Very Extraordinary Adventures of Saturnin Farandoul*). The inventions described in his novels and drawings were integrated into everyday life: his telephonoscope, both videophone and television, is mentioned in *Le Vingtième siècle. La vie électrique* (serialized and then published as a book in 1892; *The Twentieth Century: The Electrical Life*). His style was lively, satirical, and full of comic and absurd situations. During and after World War I, his style became much darker; *Les Villes Martyres* (1914; *The Martyred Cities*) for example portrayed ruined cities. *L'Ingénieur von Satanas* (1919; *The Engineer von Satanas*) is similar to *Ravage* in many ways and "express a sense of the fragility of the electric future he had once espoused" (Stableford, 2021). Claudia Aradau considers that *Ravage* is a "novel that switches from one (Robida/Vian-like) regime of verisimilitude to another (apocalyptic/post-apocalyptic) one" (Aradau 2016, 47).

Ashes, Ashes is a speculative satire and an adventure story. Barjavel emphasizes explicitly his message rather than leave it implicit. He uses a tone, which is "uncomfortably close to the mealy-mouthed propaganda of Vichy's 'National Revolution' (which can be summed up as the nostalgic urge to return to pseudo-feudal social hierarchies and supposedly natural activities)" (Lloyd 2003, 177). While narrating the apocalypse, the author describes with sarcastic, sadistic relish the impotent panic of the crowds confronted with the failure of their machines: "Everyday reality had disappeared, giving way to absurdity." (Barjavel 1967, 58). In fact, the dystopian technological world in which these people live is absurd. This world is governed by multiple ministries. Many of these ministries are presented in an ironic way, due to their strange titles. We note the Ministry of Propaganda (Barjavel 1967, 68), the Ministry of Air (Barjavel 1967, 71), the Ministry of War (Barjavel 1967, 71), the Ministry of Telephone and Telegraph (Barjavel 1967, 72), the Minister of Mental Health (Barjavel 1967, 72), the Ministry of Production and Coordination (Barjavel 1967, 75), and the Ministry of Free and Compulsory Medicine (Barjavel 1967, 75). These ministries are not similar to the ones that exist nowadays. They are more related to the dissemination of knowledge, war, mental health, and medicine. A very attractive title is the Ministry of Air. The latter becomes an element of consumption, thus, it requires a ministry to manage it. Moreover, it is noteworthy to highlight the irony in narrating the council meeting: "They had lost the habit of walking. And stupefaction, as much as fatigue, made them short of breath" (Barjavel 1967, 71). Besides their physical incapacity, the ministers are not able to find any solution to the apocalypse, despite their highly technologically advanced society and machines. More ironically, "the Minister of Sports considered himself incapable of coming on foot from Passy" (Barjavel 1967, 71). However, this irony is mixed with bitterness. This collapsing city makes us recall Babylon, where technology provides mankind with an unlimited scope for evildoing. "As in George Orwell's 1984, other continents are ravaged by war. The South American emperor 'Noir Robinson,' descendant of transported slaves, announces an all-out missile attack on the white races of North America (though probably annihilates his own people as well when the power fails)" (Lloyd 2003, 177). Furthermore, the loss of electricity is metaphorical as it implies the dependency of the civilized man on technology and machines, as well as "the benefits for those who are able to escape this dependency and re-establish a more authentic rapport with nature" (Lloyd 2003, 177).

SUMMARY

Ravage is formally divided into four parts: part one (Les Temps nouveaux) and part two (La chute des villes) are the longest; part three (Le chemin de cendres) is smaller and part four (Le patriarche) is only a few pages long.

Les temps nouveaux (The new times)

June 3, 2052, before 7 pm, François Dechamps is waiting at Saint-Charles Railway Station in Marseilles. He is about to go to Paris, a futuristic metropolis of twenty-five million inhabitants. There is an *automotrice* (a high-speed vehicle) every five minutes, and it only takes an hour to reach the capital. During the journey, François reads a newspaper and learns that, while relations between Europe and Asia are peaceful, tensions are high between South America ruled by the Black Emperor Robinson and White North America. The South is threatening to attack the North. Meanwhile, researchers are trying to find out why the world is suffering an exceptional heat wave and why the voltage of the electric current suddenly dropped for a few minutes several months ago.

While François arrives in Paris and goes to his humble dwelling in Montparnasse, his childhood friend Blanche Rouget meets with Jérôme Seita, who wants to make her a star under the stage name of Régina Vox. She has abandoned her studies without telling her family or François who she is supposed to have dinner with the next day. Jérôme feels threatened by this childhood friend; he asks Blanche to cancel their dinner so she can come and sign her contract. He also offers her an apartment in the building of the Radiant City, close to him and to the Radio-300 studios, located on the 96th Floor. He then invites Blanche to a trip in Scotland, where they have dinner. Jérôme used his influence to make François's life a nightmare: he is failed at the entrance exam, he cannot meet Blanche who has accepted to marry Jérôme, and there is no electricity in his apartment.

La chute des villes (The fall of the cities)

François goes to Legrand's apartment to watch the gala and the official debut of Régina Vox. His former classmate Legrand is rich and lives in Montmartre, one of the luxurious boulevards of the capital. They first watch the news and learn that the Black Emperor has launched a thousand torpedoes and is about to attack North America to avenge centuries of servitude and humiliation. As to Jérôme Seita, he is about to launch the Regina Gala at 9 pm, from the 96th floor of the Radiant City, when suddenly all electricity is lost. In a world entirely depending on electricity, the situation quickly descends into chaos, with people screaming and planes falling down from the sky. While everybody tries to flee the Radiant City, Jérôme invites Blanche to the safety of his apartment. She realizes that her career is already over. François immediately resolves to reach the 96th floor of the building to rescue Blanche. The sudden blackout has not only destroyed her dreams, but also the launch of the Black Emperor's war on the North. Chaos is followed by disease and cholera is beginning to spread fast. Blanche becomes ill. While going down the stairs to find a doctor, Jérôme meets François who forces him to go back to the apartment. Together they help Blanche to move down the stairs. Jérôme is killed while fighting with the gardener who refuses to sell his horse and cart. François is more successful in fighting the gardener; he puts Blanche on the cart, and they go back to his apartment where the local doctor, Fauque, takes care of Blanche. François is able to find both food and weapons and decides to recruit a few people, including Dr. Fauque, his daughter Colette, Bernard Teste, a young student in love with Colette, Georges Pélisson, a cyclist, and André Martin, the nephew of François's concierge, Madame Vélin, Fillon, a worker, Debecker, a shoemaker, Léger, a lawyer, Pierrot Durillot and his pregnant wife, five guards and five horses.

Barjavel goes on to describe the Institute of Mental Electrotherapy No. 149: The institute provides treatment to mental health patients according to the method innovated by a twentieth-century psychiatrist. However, his techniques has been improved, but the principle remains the same. The patients are labelled in numbers and locked in cells. Seated in an electric chair, the patient receives a series of high-voltage electric shocks of calculated intensity. This treatment helps in restoring "the amnesiac's memory, the depressive's optimism, the megalomaniac's modesty. [. . .] The proportion of cures [is] eighty per cent" (Barjavel 1967, 129).

Depiqueur, Minister of Medicine, was fascinated by this successful method and nationalized it. He endowed all other cities with similar institutes. With the increase of mental health disorders in 2026 with the wave of nervousness and depression that threatened the nation and engendered a massive resurgence of divorces and suicides, and as per the advice of the Mental Council, an emergency decree was issued by the government: "The entire population was subjected to the electric chair. Men, women, children, oldsters, all received their shocks from the 'deloonifier'" (Barjavel 1967, 130). Noting the age of the people who receive this treatment, we underline that Barjavel insinuates that the treatment is abusive, he says: "The results were so dramatic that a law was passed instituting a compulsory annual mental examination for everyone. After this examination, every spring, a large number of citizens underwent treatment by the deloonifier" (Barjavel 1967, 130). Even the manual and intellectual workplaces benefited from this therapy, as large firms with high demanding work has installed deloonifers between the canteen and the restroom. Workers whose production decreased went there to get a shock. For the seriously disturbed, such as the obsessives and schizophrenics, it is necessary to use a severe shock to stiffen their muscles, twist their spines, and gently boil their brains. Many recovered from this therapy, however, "those who sat down as Napoleon or God the Father arose as lathe operators, bank clerks, or ticket salesmen, and always with pleasure, which shows that man is easily reconciled to his lot" (Barjavel 1967, 130).

Le chemin de cendres (The road of ashes)

François climbs a hill before the fellowship begins their long journey to Provence and observes that the capital is on fire. The heat causes fires everywhere and they need to move fast to the South, if possible close to a river. Blanche's love for François grows; she notices how much she worries about him. At the same time, she is convinced he will save them all. Everything is burning around the survivors and François has little time to pay attention to Blanche. He turns violent and ruthless when one of the guards falls alseep during the middle of the night: as the camp is surrounded by flames, François kills him. The group barely escapes death. They build a raft, but a guard and Léger are killed by a horse gone wild. The survivors have to face not only the cholera, but the looters, the fires and starvation. Later, after François sends Pierrot on a horse to look for water, the group believes they are attacked by bats. When Colette collapses, exhausted, Bernard Teste kills her with a knife and commits suicide. Pierrot comes back and tells the survivors that there is a river and a house on a small island not far. They realize that there are no bats and that they were all victims of mass hysteria and collective hallucination.

After eating and resting, they leave the island and continue their journey. There are only five companions left (François and Blanche, Pierrot and his wife, and Narcisse) and one horse. Pierre's wife gives birth to a boy they name Victor-Pierre. Then, they finally arrive in Vaux, where François's mother is still alive, but not Blanche's parents. After a while, he summons the heads of all the families of the village; François is named chief of the village and marries Blanche. After they take care of looters, François is elected chief of the entire valley.

Le patriarche (The patriarchy)

François is now 129 years old; he is a respected leader, a patriarch. He controls an area south of Lyons way down to the Mediterranean. Blanche has died of old age. They had 17 children together. Polygamy has been authorized to repopulate the world. François had a total of seven wives, 227 boys and one daughter named Blanche, promised to Paul, the descendant of his companion Narcisse. One day, when François welcomes all the chiefs of the local villages, a man called Denis brings a steam-powered tractor. Enraged, François attacks the young man, but is killed. He is later avenged by Paul who marries young Blanche and becomes the new patriarch.

MAIN CHARACTERS

The story is told by an anonymous and omniscient narrator. During a discussion with students from the Collège de Chalais, near Angoulême in 1983, Barjavel was asked if he identified with one of the characters in *Ravage*; he said:

> En tous cas je ne suis pas du tout un héros dans le genre de François Deschamps . . . Si je m'étais trouvé dans les mêmes circonstances que lui—ça peut arriver demain—je crois que je serais tranquillement resté sur place et j'aurais attendu . . . que les toits me tombent dessus, ou que la faim ait raison de moi (http://barjaweb.free.fr/SITE/documents/chalais.html).
>
> Translation of the authors: In any case, I am not at all a hero like François Deschamps. . . . If I found myself in the same circumstances as him—it could happen tomorrow—I think I would quietly stay there and I would wait . . . for the roofs to fall on me, or for hunger to get the better of me.

François Deschamps

François Deschamps (a truly predestined family name meaning *from the fields*) is the protagonist of the novel; 22 years old at the beginning of the story, he is about to travel to Paris. He is a student in agricultural chemistry from Vaux, a small in Haute-Provence (hamlet of Vaux or Veaux, former ephemeral town, attached to Malaucène since 1794; Vaucluse department). He is in love with young and pretty Blanche Rouget, a childhood friend from Vaux; she lives in Paris and is attracted to rich and powerful Jérôme Seita who fancies making Blanche a star. François goes to Paris by train from Marseille, not only to meet Blanche, but also to learn the results of the examination he passed to enter the Superior School of Agricultural Chemistry. He is shocked to learn that he was rejected, even though he had the best results (Seita personally intervened to make François fail after Blanche naively told him about their friendship).

Son and grandson of peasants, François quickly proves to be courageous and resourceful when the tragedy occurs; François is charismatic (he leads a group of survivors, including Blanche), but he can also be ruthless as he is ready to do anything to successfully go back to his native Provence. Back in Vaux, Deschamps becomes a patriarch and vows to protect the survivors from the dangers of modernization. Driven by the desire to repopulate the world, he has 228 children, including 17 with Blanche (227 boys and one girl, named Blanche too); he lives 129 years when a well-intentioned blacksmith called Denis comes to offer him a gift: a steam-powered tractor. Enraged, François attacks the young man who kills him in self-defense. François is avenged by Paul (a descendant of one of his companions called Narcisse), who has been handpicked as his successor as well as Blanche's husband.

Blanche Rouget

Blanche Rouget is a 17-year-old girl from Vaux like François. She is in Paris to pursue her studies at the École nationale feminine (National Women's School), which trains mothers of elite families. François calls her Blanchette, probably a reference to Blanquette, Mr. Seguin's Goat, his seventh goat to be eaten by the by the big bad wolf (presumably Seita in *Ravage*) after wanting to leave the safety of the stable to go to the mountain (Alphonse Daudet, 1840–1897; *Lettres de Mon Moulin* published in 1869; English: *Letters from my Mill*). Blanche has actually left school and is trying to become a singer. Frivolous and carefree Blanche wants to live in the most luxurious district of Paris, la Ville Radieuse (The Radiant City; Blanquette's mountain), with Seita who is about to make her a star and asks her to marry him. Seita discovered Blanche when she joined a competition organized by his news channel.

Introduced to the public as Régina Vox, Blanche is about to perform live when the impossible happens: a worldwide, sudden and unexplained loss of electricity and its catastrophic consequences for a society entirely relying on this form of energy. As everything falls apart, François finds her and saves her. The cataclysmic event is followed by an outbreak of cholera. François and Blanche leave the capital and are able to cross the country on foot and to go back to Vaux after a perilous and initiatory journey. In Vaux, François's mother is still alive, but not his father; the parents of Blanche and three quarters of the village's population have already succumbed to the disease. François is appointed chief of the village and marries Blanche.

Jérôme Seita

Pierre-Jacques Seita is a wealthy media magnate who owns the largest national news channel, Radio 300. His son Jérôme is the artistic director of the channel. Jérôme is an ugly, vain, and sly man who has considerable control over money and politics; he is served by subordinates and does nothing by himself. Jérôme acts quite viciously against François, a man he is jealous of, just because Blanche mentioned him: he not only intervenes to make François fail the entrance examination, but also to cut off his water, milk and (ironically) his electricity supply. Following the disappearance of electrical power, Jérôme brings Blanche to his apartment; he realizes the gravity of the situation when he sees planes falling down. Blanche becomes suddenly ill; he tries to find a doctor and goes down to the 58th floor of the building, but he meets François on his way down and together they go back to his apartment to rescue Blanche. They finally reach the house of the gardener who owns a cart and a horse. Jérôme is shocked to hear that the gardener doesn't want to sell them the horse, whatever the price. They fight and Jérôme receives a blow to the head; he collapses and he is trampled by the horse. After successfully fighting the gardener, François takes the horse and goes back to Blanche. He does not tell her that Jérôme is dead.

PARIS IN 2052 BEFORE THE APOCALYPSE, THE TECHNOLOGY/THE SOCIETY

The novel opens on the 3rd of June 2052 at seven o'clock, at a time when the moon is about to change. The French capital showcases a remarkable technological progress: there is an automatic car every five minutes. With their slender torpedo shape, these cars are like ancient submarines. While the railways have been elevated as per the popular demand, hollow girders replaced the rails, and suspended carriages the wheeled cars. It is the turning point of the atomic age, the era of speed, during which "men had turned resolutely toward a more human way of life" (Barjavel 1967, 11). Saying this, we assume a more human society. However, we notice that atomic rockets have been given up for civilian use and in favor of comfortable planes with wraparound helixes, and that railways have been rediscovered to run wheeled trains fueled with coal and oil and driven by internal combustion. Thus, the mentioned human way of life is purely correlated to machines and technology. The society is industrialized and industry is preserved from any confusion caused by the interruption of traffic between continents, through an advanced infrastructure. We also point out that the 2052 society is not globalized through digitalization and Internet only, as continents are linked to each other by ribbons: an immense one crosses Europe and Asia, and millions of men are set to work there at the same moment. Working day and night, the workers are supervized by swarms of engineers and foremen; bent over furiously spinning tools; helped by huge machines, rock crushers, grinders of steel; encouraged by loudspeakers yelling exhortations and hymns.

Technological progress is not only limited to transportation vehicles and infrastructure, it is also noticeable in the emergence and use of electronic devices, which were inexistent at Barjavel's time, but are very popular nowadays. In 2052, the Eurasian Transport Company had installed electronic readers in each seat of public transportations to allow passengers to read at night without disturbing any of their neighbors, who preferred to remain in darkness. These devices are in the format of an adjustable plate that can be enlarged by the user to the format of his book. In the earphones, a voice reads the printed text aloud: "This voice would not only read Goethe, Dante, Mistral, or Celine in the original, but would start over at the top of each page, if desired, and give a translation in any language" (Barjavel 1967, 15). Additionally, these devices automatically broadcast the image of each page to the Reading Center of the Eurasian Transport Company, located on the outskirts of Vienna. The Center's building has been divided into ten thousand of tiny soundproof booths, in which ten thousand readers of all ages, both sexes, and all nationalities sat in front of ten thousand identical screens.

> With the happening of the apocalypse, we question the consequences of technological progress. The latter seems to be harmful and destructive. Instead of providing humans and society with growth and prosperity, it lead to ultimate destruction. Thus, Barjavel's novel remains noteworthy, however, not because it is well written (albeit in a somewhat dated style), but principally because it mirrors—in exemplary fashion—the views on science held by a majority of the French during this period and shows how they themselves tended to define this literature "of science imagination" [*littérature d'imagination scientifique*] (Bozzetto and Evans 1990, 12–13).

This viewpoint about the destructive aspect of science and technological advances demonstrates that Barjavel insinuates the importance of the human's return to the earth and simple agrarian life. Hence, we underline the author's invitation to keep in touch with our own roots, traditions, cultures, celebrations, etc. "Working the soil is the natural definition of labor, and thus of society. And such labor entails pain, but also joy" (Bozzetto and Evans 1990, 12). This return to earth and nature is symbolized in the novel through the birth scene of Pierrot's wife assisted by two old people, who live in the ruins of an ancient farm, with a few ewes, four nanny goats and a billy goat, a ram, and a shaggy dog: "They lived on the milk and cheese of their animals and clothed themselves with the wool. They were very wrinkled and very dirty" (Barjavel 1967, 171). This contrast between the technology and industrialized society on the one hand, and the simple rural life on the other hand, showcases the negative impact of the former on humans, as it resulted in controlling them by all means including in a huge apocalypse. However, the birth of the Pierrot's child in the middle of total destruction and in the valley is a sign of hope and continuity of life.

THE CENSORSHIP AND THE CONTROL, COMPARISON WITH *FAHRENHEIT 451*

Fahrenheit 451 is an American dystopian novel written by Ray Bradbury and published in 1953. It is considered as one of Bradbury's best works. It comprises three parts: "The Hearth and the Salamander," "The Sieve and the Sand," "Burning Bright." The novel depicts a futuristic society that controls free thought by means of outlawing books and burning them. To do so, firemen are hired to set fire to printed books that cross their path. The main character, Guy Montag, is an unhappily married fireman, who is satisfied with his job. However, his life is turned upside down when he meets Clarisse McClellan, a seventeen-year-old girl, who revives the thinking process in him. His recollection of the self-immolation of an old woman, who refuses to be an eyewitness to the destruction of her books, never stops to haunt him. Thus, he started saving books and decided to put an end to the political indoctrination and governmental machination. Hence, the main objective of *Fahrenheit 451* is to denounce censorship and the control of freedom, through pointing out the harmful role played by the mass media in brainwashing the individual and generating intellectual clones.

While reading *Fahrenheit 451*, we notice a similarity of the viewpoints of Barjavel and Bradbury about the technological and industrialized society and its impact on the human mind as well as on arts, literature, and freedom of expression. In *Ashes, Ashes*, the park of Versailles became newly ornamented with one hundred twenty-seven statues of the sculptor Petitbois. These sculptors represent the many glories of science. The regression of sculptor as an art is also implicitly reflected in *Fahrenheit 451*, when Granger talked about his late grandfather. He said:

> When I was a boy my grandfather died, and he was a sculptor. [. . .] And when he died, I suddenly realized I wasn't crying for him at all, but for the things he did. I cried because he would never do them again, he would never carve another piece of wood or help us raise doves and pigeons in the back yard or play the violin the way he did, or tell us jokes the way he did. He was part of us and when he died, all the actions stopped dead and there was no one to do them just the way he did. He was individual. He was an important man. I've never gotten over his death. Often I think, what wonderful carvings never came to birth because he died. How many jokes are missing from the world, and how many homing pigeons untouched by his hands? He shaped the world. He did things to the world. The world was bankrupted of ten million fine actions the night he passed on (Bradbury 2008, 116–117).

In addition to sculpting, painting became popular, noncertificated painters retained the freedom to paint, but they did not have the right to paint their work. A few of them ventured to do so, however, "the Painters' Guild prosecuted them for practicing art illegally" (Barjavel 1967, 18). The last group of these artistic rebels were condemned to die of hunger. This system highlights the monopolization of arts in 2052, while painters are marginalized in the depicted society in *Fahrenheit 451*. Just like cartographers and mechanics, they are not represented in books, plays, and TV serials. In fact, these platforms represent those who have a bigger market.

Becoming the patriarch in *Ashes, Ashes*, François met once a year which the heads of the province to compare the results of the harvests, agree on barter, and fix the dates of fairs. One of the first measures undertook by François was the destruction of books. All the books that have been found in the excavated ruins were burned on the first day of spring, in the village square. During this event, the heads of the villages explained to the assembled young people that they were burning the very spirit of the evil (see Barjavel 1967, 182). A few books of poetry have been preserved as they "are books which were not dangerous except to their authors," said François (Barjavel 1967, 182). Instead of cutting out the controversial excerpts from the books, we notice that censorship is realized through burning the whole intellectual minds and bringing them to ashes. The same censorship pattern is used in *Fahrenheit 451*, where books are burned. Adopting the following official slogan "Monday bum Millay, Wednesday Whitman, Friday Faulkner, burn 'em to ashes, then bum the ashes" (Bradbury 2008, 5), firemen burn books, the latter are considered loaded guns in the house next door, thus, they should be burnt. We highlight the firemen's role as explained by Beatty to Montag:

> Take the shot from the weapon. Breach man's mind. Who knows who might be the target of the well? read man? Me? I won't stomach them for a minute. And so when houses were finally fireproofed completely, all over the world (you were correct in your assumption the other night) there was no longer need of firemen for the old purposes. They were given the new job, as custodians of our peace of mind, the focus of our understandable and rightful dread of being inferior; official censors, judges, and executors (Bradbury 2008, 47).

Besides censorship, burning the books in *Fahrenheit 451* aims to control the human mind: "We must all be alike. Not everyone born free and equal, as the Constitution says, but everyone made equal. Each man the image of every other; then all are happy, for there are no mountains to make them cower, to judge themselves against," added Beatty (Bradbury 2008, 47–48). While François in *Ashes, Ashes* made the art of writing a privilege to the class of village chiefs, because "writing permitted speculative thought, the development of arguments, the construction of theories, the multiplication of errors" (Barjavel 1967, 182) and because of his fear that his people stay close to solid reality. Hence, we underline his manipulative approach, which aims to control literature and to eliminate any divergence or diversity in the points of views. However, the books destruction is not the only result that emanated from the excessive progress, as the whole society collapsed.

THE TECHNOCRATIC HUBRIS AND THE COLLAPSE: TOO MUCH PROGRESS SOFTENING MANKIND?

Despite the technological and industrial progress, the society and humankind did not find prosperity or stability in 2052. Humans have mastered the forces of nature, and they totally live divorced from the natural. The food they eat and the air they breathe are artificial. Not only industry offers its customers rare meats of various tastes and served in thick slices, but specialized gastronomy firms are also producing extraordinary boiled or grilled meats, without anything added. A company named Christian Abstinence Society, whose slogan is "Eat to live, don't live to eat," supplies its members with a meat which had no taste at all, to help them escape the sin of gluttony. Women have a great deal of freedom, pursue higher education, and cultivate careers. Moreover, "sociologists, engineers, scholars, and physicians methodically organized the clearing of the virgin forest, made this three-quarters-uninhabited continent into a habitable land" (Barjavel 1967, 53). In fact, and according to François Deschamps, the apocalypse happened because of the mankind's fault. He said: "They believed they were mastering nature; they called it progress. It's an accelerated progress toward death" (Barjavel 1967, 54). Therefore, and due to excessive progress, a massive catastrophe strikes this society in 2052, and forces some of its citizens to flee to Provence, a region that had been isolated from the nefarious technological, economic, and sociopolitical developments of the twenty-first century: "Some people, abandoned by garments with magnetic closures, found themselves suddenly half undressed (Barjavel 1967, 58). The cosmopolitan advanced society collapsed gradually. Thousands of planes flew over Paris, but they merely obeyed to the simple law of gravity. Those whose parachutes did not have time to open, or whose speed was not sufficient to carry them to the distant open country, fell on the city like bombs. Terrified subway passengers tore each other to shreds in darkened tunnels, the earth trembled, people died while trying to evacuate from skyscrapers, and houses fell down (see Barjavel 1967, 59–60). The "nature's restoring the balance," said François (Barjavel 1967, 60), adding: "The sudden death of motors had restored man and the terrestrial globe to their real dimensions" (Barjavel 1967, 60). However, this apocalyptic event is a connotation of nature's revenge toward its abuse and destruction by mankind, in addition to its reaction against machinism and industrialization. It is a wake-up call for mankind to return to their origin and roots. It also highlights mankind's incapacity to live separately from nature. Consequently, the survivors from the apocalypse returned to nature and created a patriarchy in Provence, in which men are all powerful, and women rear children. It is noteworthy to underline that this newly created patriarchy is the society before the technological progress, thus, we note the return to the past. In other words, the futuristic cosmopolitan society is buried in the past, and the traditional past becomes the future.

NEW PROVENCE, A PATRIARCHAL SOCIETY

As mentioned earlier, the few people who survived the apocalypse created a new society: The Patriarchy in the Provence, the native land of François and Blanche. However, Barjavel insinuates that "technophobia leads to a patriarchal backlash: describing a world where the use of any artifacts is punished by death penalty" (Hoquet 2018, 270). The patriarch has his authority extended over all the region: on the west and north by the Rhone, on the east by the Alps, and on the south by the Mediterranean. Polygamy has been made compulsory and became one of the basic laws of the new State. The cholera, fire, and famine have left a few survivors, and there were about four women for every man: "Nature, in order to repopulate the world, had multiplied the soft growing hands. She knew there would be no lack of seed" (Barjavel 1967, 179).

However, to gain acceptance of the new law among those who had known the old customs, François, the patriarch, addresses himself first to the women of his valley. When he obtains their consent, he imposes his will on the men. "Two of the most important of these laws were that which forbade a man to own more land than he could walk around from sunrise to sunset on the longest day of the year, and that which forbade more than five hundred families to live together in the same town" (Barjavel 1967, 179). Moreover, commerce was not practiced in the new world, in which the meaning of the word "merchant" is unknown, and the cult of red wine had been replaced with the cult of water. Furthermore, "the great catastrophe had left behind a frightful memory, passed on by oral tradition, of a deluge of fire and a pitiless plague, manifestations of divine wrath against the pride of man" (Barjavel 1967, 182). This patriarchal society is, however, an utopic one that followed the dystopic society that collapsed during the apocalypse. Therefore, we underline the binary utopic/dystopic society depicted in *Ashes, Ashes*. On the one hand, the technological society—the dystopian society—lead to the destruction of the mankind; on the other hand, the rural society—the utopian society—lead to the preservation and procreation of the mankind after the apocalyse. In this regard, Andrew Sobanet points out that

> [. . .] *Ravage* portrays an ideal society that has a successful post-apocalypse renaissance. That societal rebirth is founded upon a strict adherence to traditionalist priorities and values similar to those promoted by the Vichy government, such as discipline, loyality, hard work, and a high birth rate. Indeed, [. . .] Barjavel uses the utopia—a traditional convention of speculative fiction—to illustrate the potential for national regeneration and renovation promoted by those Pétainist ideals (Sobanet 2007, 2).

The patriarchy represented in *Ashes, Ashes* is a peaceful society in which citizens live happily in well-orchestrated harmony with nature and the Earth. However, despite all this, the patriarchy has not been preserved from the dangers of modernization. François Deschamps, who lived 129 years and has 228 children, is killed by a young man who built a steam-powered tractor built to reduce the amount of labor.

TRIBAL WAR AND THE INFERNAL MACHINE

The patriarchal utopian society reaches its end with the death of François Deschamps by a machine, built by a young man called Denis, the head blacksmith of Mount Ventoux. However, François wanted to destroy this machine and the brain that created it as well. Conceived to spare help in the daily labor, this machine triggered the technological and industrialized society that has been destroyed during the apocalypse, noting that the latter represents a lesson for its survivors. In this regard, François's reaction when he saw the machine was pure anger. We note his words to Denis: "Has it been so long since the catastrophe that almost destroyed the world that a man your age could have forgotten its lesson? (Barjavel 1967, 188). Replaced by machines, the pre-apocalypse society has been destroyed: "when they stopped, all at once, [. . .] men were like oysters out of their shells, there was nothing left for them to do but die . . . " (Barjavel 1967, 188). The emergence of the new machine in the Patriarchy is a symbol of the revival of the pre-apocalypse, dystopian society. It also engendered the death of the patriarch, François Deschamps, as well as a strong storm that came roaring from the depths of the valley. However, the turbulence caused by the moving machine was put to an end by Paul, whom the late patriarch had chosen as his successor and husband of his only daughter. Thus, we noted the presevation of the utopian society through the destruction of the machine that threatened its prosperity and peace.

RACISM AND SEXISM IN *RAVAGE*?

Sobanet (2007) tries to demonstrate that *Ravage* is a "Pétainist Utopia," but according to Vas-Deyres (2018), Barjavel's collaboration with anti-Semitic and collaborationist *Je suis partout* on several of his works (*Ravage*; *les Mains d'Anicette*; *la Fée et le soldat*; *Péniche*, all in 1943; *le Voyageur imprudent*, 1944), was more contextual and opportunistic than ideological. Rombaldi edition of *Ravage* in 1974 contains an interview of Barjavel, who notably answers a question about the words spoken by the Black Emperor Robinson. He says they can be likened to Hitler's behavior before and during the war:

> Oui, cette silhouette lointaine et menaçante de l'empereur noir voulait rappeler les terribles mois de 1938 (Munich) et 1939, où Hitler faisait peser sur l'Europe le poids effrayant de sa voix. Il n'y avait pas encore la télé et on entendait cette voix sauvage, à laquelle on ne comprenait rien [. . .] comme celle d'un démon noir qui faisait le bruit de la haine et de la mort. Si bien que la guerre nous apporta le soulagement. On se dit: « Enfin nous allons en finir avec ce fou! » (Barjavel 1974, préface).
>
> Translation of the authors: Yes, this distant and threatening silhouette of the Black Emperor wanted to recall the terrible months of 1938 (Munich) and 1939,

when Hitler weighed down Europe with the frightening weight of his voice. There was no TV yet and we heard this wild voice, which we did not understand [. . .] like that of a black demon which made the noise of hatred and death. So the war brought us relief. We said to ourselves: "Finally, we are going to put an end to this madman!"

Moreover, despite the fact that Barjavel was publicly denounced as a collaborator by the Comité national des écrivains (National Writers' Committee), he quickly got cleared of these charges. It should also be noted that the first draft of *Ravage* was written in 1939. He originally called the novel *Colère de Dieu* (*Wrath of god*) and showed his worked to Robert Denoël who had become his friend. Denoël did not like the title and proposed *Ravage* instead; he also gave Barjavel advice and pointed out the novel's strengths and weaknesses. That was before the defeat (22 June 1940, the Second Armistice at Compiègne) and the Vichy government led by Marshal Philippe Pétain (10 July 1940). It would be unfair and anachronistic to declare *Ravage* to be a product of Vichy France.

DURABILITY OF LOVE

In 1982, Barjavel shared a glimpse of his love life when he was a teenager; he discretely acknowledged the major influence a great love story had on the way he portrayed all his heroines:

> À ce moment-là commence la période la plus riche de mon existence, mon passage au collège et une grande histoire d'amour que je ne raconterai jamais, parce que c'est mon trésor personnel et qu'elle m'a ébloui pour le reste de ma vie . . . Toutes mes héroïnes, par la suite, en ont été des avatars, toutes mes histoires d'amour en portent la trace (*Journal d'un homme simple*, 1982; see http://barjaweb.free.fr/SITE/ecrits/JDHS/jdhs.html).
>
> Translation of the authors: At that moment the richest period of my existence begins, my time in college and a great love story that I will never tell, because it is my personal treasure and it dazzled me for the rest of my life. . . . All my heroines, subsequently, were avatars, all my love stories bear the mark.

It is significant to underline that Blanche, the heroine in *Ashes, Ashes*, represents an avatar of Barjavel's loved one. We underline Francois's strong love for Blanche. François saved Blanche's life and remained by her side during the events of apocalypse. The latter destroyed everything, except their love. They got married and lived in the created Provence, where François became the patriarch. Despite his multiple marriages, Blanche remained his best loved wife and he named his single daughter Blanche in her memory.

CONCLUSION

According to Wordcat, the most succesful works written by René Barjavel are *The Ice People*, with "175 editions published between 1968 and 2021 in 4 languages," followed by *Ashes, Ashes*, with "95 editions published between 1943 and 2019 in 4 languages" and *Le voyageur imprudent*, with 77 editions published between 1955 and 2017 in 5 languages" (Wordcat 2022). *Ravage* is not only taught at school in France, but has been successufly adapted into comics by French author Jean-David Morvan, with drawings by Filipino author Rey Macutay, and colors by Walter Pezzali (Morvan, Macutay, & Pezzali, 2016–2021). The English translation was published in July 2021 by Magnetic Press:

> Based on the 1943 novel *Ravage* by Rene Barjavel, this might have looked dated or out of its time, but the story of a society without technology is as pertinent today as it was 60 years ago. Has man become so reliant that if it all stopped most of us would die? Barjavel's and Morvan seek to answer that question while wrapping an excellent comic around it (Lennox 2022, online).

While some issues and statements in the novel might be controversial, many of its predictions are coming true in our 21st-century world, for better or worse, with war, famine, disease, and a terrible mixture of incompetence and corruption plaguing too many countries.

REFERENCES

Barjavel, René. 1943. *Ravage*. Paris: Denoël.
_____ 1944. *Le Voyageur imprudent*. Paris: Denoël.
_____ 1946. *Tarendol*. Paris: Denoël.
_____ 1948. *The tragic innocents* [*Tarendol*]. Translated by Wilkins, Eithne. London: H. Hamilton.
_____ 1967. *Ashes, Ashes* [*Ravage*]. Translated by Knight, Damon. Garden City, N.Y: Doubleday.
_____ 1971. *Future times three* [*Le Voyageur imprudent*]. Translated by Scouten, Margaret Sansone. New York: Award Books.
_____ 1974. *Ravage*. Sevilla: Rombaldi. Preface retrieved February 9, 2022 from http://barjaweb.free.fr/SITE/documents/dossiers/ravage/rava_interv.html.
_____ 1980. *La charette bleue*. Paris: Denoël.
Aradau, Claudia. 2016. Snookered. *Radical Philosophy*, issue 196. Review of *Quentin Meillassoux, Science Fiction and Extro-Science Fiction*, trans. Alyosha Edlebl. Minneapolis: Univocal. Retrieved March 10, 2022 from https://www.radicalphilosophy.com/reviews/196-reviews.

Bozzetto, Roger, and Arthur B. Evans. 1990. "Intercultural Interplay: Science Fiction in France and the United States (As Viewed from the French Shore) (Des Liaisons Équivoques: La Science-Fiction En France et Aux États-Unis [Une Vue Des Côtes Françaises])." *Science Fiction Studies* 17(1): 1–24. http://www.jstor.org/stable /4239968.

Bradbury, Ray. 2008. *Fahrenheit 451*. New York: Ballantine Books.

Durand, André. 2020. *Comptoir littéraire. Barjavel René*. Retrieved January 25, 2022 from http://www.comptoirlitteraire.com/977-barjavel-rene.html.

Geneanet 2022. *René Gustave Henri Barjavel*. Retrieved January 11, 2022 from https: //gw.geneanet.org.

Hoquet, Thierry. 2018. "Cyborgs, Between Organology and Phenomenology: Two Perspectives on Artifacts and Life." In *French Philosophy of Technology. Classical Readings and Contemporary Approaches*, edited by Sacha Loeve, Xavier Guchet, and Bernadette Bensaude Vincent, 257–77. Switzerland: Springer.

Leasor, James. 1961. *The Plague and the Fire*. New York: McGraw-Hill.

Lennox, Michael. 2022. *Review—Ashes, Ashes #1*. Retrieved March 25, 2022 from https://www.bigglasgowcomicpage.com/review-ashes-ashes-1.

Lloyd, Christopher. 2003. *Collaboration and Resistance in Occupied France. Representing Treason and Sacrifice*. New York: Palgrave Macmillan.

Morvan, Jean-David, Macutay, Rey, & Pezzali, Walter. 2016–2021. *Ravage*. 3 tomes. Paris: Glénat, coll. Grafica (Tome 01, Septembre 2016; tome 02, Octobre 2017; tome 03, March 2021). https://www.glenat.com/bd/series/ravage.

Nakayama, Don K. 2022. Social Distancing and Contact Tracing During the Great Plague of 1665. The American Surgeon, Vol. 88(2): 165–166. https://doi.org/10 .1177/00031348211065094.

Sobanet, Andrew. 2007. A Return to the Soil: René Barjavel's Pétainist Utopia. *French Forum* 32(1/2): 171–88. http://www.jstor.org/stable/40552454.

Stableford, Brian. 2021. "Robida, Albert." The Encyclopedia of Science Fiction. Retrieved February 10, 2022 from https://sf-encyclopedia.com/entry/robida_albert.

Vas-Deyres, Natasha. 2018. Anticipation et science-fiction dans la France occupée: entre Résistance et Collaboration. *Le journal de Quinzinzinzili, 33*: 10–13. Retrieved March 25, 2022 from https://www.academia.edu/38337404/_Anticipation_et_ science_fiction_dans_la_France_occupée_entre_Résistance_et_Collaboration_.

Wordcat. 2022. Barjavel, René 1911–1985. Retrieved March 20, 2022 from https:// www.worldcat.org/identities/lccn-n50017785.

Chapter Seven

Dystopia as the First-Person World

Rereading E. M. Forster's The Machine Stops as a Pandemic Novel of a Global Society

Akiyoshi Suzuki, Nagasaki University, Japan

No one can exist with a respirator out of doors. Hygienic clothing and medicines make them safer. Physical contact is avoided except for reproductive purposes, and direct communication is also avoided. Everyone stays in their homes, where they do everything, including shopping and working, using a "machine." Using the machine, they communicate by sending and receiving messages and by talking while looking at each other's faces on the screen using the remote communication system of the machine. Through these styles of communication, some of these individuals have connections with thousands of people. The machine offers various suggestions and asks questions, and people respond to them to receive varied services that suit their tastes and thoughts as well as for safety. Education in this world encompasses online distance learning. "The clumsy system of public gatherings had been long since abandoned; neither Vashti nor her audience stirred from their rooms. Seated in her armchair she spoke, while they in their armchairs heard her, fairly well, and saw her, fairly well" (Forster 1909, 4). In this society, if people are not proficient in using the machine, they will become homeless. Moreover, they will die without any support from others.

This is not a description of a society in the 2020s, but the world of E. M. Forster's 1909 story, *The Machine Stops*. Forster did not write a story about a plague. *The Machine Stops* is a short story written during a period when the London subways were running, telephones were spreading, and airships were flying. It is generally believed that the story criticizes the development of science and the optimistic attitude toward mechanistic civilization as an early version of science fiction.

In this fictional world, the machine is worshipped as God by everyone, including Vashti. Her son, Kuno, is uncomfortable in a world wherein the machine guarantees human life and happiness and is worshipped as God and with people like Vashti who have no doubts about this world. When the machines finally stop, the human race perishes, except for a few people who are exiled to a world without machines. The story concludes with Kuno leaving this world hoping that the world will regain its humanity and start anew with these remaining inhabitants.

I have briefly summarized *The Machine Stops*. However, the question posed is as follows: Am I alone in thinking that this science fiction can be read not only as an allegorical story of a contemporary society with advanced information and communication technology, as Silvana Caporaletti (1997) and Marcia Bundy Seabury (1997) refer, but also as an allegorical story of the world in the 2020s when COVID-19 is spreading? When discussing the use of unrealistic depictions and stories in fantasy, Forster emphasized them in a fictional story by asking "how much they may mean to him?" (Forster 1927, 102). Therefore, I attempt to consider "how much they may mean" in *The Machine Stops* to current readers. This reading is similar to reading Camus's *The Plague* (1947) not as a story of the plague but as a story of human absurdity and of a world in which COVID-19 is spreading. In fact, in 2020, *The Plague* was read globally as a story of the present age in which COVID-19 is spreading. It seems that the effect of a history book was expected for *The Plague*. As Longxi Zhang (2015) persuasively explains, reading with the expectation of the effects of historical books means reading texts that record certain historical events for future lessons and warnings and transforming them into wisdom (Zhang 2015, 87–102). Insofar as we read the past as the present, reading with the expectation of the effects of historical books is also a form of allegorical reading.

In allegorical reading, the entire text is rhetorically connected in the reader's mind to individual or collective ideals, experiences, or facts that exist outside of the text (aside from the world in which it is written). According to Heidegger, the major factors called "fore-structure for understanding" determine the individual horizon as well as the rhetorical meaning and effect of words. Nobuo Satō, a Japanese linguist, considers it an illusion to assume that language is a tool for faithfully transcribing and conveying facts and states that the art of rhetoric is necessary in order to express our perceptions as they really are (Satō 1992, 25–26). By contrast, a text can be read with a realistic sense, considering it as a metaphor that refers to something different from the literal meaning of the text, even if one reads it literally. Camus's *The Plague* was widely read in 2020 because the description in the text was read with a realistic sense as a metaphor for the present.

The Machine Stops can be read as a literal warning against a mechanistic civilization, or, as John Beer (1979, 262), Wilfred Stone (1966, 18), and Lionel Trilling (1965, 47–49) have highlighted, as Forster's desire to escape from his mother. In this chapter, I read *The Machine Stops* allegorically and a posteriori as a dystopia novel intended as a warning to the world in the 2020s. However, *The Machine Stops* contains no mention of disease or suffering from a disease. Nevertheless, it can be read as a story of a world wherein disease is rampant, which is a poignant characteristic of this story for readers living in the midst of a pandemic. Susan Sontag once discussed reading the pain of others based on the natural assumption that humans turn away from things that make them feel bad and ignore tragic events (2003, 116–18). *The Machine Stops* is significant in that it can be read as a story of a world in which disease prevails without describing sickness or the suffering of a disease. Therefore, the novel has a greater potential to make readers confront the suffering of others. Moreover, as Trilling (1965) suggested, the stories written by Forster have been evaluated as containing wisdom for living in a world of confusion while maintaining a sense of equilibrium (Tsutsui 1983, 3).

However, it would be clumsy to connect the story of 1909 to the world of the 2020s without any assumptions. Therefore, I will first read the novel from the perspective of both utopia and its negative mirror, dystopia, in light of Forster's thought and the society of the time in which it was written. From the perspective of the social and political criticism of that time, the warning of *The Machine Stops* is reconsidered as a story constituting elements of dystopia. This is followed by a genealogy of critique considering Mark E. Hillegas's perspective (1967, 82) and contemporary scholars such as Marcin Tereszewski (2020). Nevertheless, the story is initially read from both utopian and dystopian perspectives because there exist elements of utopia and dystopia in this story. For instance, there is a reference to Orion in *The Machine Stops*, and as Judith Scherer Herz (1979, 19) and John Beer (1962, 90–93) suggest, Forster often used Orion as "a symbol of the ambivalent meaning" of promise or hope and its negation. Furthermore, the inhabitants of the world of *The Machine Stops* live in a beehive-like room. As Seabury (1997) and Cristopher Hollingsworth (2001) indicate, since the rhetorical meaning of the beehive has changed from positive or neutral to negative from the ancient Greek period to the present, *The Machine Stops* has positive and negative connotations (Seabury 1997, 68). Therefore, both meanings require discussion. Following the discussion, this story will be identified as a dystopian novel. Subsequently, I will argue for the modernity of the warning in *The Machine Stops* based on the similarity between the society depicted in the story and contemporary society with the development of information and communication technology. This argument is predicated on the similarity to contemporary society, as it emphasizes the spread of infectious diseases.

EQUALITY AND SECURITY: THE UTOPIAN NATURE OF *THE MACHINE STOPS*

The period in which the short story was written has been previously mentioned; however, if the story emerged from a criticism of the science and mechanical civilization of the time, it can be considered a criticism of the capitalist British society during this period. In fact, the division between the rich and the poor was vast in the UK at that time. In the novel, people are freed from labor and the society is economically equal: they can acquire what they want through the machines in their homes; they have jobs (such as lecturing at Vashti or working as a flight attendant on an airship) and they do not receive payment for them. Sachiko Abe, a Japanese scholar of Forster, asserted that although the author was a member of the Bloomsbury Group, he was indifferent to the problems of the working class and social welfare (1989, 202). However, it is impossible to assert that he was indifferent to the problems of a capitalist society as long as an economically equal society is depicted in contrast to a capitalist society.

In the story, equality finds expression in various things such as houses. Perhaps influenced by his father, an architect—although he died when he was a child—Forster often wrote detailed descriptions of houses, including *Howards End* (1910). *The Machine Stops* also begins with a description of people's houses. The French sociologist Pierre Bourdieu observes few markets as state-controlled and state-constructed as the housing market (Bourdieu 2000/2006, 125). Thus, it is valuable to confirm the equality in terms of housing and other buildings. According to Stuart Lowe (2011), an expert on British housing, Britain in the late 19th and early 20th centuries was riddled with various housing problems, including unsanitary housing for workers. The quality of housing declined due to overcrowding by low-wage workers, especially in the cities. During that time, the housing supply was financed by private real estate investors. With the emergence of problems of liability for unsanitary housing and taxation as well as the maturing of new joint investment companies and banking systems, private investors gradually withdrew from the real estate business at the end of the 19th century. Consequently, municipalities began to provide public housing. Furthermore, the wealthy began to own houses and a large gap between the wealthy and the underprivileged remained in the new housing situation (Lowe 2011, chap. 2). The homes of the wealthy during this period are described in detail in *Howards End*, in contrast to the lives of the lower-middle class busts.

In the world of *The Machine Stops*, housing inequality has been solved. Everyone lives in "a small room, hexagonal in shape, like the cell of a bee" (Forster 1909, 1). Moreover, "thanks to the advance of science, the earth was exactly alike all over" (Forster 1909, 6), and equal housing has been achieved globally.

Notably, the entrance door of the house in *The Machine Stops* has "a sliding door" (Forster 1909, 10). Although this may not be unusual to contemporary readers, such a sliding door differs from the traditional European construction of entrance doors and windows. According to Takashi Hamamoto (2011), an expert on Japanese and European architectural representations, most traditional European entrance doors and windows are designed to be pushed from the outside into the inside. This construction was born out of a sense of safety to easily protect oneself from external enemies by putting blocking objects, a consciousness that spread especially in England during the Industrial Revolution of the 17th and 18th centuries. In addition, this is connected to the culture of private rooms and locks that reached its peak in the 19th century (Hamamoto 2011, 16–18, 113–14; Tuan 2018, 300). As Hamamoto states, the "push culture" of pushing doors and windows to enter people's living spaces is also connected to the behavioral principles of colonialism and imperialism (Hamamoto 2011, 18–21). The "push culture" has disappeared in the world of *The Machine Stops*. Even if people do not consciously lock their doors, they will be protected by a mechanically controlled automatic lock. In a world filled with these houses, wars and invasions exist only in history classes, and no colonial policies or battles exist. At the end of the story, the situation where "Someone is trying to make himself king, to reintroduce the personal element" is regarded as an emergency, and there is a call to "Kill the man!" (Forster 1909, 22). This suggests that the power relations among people are equal. It is also a society of equality without class, insofar as it denies the idea of being a "king."

Although in his World System Theory, Immanuel Wallerstein explained imperialism and colonial policy as the structure of world capitalism, the world of *The Machine Stops* lacks several elements of capitalization at the popular level. For example, one of the characteristics of the buildings in the novel is their lack of windows. In his unfinished lifework *Das Passagen-Werk* (*The Arcade Project*, 1927–1940), Walter Benjamin once highlighted that capitalization and the desire for commodities are linked to glass and light. A concrete example of this is a shopping street. A shopping street displays a variety of materials to stimulate the material desires of passersby. The key elements that facilitate this are windows and light. This world is non-existent in Forster's story. However, the inhabitants of the world of *The Machine*

Stops do not require shopping malls because they can acquire everything they want by operating the machine in their houses. In fact, they do not leave their houses in the first place.

The world of *The Machine Stops* is not capitalized, the inhabitants are free from labor, and the power relations between people are equal economically and in terms of class. The structure of the houses and the living spaces indicate gender equality. The houses of Vashti and Kuno, who live on the opposite sides of the globe, are similarly constructed internally and externally, indicating that the inhabitants of the world of *The Machine Stops* live in structurally similar houses. In their houses, there are no kitchens, but only machines, desks, and armchairs. Childcare is left to public infant nurseries immediately after birth. In his book *Le sens pratique* (1980), Pierre Bourdieu discusses the Kabyle people's house and indicates that the material values and forms of architecture are connected with abstract values. He highlights that the interior of the house and various activities are organized in connection with dichotomous elements such as inside/outside, front door/back door, light/dark, east/west, and food storage/storage (Bourdieu 1980/1990, 209–31). This is, of course, not only pertinent to the Kabyle people. It is a global reality that the house is organized in such a way that the dichotomy of man/woman is associated with, for example, that of the living room/kitchen, entrance/kitchen door, and main/back. However, given the internal structure of houses in the story, daily activities (with the sole exception of childbirth) are gender-neutral. Considering the fact that Forster was homosexual, the world of the "machine" may have been an ideal society for him. In the latter half of the 20th century, Donna Haraway (1985) and Kōjin Karatani (2000) believed that the development of a computer as a machine could destroy capitalism and gender differences. As the most effective means to achieve this, the power of cyberspace was nominated and expected to bring benefit to people through its ability to diversify a self-image without codes or centers. In the world of *The Machine Stops*, a similar world is realized by the machines.

Through focusing on the buildings, the world of *The Machine Stops* reminds us of a utopia. The essential element of a utopia is "the desire for a better way of being" (Levitas 1990, 191), and a utopian novel is a story that concretely represents this desire at a conceptual level. Provided it is a representation of "the desire for a better way of being," a utopian novel can be a measure for judging and criticizing the real society. In fact, it is used as a measure (Zhang 2005, 165–67). Hence, the discourse on utopia always has a critical function because it transforms social allegory into a measure of the quality of life (Zhang 2005, 175). The equal and secure society of *The Machine Stops* seems to be a critique of English society during the period in which it was written. Hence, it can be considered a social allegory for an ideal society.

If the world of *The Machine Stops* is a utopian society, then the inhabitants of that world have great faith in science and machines. This is because the optimistic attitude toward science and machine civilization was shared by those who supported capitalist society and by those who expected an anti-capitalist society. Erika Gottlieb describes the expectations and utopias for the solution of the problems created by the Industrial Revolution, explaining that across the nineteenth century, there was desire to ameliorate the social ills caused by the Industrial Revolution, through both science, which was to end poverty, and socialism, which was to end injustice (Gottlieb 2001, 119). Zhang also highlights—using Soviet literature as an example—the following: early Soviet literature was saturated with utopian aspirations that imagined a world created by the proletariat and based on industrialized technology, scientific advancement, and Lenin's theories of communism (Zhang 2005, 204). The arrival of science and machines was greatly anticipated as a savior that would help the poor and eliminate social disparities. Therefore, even in the world of *The Machine Stops*, the machine is revered as "Machine" beginning with a capital letter, and "the Book" about this "savior" is cherished like the Bible.

SELF-INTEREST OVER LOVE: THE DYSTOPIAN NATURE OF *THE MACHINE STOPS*

However, Forster never portrayed the world of *The Machine Stops* in a positive light. As an endorsement, according to Nicola Beauman, a writer of Forster's biography, in January 1908, when Forster wrote his novel, he criticized the successful flight of a heavy airplane, stating that science did not make humans free but a servant of the machine (Beauman 1993, 214). In addition, Forster espoused democracy but rejected an efficiency regime that divides its citizens into the bossers and the bossed as well as totalitarianism that devalues "the individual" (Forster 1939, 70). However, probably due to the influence of Dickinson, Foster did not dogmatize democracy by expressing two cheers for democracy instead of three cheers.

One of the great influences on the formation of Forster's thought was Goldsworthy Lowes Dickinson, a British political scientist and philosopher, who helped to promote the establishment of the League of Nations. He emphasized harmony. As a Japanese scholar of E. M. Forster, Jirō Fukuda summarizes that since the claims of capitalism, imperialism, and socialism based on national interests and power relations all lead to conflicts with "anti" beliefs, and both sides continue to assert their own legitimacy, Dickinson believed that a constant search for mutual recognition based on a spirit of tolerance was essential (Fukuda 2014, 76). In June 1908, when Forster was writing *The Machine Stops*, he read American poet Walt Whitman's *Leaves of Grass* (1855) and was impressed by the theme of "connect" in the poem. Reflecting the theme, in *Howards End*, Forster depicted the reconciliation of people with different ideas, and he continued to develop the themes of "union," "reconciliation," and "harmony."

Forster emphasized the importance of a society in which the individual is respected and in which all individuals coexist harmoniously. Therefore, even if Forster, as a marginal member of the Bloomsbury Group, lacked interest in the working class and social welfare issues, it does not mean that he had a positive perspective of British society at the time, where the income division was such that few individuals lived happily. Simultaneously, Forster did not have a positive perspective of an equal society such as communism.

What, then, is the problem with the society of *The Machine Stops*? Unlike most dystopias, Forster's story does not foreground a society in which equality is associated with totalitarianism and in which individual values, humanity, and freedom are overwhelmingly devalued in the cause of the collective. This is because in such a society, each individual is confined to his or her house; there is no collective, collaborative, or cooperative spirit. In the world of Forster's story, there are restrictions on going out, similar to Thomas More's *Utopia* (1516). In the case of *The Machine Stops*, people are restricted in their activities because they are in a situation where they cannot go out (to the ground) without a ventilator, and it is not a consequence of purely social characteristics. Anyone who is deemed to have the physical strength to destroy the machine is eliminated, even at birth. The machine is not only the savior of the people but also the social infrastructure that guarantees their daily life, such as order and safety. When machines are personified (as in the former case), the elimination of those who destroy them means the prohibition of rebellion against the dictator. Therefore, the society is totalitarian. In the latter case, it means the elimination of those who may disturb the social order and disrupt the society of *The Machine Stops*. While it is quite normal for any society to socially exclude such people as dangerous molecules, the society in this story ignores the humanity of individuals through their exclusion from birth. Nevertheless, it differs from a common dystopia in that individual freedoms and values are not ignored in favor of group cooperation and the public good, but rather, individual freedoms remain. As Laurence Blander mentions, they do not live in a surveillance society where criticism of machines can be heard by the machine (Blander 1970, 213). Criticism of the machine is also possible. Many scholars have contended that the short story highlights how science and machines remove human freedom based on Forster's statement that science makes man a servant of the machine. Certainly, humans are crippled insofar as they cannot live without machines, but the machines in *The Machine Stops* provide humans with everything, and humans are free to choose and obtain what they want while at home. In this sense, the residents have relative freedom. If this is the case, what is the issue with this situation?

Such a situation itself is a problem. In the world of *The Machine Stops*, "[t]he better a man knew his own duties upon it, the less he understood the duties of his neighbor" (Forster 1909, 20). Stephen K. Land describes it as a society in which individualism is swiftly disappearing (Land 1990, 138); in fact, it is the opposite: it is a society of ultimate individualism, and the problem with this society is that each individual lives in a shell, where they are free to choose what they want in their own room and the machine provides it. In addition, the machine guarantees safety and security—that is, where others are unnecessary as long as there is a machine. In fact, as Avtar Singh highlights, the modern problem of coexistence of the individuals was already important in England (Singh 1986, 122). In light of Forster's emphasis on a society in which the individual is valued and in which all individuals coexist in harmony and cohesion, the overly "individual" life (and the way of being closed to the individual without connection to others) is considered a major element of the dystopian nature of *The Machine Stops*. In the story, people are not connected to others, as if reflecting the British society of the time, but they are connected conceptually by the machine—including the screen and the information and communication technology. If they drop a book in an air-ship, no one picks it up for them: within this society, cooperation and harmony are just conceptual matters, not physical realities or actions.

A society that prioritizes the self over others is a dystopian, as is a society that prioritizes the group over the individual. The word "dystopia" typically reminds us of a society where the group presides over the individual. For instance, in *We* (1924), the author Yevgeny Zamyatin questioned the socialist ideology and the uncompromising scientism that prevailed in the socialist states he witnessed at the time. He warned readers of the danger of sacrificing individual freedom and erasing humanity for the greater good of the collective or the dangers of specious utopian claims of rationality, scientific progress, and the public good. Historically, a dystopia also includes societies filled with people who think only of their own self-interest, and a number of such dystopian novels were written in the 19th century. This type of dystopia was developed in the 19th century. As Zhang (2005) explains, dystopia—the inverse of utopia—first emerged in the nineteenth century and, in the twentieth century, became an important response to the inherent malleability of human nature, the unrealistic expectations of social improvement, and the confidence in machines and technological advances. For instance, the French

Charles Nodier published several dystopian novels in the 1830s, and Emile Souvestre's *Le Monde tel qu'il sera* (1845) warned readers about the risks of industrialization, thought control, and materialism. Therefore, as early as 1845, there was overt concern about potential human enslavement to the machine and the replacement of love with self-interest. In England, Richard Jefferies's *After London* (1885), Ignatius Donnelly's *Caesar's Column* (1890), and Eugene Richter's *Pictures of a Socialist Future* (1893) were similar dystopian novels that offered social commentary (Zhang 2005, 204–205).

Following Zhang's perspective, *The Machine Stops* follows the lineage of the 19th-century dystopian novels. The houses of the people are underground and described as "cells." This implies that they do not live a happy life in houses like a prison, where they keep to themselves and put themselves before others.

However, since machines were created by human beings, the situation in which the self is given too much priority over others is also born from overconfidence in human power. Intrinsically, humans were powerless in the Western Christian world. Due to the influence of theologians and philosophers—especially St. Augustine—it was believed that human beings could not be happy in this world no matter how hard they tried because God commanded the fate of human beings, who were burdened with original sin. Gradually, this was replaced with the optimism that human beings could make society and life better and attain happiness through their own power, without the help of God. This change occurred in the age of religious secularization and the Age of Discovery (Zhang 2005, chap. 4). Therefore, to compare a human-made machine with God would indicate that the trust in human ability has turned into overconfidence. Thus, most of the people in the story are living individually without any doubt of their inability and powerlessness. If each of them is powerless, they must join forces. Human beings can live without the help of others because they can live (or think they can) solely by their own power. The machine has made this situation possible. Therefore, the world of *The Machine Stops* is dystopian owing to the excessive worship and overconfidence in the power of the individual, as opposed to dystopia due to the primacy of the collective over the individual. The story is dystopian due to the delusion that humans can live alone without the existence of others if only they had machines. Pointing once to the elements of Greek mythology and Italian Renaissance, Wilfred Stone documents that Forster's early short stories are characterized by gods entering among people or by people growing taller and becoming gods (Stone 1966, 130). From the perspective of overconfidence in human power, Stone's perspective applies to Forster's story despite the fact that at first glance, the story seems to have nothing to do with Greece or the Renaissance.

The machine in the novel achieves equality in many ways and provides people with a safe and comfortable life. Conversely, the individual is given too much priority, and people live in a world as if there were not any other people. The former is the utopian element, and the latter is the dystopian one. In Forster's story, the latter element is dominant because of his emphasis on coexistence with others and because the concept of equality itself cannot be established unless there are other people in the world.

The dystopian nature of story is not only a feature of the society presented as a warning in the early 20th century but also a feature of the world since the late 20th century. In fact, the world in which people live in isolation and value self-interest over love through the extensive use of "machines," especially those related to information and communication technology, was critically depicted in science fiction and fantasy in the latter half of the 20th century—especially in cyberpunk. For instance, in the society of Bruce Sterling's novel *Islands in the Net* (1988), which depicts a world with the slogan "from loneliness to symbiosis," solidarity is constantly emphasized; however, the reality of that society is a multinational corporation that pursues self-interest by making complete use of computers. Laura, a "corporate girl" (Sterling 1988, chap. 10), who finally realizes this reality, says "We had bad luck. [. . .] We stumbled over something buried, and it tore us up" (Sterling 1988, chap. 11). In contrast, the other main character, Gresham, tells that the net pulled them to pieces just as money, politics, and multinationals ripped them apart (Sterling 1988, chap. 11). They listen to a song sung by people who call themselves the "Indian Cultural Revolution," who say that the lives of their fathers and grandfathers were better, comparing to the contemporary people who live in the cities, in the world of "numbers and letters," and "eat magic food from tubes in camp" (Sterling 1988, chap. 10). People live in a world of numbers and letters or computer-connected "islands in the net," with no physical movement between people, no direct delivery of messages, and individual meals served through tubes in a camp. If we read "camp" as "a small room, hexagonal in shape, like the cell of a bee," it is the world of *The Machine Stops*.

Of course, there is a difference between *The Machine Stops* and science fiction of the latter half of the 20th century: in the former, the inhabitants are freed from labor thanks to the machine, and in the latter, the inhabitants are engaged in global labor thanks to the machine. However, there are similarities in that each individual lives separately and lives for self-interest rather than love. In other words, the dystopian elements of the latter half of the 19th century are common to the dystopian nature of the society of the latter half of the 20th century, and this dystopia is not a fiction.

In this sense, Forster's short story illuminates the reality of the early 20th century and represents contemporary society with its advanced information and communication technology. Furthermore, the world of *The Machine Stops* can be read allegorically as the reality of the world in the 2020s; when COVID-19 is prevalent, the majority of the global community are restricted from leaving their homes during the pandemic, physical contact is avoided, and talking through a screen using a machine is normalized without choice. However, the situation of the real world is somehow more complicated. In the contemporary business world, face-to-face negotiations, known as F2F, are not favored, and negotiations on the computer using the Internet are preferred. The physical division of people—a "Machine Stops" dystopian society—is not an abomination, but it is recommended as a desirable one. First, living in contemporary society—with computers and communication through information and communication technology—using the Internet is considered so indispensable that it is even taught in school. Thanks to this, in 2020, when COVID-19 became prevalent, lectures by teachers were provided online, similar to the world of *The Machine Stops* where physical contact is avoided. Therefore, the warnings issued in the story are significant for people living in contemporary societies, where dystopias are encouraged and dystopian elements are reinforced for pandemics. The contemporary significance of Forster's story and the modernity of its warning will be examined in detail in the following section.

A SOCIETY OF CLONELINESS: THE MODERNITY OF *THE MACHINE STOPS*

The story begins with a reference to the beehive-shaped dwellings of the inhabitants of the world, followed by a scene in which Vashti, who deifies the machine, and her son Kuno talk through a screen using a remote communication system. With the machine, they can talk face to face with people around the world. The machine also provides all the necessities of life so that humans do not have to step out of their rooms.

> There were buttons and switches everywhere—buttons to call for food for music, for clothing. There was the hot-bath button, by pressure of which a basin of (imitation) marble rose out of the floor, filled to the brim with a warm deodorized liquid. There was the cold-bath button. There was the button that produced literature. And there were of course the buttons by which she communicated with her friends. The room, though it contained nothing, was in touch with all that she cared for in the world (Forster 1909, 3–4).

Occasionally, the inhabitants will release the "isolation switch," read messages sent to them, and respond if necessary.

Vashti's next move was to turn off the isolation switch, and all the accumulations of the last three minutes burst upon her. The room was filled with the noise of bells and speaking tubes. What was the new food like? Could she recommend it? Has she had any ideas lately? Might one tell her one's own ideas? Would she make an engagement to visit the public nurseries at an early date?—say this day month. To most of these questions, she replied with irritation—a growing quality in that accelerated age (Forster 1909, 4).

Such a description functions rhetorically as a representation of the contemporary world with its advanced information and communication technology. It may not be possible for a bath to appear inside a house at the touch of a button, but it is now possible to fill the bath inside a house externally with a "smart phone." Literary texts can also be read at the click of an icon, whether on a smartphone or a computer. Furthermore, music, clothes, and meals can be delivered at the touch of an icon, which is also made possible by Amazon and Uber Eats. *The Machine Stops* says that these services were created owing to "the civilization that had mistaken the functions" of "the communication-system" and "had used it for bringing people to things, instead of for bringing things to people" (Forster, 1909, 5). This is also the idea behind Uber Eats and similar services that reversed the idea of people going to restaurants to eat and drink. When we use various services with machines, we receive messages asking us what we think of the food and whether we would recommend the service to others. This is also an ordinary state in which algorithms (as represented by GAFA) govern people in contemporary society and where information and communication engineering and daily human life are closely related. As those services are available with computers and smart phones (especially in urban areas, at least in Tokyo, Japan), people are increasingly living in small rooms with almost nothing. The houses of the people in *The Machine Stops* also contain "a small room, hexagonal in shape, like the cell of a bee," where an "armchair is in the center, by its side a reading-desk—that is all the furniture" (Forster 1909, 1). Furthermore, with use of the remote communication system of the machine, some individuals have connections with thousands of people. For instance, Vashti "knew several thousand people, in certain directions human intercourse had advanced enormously" (Forster 1909, 1), which is another characteristic of human relations in contemporary society. It may not be common to have "several thousands" of acquaintances through e-mail, LINE, Facebook, and other social networking sites, but it is not unusual to have "hundreds."

Considering this situation, the people in the world of *The Machine Stops* and the people of today, with the development of information and communication technology, share the common characteristic of living in physical isolation while forming conceptual groups. The acquaintances in the short story are similar to the acquaintances on contemporary social networking sites: the fact that they are connected to each other as acquaintances is not something that can be physically confirmed, but it is a connection that can be recognized by conceptually imagining the connection in the communication network (in cyberspace). In addition, the act of meeting is not an act of the whole body but is equivalent to the movement of a fingertip, such as pressing a button or clicking a mouse in an environment with an Internet connection. This situation of bodily fragmentation is clearly reproduced in *Vox* (1992), an American novel written by Nicholson Baker, which comprises only telephone conversations between a woman and a man. In the novel, a woman and a man, ordinary citizens leading ordinary lives, who do not know each other's names or faces, talk endlessly on the phone to each other in the language of a similar middle-class material world. Their conversations center on sex, and while they share tastes and thoughts, their conversations reveal a physical solitude in which the most intimate physical contact has been removed. In 1940, the American writer Carson McCullers published a novel entitled by *The Heart Is a Lonely Hunter*, but since *The Machine Stops* and the end of the 20th century, people have been living in the situation of "The Body is a Lonely Hunter."

In contemporary society, people are considered to be governed collectively by algorithms. As represented by Google, Apple, Facebook, and Amazon, or GAFA, information about individuals is collected through "machines," and people are clustered according to their preferences and thoughts. Individuals are frequently asked "How about this?" This happens without any special skills, as long as the "machine" is active. Therefore, people of all ages and genders, if they have the "machine," form an algorithmic crowd. Besides, the reliance on and the value of computers in contemporary society is unparalleled, and contemporary people are united in the thought that using computers, using English, and excelling in ideas are essential. People living in the society of *The Machine Stops* also use English (as it is natural because the text was written in English), and people are "almost exactly alike all over the world" (Forster 1909, 8), using "machines" to exchange "ideas" (Forster 1909, 2ff.). If it may be impossible to construct a system other than the current algorithm in which "machines" ask individuals for their impressions and opinions and provide them with appropriate ones, then even in the world of *The Machine Stops*, people would be physically alone in principle. But they would be clustered by preference and thought because they answer questions from "machines" and are provided with the most appropriate ones.

Michael O'Sullivan (2019) calls the situation of identification of people's tastes and thoughts and conceptual grouping and physical loneliness caused by machines (or information and communication technology) "cloneliness." People are connected to others in cyberspace, but the encounter involves single click of the mouse. They live as solitary entities in their physical bodies and continue to be reproduced as clones whose tastes and thoughts are clustered in a world where machines, English, and the exchange of ideas are equally important and controlled by algorithms. Psychiatrist Daniel Zagary warns that people in such an environment lose their sense of the actual other, not to consider the position of others, and to think and act like criminals and murderers (Zagary 2018, 111). Here, the danger of a dystopian contemporary society, which can be read as an allegory, emerges. That is the danger of a society full of people who, by placing importance on machines, devalue the existence of others and place too much importance on the self. However, we should not forget that such a society is not an abomination but perceived as a desirable one in the contemporary world. In addition, the world of *The Machine Stops*, in which those who cannot live or eat in such a society are called "homeless" and expelled from society, indicates the world of contemporary neoliberalism, in which the homeless are avoided and discarded.

THE NIGHTMARISH REVERSAL OF SAFETY: THE "OBJECTIFICATION" OF OTHERS AND THE WORLD

I have previously mentioned that cloneliness leads to a loss of a sense of actual otherness. In the novel, Kuno states the following to his mother: "I see something like you in this plate, but I do not see you. I hear something like you through this telephone, but I do not hear you. That is why I want you to come. Pay me a visit, so that we can meet face to face, and talk about the hopes that are in my mind" (Forster 1909, 2). Furthermore,

> the Machine did not transmit *nuances* of expression. It only gave a general idea of people—an idea that was good enough for all practical purposes, Vashti thought. The imponderable bloom, declared by a discredited philosophy to be the actual essence of intercourse, was rightly ignored by the Machine (Forster 1909, 3).

Of course, this does not mean that the communication lines are in bad condition. But it signifies a loss of a sense of the actual other, a lack of a sense of reality.

According to Zagary, as mentioned earlier, there is a danger that the loss of a sense of the actual other and the lack of a sense of reality will make people think and act like criminals and murderers. However, according to the novel, the machine asks people many questions to ensure their safety and comfort. In addition, people cannot easily walk out of doors. Hence, thanks to the machine, human life is protected, and safety is guaranteed. It is a kind of nightmare where the guarantee of safety leads to such a dangerous situation as Zagary highlights, but how does the safety provided by machines reverse into danger? In order to delve into the dystopian nature of *The Machine Stops* and contemporary society, this nightmarish reversal of security will be argued here from two aspects: the problem of systematic security and of conversations through screens, where the senses of sight and hearing are independent from the other senses.

The security provided to people by the machine in the novel is similar to the rational functioning systems that surround contemporary society, in that security is guaranteed without human experience or thought. The rational functioning system comprises safeguards or insurances that guarantee (or provide the impression of guaranteeing) a quick solution (provided an individual places their trust in the system), instead of living through the steps of confronting, pondering, attempting to solve, and overcoming difficulties in society. Satoshi Tanaka (2003), a Japanese pedagogue, explains the state of people of today who are "parasites" on the radical functioning system. According to Tanaka, in caricature form, it is a way of life in which, when one becomes ill, one immediately clings to a medical system that regards health as absolute; when one has a child, one immediately clings to an educational system that regards development as absolute; when one becomes anxious, one immediately clings to a religious system that regards faith as absolute; one immediately buries oneself in an economic system to the point of rejecting gifts that are not exchanges; and one immediately trusts a political system to the point of not being able to doubt the representative system (Tanaka 2003, 266). People might argue that it is better not to be a parasite on the radical functioning system. However, living in contemporary society is almost synonymous with living in the functioning system. As Ryōhei Matsushita (2006), a Japanese educationist, highlights, the rational functioning system is covering all aspects of life, both public and private, and people are able to live without experiences. In order to avoid problems and increase efficiency and predictability, rigorously calculated codes are proliferating to the extent that they are filling in every hole and corner of in people's lives, attracting them with their aesthetic taste and consummatory sense. Thus, in both public and private life, people can enjoy the here and now in their own way while subordinating themselves to the rational functioning system, so that they do not have to think about not only the purpose of their lives and activities but also the means to realize them (Matsushita 2006, 240).

The machine, which is an accumulation of rigorously calculated codes, guarantees the safety of human beings. In this sense, the surrender to the security of machines and subordination to the rational functioning system of contemporary society can be regarded as similar actions. From this perspective, what Matsushita explains later as a result of subordination to a rational functioning system can be read as a consequence of submitting oneself to the security of machines. According to Matsushita, when people of today are subordinated to a rational functioning system, they have more opportunities to use the world around them (things, nature, events, and other persons) unilaterally for their own benefit, but less opportunities to interact with them. This leads to phenomena such as a diminished sense of reality (not seeing the world as actual), indifference to others, and lack of historical awareness (indifference to the past and future) (Matsushita 2006, 243–44). Moreover, thinking well is left to the functioning system, and meanings are only received unilaterally through experience, and hence, they are not interrelated or ordered. In exchange for the safety and security guaranteed by relying on the rational functioning system, people of today do not have deep thoughts and impressions, and they do not become deeply involved with others and the world (Matsushita 2006, 243–44). Indeed, the inhabitants also "seized with the terrors of direct experience" (Forster 1909, 5, 7). Thus, "in all the world, there was not one who understood the monster [the Machine] as a whole. Those master brains had perished. They had left full directions, it is true, and their successors had each of them mastered a portion of those directions. But Humanity, in its desire for comfort, had over-reached itself. It had exploited the riches of nature too far" (Forster 1909, 20). Having "understood the monster [the Machine] as a whole" is equivalent to looking at one's own life with an objective and deep understanding of society itself, which Laura in *Islands in the Net* calls "something buried" and which influences the way people live, think, and value. However, for people in the novel, it has become more important to live comfortably and safely, having machines literally "mechanically" guarantee our safety.

The asymmetrical relationship with the world, in which the surrounding environment is only used by oneself, was the theme and style of naturalistic literature in North America during the same period in which the novel was written. The nature of object recognition described in these novels, both in content and style, is the same as that of *The Machine Stops* and that in contemporary society where information and communication technology has developed. The nature of object recognition is, according to Masashi Orishima, a Japanese scholar of American literature, characterized by lack of a common sense. Relying on a Japanese psychopathologist Satoshi Kimura, Orishima explains as follows: Kimura calls as a common sense "something like a third medium" that works when one acts on the other in a world where people share a common world as a social organism, but do not face each other one-on-one as parts. It is a function that connects individual senses and individual things, a function that makes the world shared, and a function that gives individual situations and things a meaning filled with a sense of being alive. The act of perceiving things is not performed only by the individual senses, such as sight, hearing, touch, taste, and smell. There is some kind of integrated sense that serves as a common basis for these individual senses and, in that sense, is higher than the individual senses. It gives meaning to life in our world (Orishima 2000, 30). Orishima continues to explain further, borrowing Kimura's perspective (Kimura 1994, 13). The world people live in is not only composed of light rays, colors captured by lenses, and sound waves collected by microphones. The world people live in is first and foremost a world that is meaningful to their life in a way that is both favorable and unfavorable for their living, a world that shapes each and every frame of their lives, before it is meaningful in a way that can be understood in a linguistically segmented way. Such meanings cannot be captured by individual senses. It is the common sense that plays the role of capturing such meanings directly or intuitively prior to their intellectual reconstruction.

Orishima concludes that this lack of a "common sense" is a characteristic of American naturalistic literature. Orishima indicates that the nature of object recognition in American naturalism, which lacks a "common sense," is similar to that of a machine (Orishima 2000, 51). For instance, in an author of American naturalism Stephen Crane's text, either reality or "objects," as the object of perception or actuality or "events" that appeals to sensibility and experience in the field of action, is almost forcibly removed. The independence of a sense of vision is correlated with the body's disconnection from the physical other, the subject's disconnection from the social other, and the senses' disconnection from the other senses (Orishima 2000, 216). Hence, Crane's text presents a severing of the linkage between the cognizing subject and the cognized object, and hence a lack of the meaning of living, and instead a bruising individual sense impression separated from the totality of impressions (Orishima 2000, 216).

This may be the reason why the inhabitants of *The Machine Stops* are the servants of the machine although they are relatively free. That is, the actuality is removed, and only the "objects"—as object of perception—are present. Therefore, sight, or sight and hearing, has been cut off from the other senses so that humans themselves become similar to machines. The sense of discomfort Kuno experiences when talking through a screen is caused by the fact that communication through a screen does not become a place of action and that the higher integrated senses do not function because of the reliance only on sight and hearing.

According to Orishima, the object of perception depicted in American naturalistic literature is similar to that of people living in contemporary consumer capitalist society. This is not due to the influence of information and communication technology but due to the influence of capital economy, indicating that contemporary capitalist society is equivalent to a dystopia where self-interest presides over love, relying on machines. Therefore, the world of *The Machine Stops* can be an allegory of contemporary society in which capitalism is global. Relying on Frederic Jameson (1981), Orishima states that the process of fragmentation of mental faculties proceeds within the limits inevitably imposed by the rationalization, materialization, and fragmentation of human social life by the market economy. He mentioned that each mental faculty becomes relatively independent, as, for example, the faculty of measuring and rational reasoning develops and is highly valued, while the sensory faculty is regarded as low. The representation of the senses that achieve such relative independence is sight. It is a place where, with the desensitization of science, a great deal of perceptual energy is concentrated (Orishima 2000, 219–20). As a result, the subject and the environment, which used to be considered as unarticulated and monolithic entities, can now be broken down into measurable dimensions and the notion of color as single concept (rather than different colors, such as brown or blue). That is, the psyche and the world are simultaneously fragmented. Its typical example is a genre of landscape painting, which no longer depicts the natural world as we see it but rather emphasizes sensory processes (Jameson 1981, 229–30). This implies the indifference of contemporary people to the external world and the self-objectification of their senses (Orishima 2000, 220). The passage in the novel that refers to the "imponderable bloom, declared by a discredited philosophy to be the actual essence of intercourse, was rightly ignored by the Machine" (Forster 1909, 3), can be read as a warning of a situation where a fragmentation of the world and of the psyche occur together.

Here, it is important to note that Forster also emphasized the integration of the senses in his 1927 essay, "The Bunch of Sensations." Hitoshi Tsutsui (1983), a Japanese specialist of Forster's literature, explains the expression of "experience" as seen in this text in relation to "world sense" as follows. First, "experience" means "what is felt in the body and the feeling of it." It is "what is felt by all the five organs and what is sensed by the simultaneous activity of both the body and the mind" and "the physical and mental feeling" that can only be called experience which is not merely the functioning of individual senses among the five senses, such as sight and hearing, but the activity of all the five organs and the integration of them. Forster emphasized the importance of such sensations. To paraphrase the words of Yoshio Abe, a Japanese scholar of British literature, Forster idealized the "whole man" (Abe 1983, 71).

To this extent, Forster is critical of the lack of a common sense, or the independence of sight (or sight and hearing), which is a characteristic of American naturalistic literature and contemporary society. The situation, in which individual living places appear as "objects" of perception rather than "events" that appeal to sensibility and experience, is considered to be contrary to

Forster's ideal. Systematic security also makes people unilaterally involved in the world so that the world and others appear as "objects." If others are only "objects" to a person, there is no way for them to coexist with others.

For reference, it would be interesting to compare, for instance, Rebecca Brown's collection of short stories *The Gifts of the Body* (1994) and *The Machine Stops* with regard to the body. The novel lacks physicality. By contrast, the people in the world of *The Gifts of the Body* value the body and care for others. In the short story "Plague," the saddest thing in a world where plague is spreading is that people are dying one after another, and the story ends with a friend who is dying of plague saying, "I miss you too." The story suggests that it is only through the presence of others that one feels alive.

ON THE DISCOMFORT OF DISTANCE EDUCATION: FOR THE RESTORATION OF THE BODY

The previous section also highlighted the problem of online distance education in the world of *The Machine Stops*, a world where physical contact with others is avoided. In *The Machine Stops*, Vashti lectures on history online, and Kuno has also learned many things online. In his book *On the Internet*, Hubert L. Dreyfus (2001) reveals the problems of distance learning through chapters such as "How Far is Distance Learning from Education?" as if he were following Tanaka, Matsushita, and Orishima's arguments and Forster's opinion in "Bunch of Sensations." Similarly, Dreyfus believes that *The Machine Stops* foresaw the problems of contemporary distance education.

According to Dreyfus, online distance learning provides the facts, rules, and training necessary for beginner students. However, the experience of making incorrect interpretations and then learning from one's mistakes is essential for gaining skill in a field (Dreyfus 2001, 121–22). Dreyfus continues to explain that the Web allows us to store large amounts of information, to remain connected with each other, to learn about distant places, and to experiment virtually without risk to the actual world. We also, though, need to use our own physical powers to learn skills, to understand the world, to encounter risk, and to experience shared feelings—all of which bring meaning to our lives (Dreyfus 2001, 124–25). Similarly, Tanaka and Matsushita highlight that in exchange for safety and security (i.e., without any risk at all), people lose their ability to think deeply, to be moved, and to engage deeply with others and the world. Risks are avoided by a rational functioning system that is an accumulation of strictly calculated codes, but because of this, humans only work with the world around them in a one-way manner and do not negotiate with the world. Consequently, the world becomes "objects" as objects of perception, and we lose deep thoughts, impressions, and deep relationships with others and the world. In order to avoid such a situation, we need to negotiate directly with the world, always bearing the possibility of risk. To do this, it is not enough to use only our eyes and ears. As Dreyfus indicates, our body and our psyche are essential for understanding what is relevant around us and what matters to us, for acquiring skills, for learning to trust others and to make commitments to others, and for cultivating the intercorporeality. Because all of this gives focus to our lives, it would be a grave error to think we could jettison our embodied experiences by relying on the opportunity that the Internet gives us to become increasingly disembodied and detached (Dreyfus 2001, 121).

In essence, in online distance learning, "events" (i.e., actuality) that appeal to the senses and experiences in the field of action are removed, and only "objects" as objects of perception are present. Therefore, the total senses, which are higher than the individual senses, do not function, and the connection between the cognizing subject and the cognized object is severed. In this case, as Kuno experienced, we can only see and hear others to a certain extent. Because the class is taught through a screen, learning that appeals to the senses and experience in the place of action is not possible. Therefore, learning embedded in the situation is difficult, knowledge is suspended, and a gulf is created among knowledge, understanding, and the body. Thus, Kuno is able to feel the connection between learning and reality only when he leaves the world of the screen and goes out on the ground.

> The sun grew very feeble, and I remembered that he was in Scorpio—I had been to a lecture on that too. If the sun is in Scorpio, and you are in Wessex, it means that you must be as quick as you can, or it will get too dark (This is the first bit of useful information I have ever got from a lecture, and I expect it will be the last) (Forster 1909, 15).

Kuno is also moved by the sense of actuality, saying "I have seen the hills of Wessex as Ælfrid saw them when he overthrew the Danes" (Forster 1909, 15). As such, Kuno says that what is "humanity" basically "seems naked" (Forster 1909, 13), without clothes, tubes, or anything else, and argues that humans should live based on the human body. The emphasis on the human body itself means the recovery of "events" (i.e., actuality) that appeal to our senses and experiences in the field of action that have been removed. Kuno says "[The Machine] has robbed us of the sense of space and of the sense of touch, it has blurred every human relation and narrowed down love to a carnal act" (Forster 1909, 15). He also states the following:

> We have lost a part of ourselves. I determined to recover it, and I began by walking up and down the platform of the railway outside my room. Up and down,

until I was tired, and so did recapture the meaning of 'Near' and 'Far.' 'Near' is a place to which I can get quickly *on my feet*, not a place to which the train or the air-ship will take me quickly. 'Far' is a place to which I cannot get quickly on my feet [. . .] Man is the measure. That was my first lesson. Man's feet are the measure for distance, his hands are the measure for ownership, his body is the measure for all that is lovable and desirable and strong (Forster 1909, 11–12).

What "[w]e have lost" are "events" that appeal to our senses and experiences in the place of action. That is why Kuno tries to regain "[w]e have lost" through the act of walking. Simultaneously, by doing so, he recognizes the body more clearly. This is tantamount to regaining the sense of the world, the physical and mental sense that Forster emphasizes. This is because "objects"—as objects of perception—can be recognized by appealing to the senses and experiences in the field of action, and simultaneously, in reality, without "objects" there is no appeal to the senses and experiences. In other words, there is no such thing as reality that is not supported by actuality, and as long as people are actually experiencing events, they are usually supported in some way by objects (Kimura 1994, 131).

In order not to remove either "objects" or "events," reality or actuality, it is necessary to use higher-order integrated senses and direct experiences rather than individual senses and to encourage learners to think deeply in risky situations. In an environment where we cannot but rely on "machines," we should, at least, remember this and clearly indicate the limitations of online classes to learners. Otherwise, online distance learning will provide learners with the same experience as Kuno. If their experience is closely related to *The Machine Stops* and the dystopian nature of contemporary society, online distance learning can even educate students to become familiar with life in a dystopia.

Claude J. Summers states that Kuno's emphasis on human nakedness and the body probably derives from Thomas Carlyle's *Sartor Resartus* and hence concludes that "'The Machine Stops' offers an optimistic view of Carlyle's belief that we can regain our humanity despite our dehumanizing society" (Summers 1983, 258). However, Summers overlooks an important point. That is, at the conclusion of the story, many people leave the world. If many of the people who make up the dystopia depart from the world, naturally the dystopia will collapse and humans may resurrect phoenix like from the ashes of a dehumanizing society. Therefore, the characteristic of the novel, as seen from its conclusion, is not optimism but intense irony and pessimism in the expectation of death for the humans who populate the inhuman society. Contemporary society encourages dystopia. Can we not expect the end of that society being devoid of something similar to the events in *The Machine Stops*?

CONCLUSION

E. M. Forster's *The Machine Stops* can be considered a dystopian allegory for our time due to the modernity of its warning. Initially, machines were generally designed to improve human life and society. In the early 20th century, when the story was written, science and machines were expected to be the savior that eliminated disparity among people. In the Western Christian world, this expectation derived from a shift in thinking from human original sin and helplessness before God to the ability of humans to be happy on their own without the help of God. However, the machine transforms the ideal society, or utopia, into a dystopia. The dystopia of the novel lies in the fact that it puts too much priority on the self and eliminates the actual other and the world. This is also true of contemporary society, which has developed information and communication technology since the latter half of the 20th century. While people are connected to others in cyberspace, their encounters are limited to a single click of the mouse. Each life is a solitary physical being, placing equal importance on exchanging ideas with "machines" and in English and continuing to be reproduced as clones, whose tastes and thoughts are clustered in a world controlled by algorithms. In such an environment, human beings lose their sense of the actual other because they live by relying only on senses of sight and hearing, which are separated from the other senses. Furthermore, the "events" that appeal to their senses and experiences in the field of action (i.e., their "actuality") are removed, and only "objects" as objects of perception become present. However, as Kuno notices, human beings regain their actuality based on the body. According to *The Machine Stops*, the re-emergence of such a society of human beings will eventuate only after the majority of people inhabiting the dystopia pass away.

In the early 2020s, following the global impact of COVID-19, physical contact must be avoided and daily life, work, and education must be conducted through "machines." The "machine" is a savior that can stop the infection by avoiding physical contact between people. As long as the pandemic continues, we must consider that everything will become an "object" to be recognized, that actual others and the world will increasingly disappear, and that we will be confined to our own world. The concern is that people will no longer consider the perspective of others and will start to think and act like criminals and murderers as Zagary highlights. Can we expect to see a world full of hope only after many people have left a contemporary society as the dystopian world due to the pandemic of COVID-19? Now, because of the pandemic, humans must rely on "machines" more than ever before. Consequently, society is becoming increasingly dystopian. Thus, the majority of people should remember what Forster emphasized—the importance of the individual and a society in which all individuals coexist in harmony—and remember to live daily lives that emphasize ideas, the body, and the integration of the five organs. If we remember this, there is a possibility that after the pandemic ends (or after the factors that promote dystopia have left this world), the desire for a society in which the body is valued and individuals coexist may dissolve the dystopian society. Ultimately, this reminds us that "we are together," Dr. Rieux's emphasis in Camus's *The Plague*. Is this not also the contemporary significance of the warning in *The Machine Stops*?

ACKNOWLEDGEMENTS

This work was supported by JSPS KAKENHI Grant Number JP18K00781 and JP20K02795.

REFERENCES

Abe, Sachiko. 1989. *E. M. Fōsutā kenkyū.* [*Study on E. M. Forster.*] Tokyo: New Current International.

Abe, Yoshio. 1983. *E. M. Fōsutā kenkyū: Heikō kankaku no bungaku.* [*Study on E. M. Forster: Literature of equilibrium.*] Tokyo: Seibidō.

Beauman, Nicola. 1993. *Morgan: A Biography of E. M. Forster*. London: Hodder and Stoughton.

Beer, John. 1962. *The Achievement of E. M. Forster*. London: Chatto & Windus.

———. 1979. "'The Last Englishman': Lawrence's Appreciation of Forster." In *E. M. Forster: A Human Exploration: Centenary Essays*, edited by G. K. Das and John Beer, 245–68. London: The Macmillan Press.

Blander, Laurence. 1970. *E. M. Forster: A Critical Study*. London: Rupert Hart-Davis, Rept.

Bourdieu, Pierre. 1980/1990. *Jissen kankaku 2.* [*Le sens pratique 2.*] Translate by Hitoshi Imamura, Norihiko Fukui, Fumi. Tsukahara, and Takashi Minatomichi. Tokyo: Misuzu Shobo.

———. 2000/2006. *Jūtaku jijō no shakaikeizaigaku.* [*Les structures sociales de l'économie.*] Translated by Toshio Yamada and Junko Watanabe. Tokyo: Fujiwara Shoten.

Brown, Rebecca. 1994. *The Gifts of the Body*. London: HarperCollins.

Caporaletti, Silvana. 1997. "Science as Nightmare: 'The Machine Stops' by E.M. Forster." *Utopian Studies* 8(2): 32–47.

Dreyfus, Hubert L. 2001. *On the Internet*. London and New York: Routledge.

Forster, Edward Morgan. 1909. "The Machine Stops." *Oxford and Cambridge Review*, November 1909. Retrieved June 25, 2021 from https://www.ele.uri.edu/faculty/vetter/Other-stuff/The-Machine-Stops.pdf.

_____. 1927/2021. "Bunch of Sensations." In *Delphi Complete Works of E. M. Forster*. East Sussex: Delphi Classics. Kindle.

_____. 1939/1951."What I Believe." In *Two Cheers for Democracy*, 67–76. New York: Harcourt Brace.

_____. 1961. *Aspects of the Novel*. London: Edward Arnold.

Fukuda, Jirō. 2014. "E. M. Fōsutā no shisō keisei: Kenburijji to G. L. Dikinson." ["Formative Years of E. M. Forster: Cambridge and G. L. Dickinson."] *Surugadai University Studies* 48: 61–84.

Gottlieb, Erika. 2001. *Dystopian Fiction East and West: Universe of Terror and Trial*. Montreal: McGill-Queen's University Press.

Hamamoto, Takashi. 2011. *"Mado" no shisōshi: Nihon to Yōroppa no kenchiku hyōshō ron*. [*The History of the Idea of the Window: Architectural Representation in Japan and Europe.*] Tokyo: Chikuma Shobō.

Haraway, Donna. 1985. "A Manifesto for Cyborgs: Science, Technology, and Socialist Feminism in the 1980s." *Socialist Review*, 80: 65–108.

Herz, Judith Scherer. 1979. "The Narrator as Hermes: A Study of the early short fiction." In *E. M. Forster: A Human Exploration: Centenary Essays*, edited by G. K. Das and John Beer, 17–27. London: The Macmillan Press.

Hillegas, Mark E. 1967. *The Future as Nightmare: H. G. Wells and the Anti-Utopians*. London: Oxford University Press.

Hollingsworth, Cristopher. 2001. *Poetics of the Hive: Insect Metaphor in Literature*. Iowa City: University of Iowa Press.

Jameson, Frederic. 1981. *The Political Unconscious: Narrative as a Socially Symbolic Act*. Ithaca: Cornell University Press.

Karatani, Kōjin. 2000. *NAM genri*. [*NAM Principium.*] Tokyo: Ōta Shuppan.

Kimura, Satoshi. 1994. *Kokoro no byōri wo kangaeru*. [*Considering the Pathology of the Mind.*] Tokyo: Iwanami Shoten.

Land, Stephen K. 1990. *Challenge and Conventionality in the Fiction of E. M. Forster*. New York: AMP Press.

Levitas, Ruth. 1990. *The Concept of Utopia*. New York: Philip Allan.

Lowe, Stuart. 2011. *The Housing Debate*. Bristol: Policy Press.

Matsushita, Ryōhei. 2003. "Posutomodan shakai to Dyūi: Keiken no fukken no tameni." ["Postmodern Society and Dewey: Toward the Restoration of Experience."] In *Gendai Dyui shiso no sai hyoka* [*Reevaluating Dewey's Thought of Today*], edited by Hiroshi Sugiura, 214–46. Tokyo: Seakai Shisōsha.

O'Sullivan, Michael. 2019. *Cloneliness: On the Reproduction of Loneliness*. New York: Bloomsbury.

Orishima, Masashi. 2000. *Kikai no teishi: America shizensyugi no shōsetsu no undō*. [*Stopping the Machine: Movement/time/Perception in the American Naturalist Novels.*] Tokyo: Shōhakusha.

Satō, Nobuo. 1992. *Retorikku kankaku*. [*Sense of Rhetoric.*] Tokyo: Kodansha.

Seabury, Marcia Bundy. 1997. "Image of a Networked Society: E. M. Forster's 'The Machine Stops.'" *Studies in Short Fiction*, 34 (1) (Winter): 61–71.

Singh, Avtar. 1986 *Ten Novels of E. M. Forster*. New Delhi: Atlantic.

Sontag, Susan. 2003. *Regarding the Pain of Others.* New York: Farrar, Straus and Giroux.

Sterling, Bruce. 1988. *Islands in the Net.* New York: Open Road Integrated Media. Kindle.

Stone, Wilfred. 1966. *The Cave and the Mountain.* Redwood City: Stanford University Press.

_____. 1982. "E. M. Forster's Subversive Individualism." In *E. M. Forster: Centenary Revaluations*, edited by Judith Scherer Herz and Robert K. Martin, 15–36. London: The Macmillan Press.

Summers, Claude J. 1983. *E. M. Forster.* New York: Frederick Ungar.

Tanaka, Satoshi. 2003. "Poppu kankakaku kara fuyū kankaku e: Shisutemu ni hibiku fukyō waon." ["From a Pop Sensation to a Floating Sensation: A Cacophony Echoing through the System."] In *Kyoiku to seiji: Sengo kyoikushi wo yominaosu* [*Education and Politics: Rereading Postwar Educational History*], edited by Naoto Morita, Nobuko Morita, and Yasuo Imai, 250–81. Tokyo: Keisō Shobō.

Tereszewski, Marcin. 2020. "Dystopian Space in E. M. Forster's 'The Machine Stops.'" *Language and Literary Studies of Warsaw*, Nr 10: 225–36.

Trilling, Lionel. 1965. *E. M. Forster.* New York: New Directions.

Tsutsui, Hitoshi. 1983. *E. M. Fōsutā no "Tochi no Rei."* [*The Spirit of the Land in E. M. Forster's Works.*] Tokyo: Eichōsha.

Tuan, Yi-Fu. 1982/2018. *Kojin kūkan no tanjō: Shokutaku, kaoku, gekijō, sekai.* [*Segmented Worlds and Self: Group Life and Individual Consciousness.*] Translated by Hajime Abe. Tokyo: Chikuma Shobō.

Zagary, Daniel. 2018. *La Barbarie des hommes ordinaires: Ces criminels qui pourraient être nous.* Paris: Éditions de l'Observatoire/Humensis.

Zhang, Longxi. 2005. *Allegoresis: Reading Canonical Literature East and West.* Ithaca: Cornell University Press.

_____. 2015. *From Comparison to World Literature.* New York: SUNY.

Chapter Eight

Orwellian Themes and Echoes in Today's World—A Perspective

Beena Giridharan, Curtin University, Malaysia

Demand for Dystopian novels and television series have never been high as it has been since recent times. We are cognizant that "Dystopia" is imaginary and foretells bad governance. Nevertheless, dystopic contemplations surface in people's minds when modern democracies display seemingly autocratic manoeuvres taking the populace by surprise. While governments may not be perfect, most citizens in western democracies expect clear democratic systems to check the overly powerful and establish accountability. This chapter explores the upsurge of Orwellian themes and echoes in the language and actions by governments in western democracies and attempts to highlight the rise of distortion of facts by leaders of the free worlds both in developed and developing worlds, and propaganda policies used to oppress free thought among average middle class citizens. It will draw comparisons and analysis between characters and events in Orwellian novels, *1984* and *Animal Farm,* Huxley's *Brave New World,* and other novels, to modern day democratic government actions and measures, in an effort to create a nuanced understanding of the "Big Brother is watching you" concept, and the rise of imperious actions and events in democratic countries.

DYSTOPIAN NARRATIVES

Dystopian fiction allowed for cautionary parables to expound political, social and cultural trajectories that could potentially lead to chaotic existences or states of possibilities. There has been a lot of demand for Dystopian fiction such as George Orwell's *1984* and Margaret Atwood's *The Handmaid's*

Tale since 2016, as well as young adult dystopias. For instance, *The Hunger Games* by Suzanne Collins and *Divergent* by Veronica Roth are hugely popular bestsellers and television shows (Shames & Atchison, 2020). Shames & Atchison (2020) contend that the definition of dystopia is not political, and that it is reflective of government shortcomings, and argue that understanding dystopia begins with initiating the fundamentals of good governance, and how the governments protect citizens in a "non-coercive way and are well positioned to plan and guard against natural and human made horrors." Other Dystopian researchers like Adam Stock (2019) profess that we live in dystopian times, and that 'Dystopia' has not only attained representational cultural value in exemplifying fears and apprehensions about the future, but has also become a reference for discussing topics such as governance, popular culture, security, structural discrimination, environmental disasters and more, for grappling patterns with understanding geo-political problems, economic anxieties, and social fears. In his recent publication, Stock (2019) highlights the emergence of dystopian fiction as a genre for critiquing socio-political events and discourses across the first half of the twentieth century and analyses how a sequence of scripts from an era of political extremes have been furthering the semantics in present settings and have been the cause of cultural anxieties.

RISE OF TECHNOLOGY

Aldous Huxley's *Brave New World* (1932) portended the perils of genetic engineering, and warns us about how much technology should be adopted by society. Huxley's *Brave New World* contents that the world state uses extremely powerful technologies such as '*hypnopaedia conditioning'* (learning through hypnopsis), extreme contraceptive measures, and other significant medical interventions in the name of progress while implementing advanced science, failing to disclose their true purpose of controlling society (Boyle 2015).

Huxley derides the use of '*hypnopaedia'* procedures by the control state, while talking about the '*Bokanovski'* process which resembles genetic engineering in modern day contexts, to reproduce humans in labs with embryo preferences from Alphas to Epsilons who would then be assigned a particular place in society through continued conditioning, and further states that prolonged conditioning and extreme use of technology, may compel humanity to move into a genetically modifiable future where individuals behave in the manner in which control states would expect them to.

In *Brave New World*, ironically the world state relies on science and technology for controlling human behaviour, but does not support actual science for advancement of society. The moral compass of society which under normal settings is fashioned by our belief system, values, religion, and parental upbringing, is now impelled by industry, economy and technological growth in *Brave New World*, and instead humans live in a world where they have no value as individuals but are conditioned to see the world through a collective and technology oriented perspective (Miller, 2011). The question to raise here is, how close are we to the precipice of falling into a technological chasm whilst Machine Learning (ML) and Artificial Intelligence (AI) are rapidly gaining ground? Among the drivers of massive change occurring in an expeditiously transforming world are AI and ML, and with not all changes being positive; some deem AI and ML sceptically with the potential for creating bias that could lead to exploitation, while others see them as an inevitable and inescapable part of future. AI and ML are already revolutionising the world of business and medicine and being entrenched into every aspect of our lives.

ORWELLIAN TONES IN GLOBAL RESPONSES TO COVID-19

COVID-19 has furthered disbelief in global administrations with many drawing references to the power of media in fuelling anxiety in the general public. The emergence of COVID-19 under mysterious circumstances in Wuhan, China engendered numerous conspiracy theorists to speculate on its origins. In Orwell's *Nineteen Eighty-four*, the 'Ministry of Truth's' official language 'Oceania' used 'Newspeak' to dilute the intellect of the denizens of the totalitarian state similar to the contemporary media's constant references to the staggering number of fatalities occurring daily in each country (Razaq, 2020), inducing panic and high anxiety among the masses. Citizens around the world watched their health minister or health representative provide statistics of daily COVID-19 cases and loss of lives to the illness, invoking fear and helplessness to an extent never seen before. The incessant blitz related to COVID-19 data on the number of daily new cases and fatalities defined life as it were for nearly 20 months for the majority of citizens. This was followed by the speculations on the severity of the virus variant and the despondent wait for vaccines. Daily lives of the general public were impacted distressingly due to the strict lockdowns and movement restrictions announced globally. Schools and universities resorted to fully online learning and teaching with little preparation, while businesses and organizations scampered to send their work force home. Life as we knew it vanished abruptly, and was replaced by restricted freedom and controlled governance.

Extensive media coverage on the COVID-19 pandemic, and swift responses from public on multiple social media platforms, meant that governments were left to quickly compare notes on what procedures to implement based on the severity of cases in neighbouring countries, before taking tough stances themselves. Governments warned against "multiple waves" sweeping through the lands which would decimate citizens in such devastating numbers that were overwhelming to comprehend, prompting writers and experts to raise warning signals against the rise of totalitarian states.

> Keep this studiously in mind and impress it as an important part of the scheme of organization, that they [the Black people] must have money, if they want to get free. Money will obtain them every thing [sic] necessary by which to obtain their liberty. The money is within all their reach if they only knew it was right to take it. . . . You must teach them to take all the money they can get from their masters, to enable them to make the strike without a failure. . . . Bear this in mind; it is your certain passport through the white gap, as I term it (Delany 2017, 44).

Amidst the angst of the deaths and severity of the disease, researchers and scientists were unable to provide plausible explanations on the spread of the disease nor could they predict reasonable time lines for the slowing down of the pandemic. This led to several epidemiologists to caution that societal, economic and psychological damage from the extraordinary lockdowns were likely to be far greater than the perceived risk of death but such views were dismissed and treated like Orwellian "Thought crime" (Razaq, 2020).

There is a prevalence for distorting truth in contemporary times, comparable to how in Oceania, the Ministry of Truth relentlessly tries to redraft history, with the belief that if the past was erased, it was easy to forget the past, and falsehoods soon became the truth; in some countries like China, Orwell's *1984* itself has been erased from the Internet (Cohen & Kidman, 2022). The emergent power of the control state in developing and developed countries as COVID-19 raged through the lands, was distinctly observable. Although mask mandates and restricted movements were acceptable to the masses in the absence of medical antidotes and vaccines, the prolonged border closings were largely applied to ordinary citizens, while powerful politicians and business tycoons continued to cross borders effortlessly in their private jets.

POWER PLAY POLITICS

Animal Farm reminds that totalitarianism and hypocrisy are rife to the human condition. Orwell contends that if lower classes are not educated and not empowered, society will constantly default to tyranny. Orwell demonstrates how powerful language and propaganda is used to control people in *Animal*

Farm, and how songs, slogans are used to evoke emotional responses that reinforce the animals' loyalty to the state authorities.

A week after President Donald Trump's inauguration, George Orwell's *1984* became the best-selling book on Amazon.com, to the delight of probably countless English teachers that people had to reach out to a novel published in 1949 for understanding how to cope with their present life, stated Broich, (2017) in his article "2017 isn't 1984—it's stranger than Orwell imagined." Other journalists and writers such as Gopnick (2017) who did not think much about Orwell's *1984* and had considered the novel to be too brutal, primitive and constrained in its imagination of the relation between authoritarian state and helpless citizens, was forced to rethink his beliefs of the book in the aftermath of Trump's presidential election.

In January of 2017, weeks after Trump was sworn to the office as the next president of the United States of America, Gopnick (2017) wrote that Orwell was actually right about his representations of monstrous authoritarianism, in his *1984* in that it was fundamentally based on lies repeated so often that it was more exhausting to fighting the lie than it was to repeat it, and that Orwell's understanding of doctoring reality was only next to changing perceptions in that it was the most influential a way of asserting power. This was in response to the litany of lies being repeated by President Trump. Gopnick (2017) went on to state that these repeated lies meant to intimidate the public and was a deliberate challenge to the larger picture of sanity. This sentiment was echoed throughout Trump's presidency on multiple occasions. The voices of reason that one would expect would soon prevail in a western democracy like the United States, were muted to the extent that alarm bells rang in the minds of intellectuals and educated public, and it became soon clear that this presidency would be an outlier in the scale of politics.

Many observers of US foreign policy, were alarmed by Trump's national security strategy of continued insistence on American global dominance which has been criticized by observers of the US foreign policies as "Orwellian" and "military first." Seaton, Crook & Taylor (2017) draw parallels between key messages in *1984* and Brexit, and Trump's propaganda language, which seeks to limit human consciousness, confuse human conscience, and control range of thinking in people through the use of "alternative facts" and deliberate untruths.

Trump's presidency was tarnished by the unceasing lies and truth distortions that was sadly accepted by his supporters and to a greater extent the American people who remained immune to his faults which prompted political writers like Ricks (2017) to avow that Orwell's writing spoke to contemporary problems accurately, despite the fact that Orwell had never visited the United States in his lifetime. Orwell's own experiences and events that occurred in his life had led him to develop strong beliefs against totalitarianism and to stand firmly against it, and inspired him to write novels like the *Animal Farm* (1945) and *1984* (1949), through which he sought to foster democratic socialism. His writing continues to direct us to be observant of the stunning pomposity of government declarations, of ubiquitous official and commercial surveillance, and most of all, of interferences by both public and corporate powers into the domain of the private person (Ricks, 2017).

From the onset of President Trump's presidency to his final days in office, Trump seemed to exult in political fights. Trump often used his presidential amplifier to censure and critique his perceived opponents, ranging from media personnel to representatives from his own administration, elected administrators in both political parties, and foreign heads of state. His un-presidential behaviour is further evidenced through the more than 26,000 tweets he sent as president that were blatant, real-time records of his opinions and beliefs on a wide range of issues, that was ultimately deemed to be so provocative, that his account was disabled and Twitter permanently banned him from its platform. Towards the end of his term, Trump became the first president ever to be impeached twice—the second time for inciting an uprising at the U.S. Capitol during the certification of the election he lost. Infamously, he became the first chief executive of the United States in more than 150 years who declined to attend his successor's inauguration (Dimoch & Grmalich, 2021).

THE ESCALATION OF DEGRADING RACE RELATIONS AND BIAS

It is widely accepted that Science Fiction helps to promote critical thinking and a greater understanding of present day world portrayal as well as projections of events to come. However, when race relations are depicted in futuristic scenarios, readers are compelled to examine its significance and the need to construe whether racial representations are reflective of the existent situation, as well as deliberate upon the manner in which racial distinctions are portrayed in the creative work (Harnett, 2018). Dystopian literature provided a space for characters from different backgrounds to reflect their uniqueness. Although many of the dystopian novels created novel and unique worlds, there are significant similarities in the way political structures are used to procure and exert power, and in the way interpersonal relationships are manipulated and degraded, and unity is created to integrate citizens into the society (Kalafut, 2019). We see dystopian reflections in the way the state treats different sections of society, particularly immigrant populations and minorities. In the United States in particular, race relations deteriorated even further during the presidency of Donald Trump. The "Black Lives Matter" movement though existent prior to the events of 2020 was exacerbated by the death of George Floyd and others in 2020, and may yet be one of the largest movements in the history of the United States. Academics studying social movements in the US reported that almost seven million people had partici-pated in protests and demonstrations across the US; moreover, the belligerent stance taken by the Trump administration on issues like guns, climate change, and immigration has led to more protests than under any other presidency since the Cold War (Buchanan, Bui & Patel, 2020). While each novelists deals with the issues they feel strongly about or have experienced most, their fictitious predictions warn the global community of the dire consequences if tangible changes are not effected by those in power. The world witnessed how leaders of nations tended to be dismissive of racial apathy by the police or law enforcement, stating a particular community is prone to violence and crime and that justified the police response. Dystopian novels help us understand concerns regarding power struggles, gender inequality, conflicts, and igno-rance of events in other parts of the world. Each dystopian novel presents its narratives not in indiscriminate likenesses about human nature but take us on a nightmarish journey with striking details (Kalafut, 2019).

FIGHTING THE GROWING INCOME
AND POWER DIVIDE

In "Parable of the Sower," author Victoria Butler illuminates a dystopia of widespread paucity, intensified class and racial hostility, the collapse of local communities, the expansion of private power, and governmental degeneration (Stillman, 2003), and denotes how being in a dystopic environment, indi-viduals' struggles for advancement are inhibited at resident, domestic, and global levels. The dystopian scenario of the *United States of 2024* featured in Butler's novel, "Parable of Sower," seems to originate from extremes of economic wealth and resultant inequality of political power, and in which the private power of the wealthy and that of corporates dictates governance (Stillman, 2003). Although the depictions and novel settings are related to that in fictitious United States, one could easily imagine that situation being transposed to any country where the expeditious growth of wealth disparity has pitted sections of populations against each other. The percentage of popu-lations pushed to the fringes of society are on the uptick. Decades of conflicts and inequalities are forcing people to flee from their countries ranging across the Middle East, Africa, South America, and parts of Asia to seek refuge in safe havens. Interestingly, inequality in countries is recorded in more than two thirds (71 percent) of the world population (World Social Report, 2020). In "Parable of the Sower," Canada is portrayed as the new utopian frontier as it has become fertile due to global warming and is unaffected by US economic and political decline, although the journey to reach Canada is arduous and dangerous and the border remains closed (Stillman, 2003), similar to conditions in many promised lands to which immigrants embark in increasingly dangerous journeys by sea and land. It is notable that the novel exemplifies that the fecundity of the land was caused by environmental decay and global warming. In a growing trend, although countries are progressing, income and wealth are progressively limited to a small group with the share of wealth concentrated among the top 1 percent of the global population in 46 out of 57 countries and regions, analysed in data from 1990 to 2015 (World Social Report, 2020).

Digital innovation and artificial intelligence are creating tremendous prospects for sectors such as education, health and banking, with widespread extrapolations for equality, however, we are aware that the potential of new technologies to cultivate promote sustainable development can only be fulfilled if everyone has access to them. Sadly, new technologies are bolstering various forms of inequality and creating new "digital divides" (World Social Report, 2020).

ENVIRONMENTAL DYSTOPIA

Ironically, the tremendous power and advancement of Science and Technology has not ebbed the unprecedented environmental degradation and damage due to anthropomorphic activities and influences in the present day. Climate change looms largely as one of the biggest threat against mankind's very existence. It was in 1962 that climate fiction writer, JG Ballard wrote his novel, *The Drowned World* in which he examined potentially the worst effects of global warming, and initiated a genre of writing termed "cli-fi." The novel which is set against the backdrop of a futuristic and incongruous, tropical London that is prone to flooding in the year 2145, is one of the first novels to be published in the climate-fiction genre. The novel tracks a group of scientists who are investigating the flora and fauna in what was once the UK's capital, but, due to extreme environmental changes wreaked by solar storms, has instead become a sweltering swamp (Whiting, 2019).

Scientists continue to raise alarms on how the rapid ice melting in the Arctic could have deleterious effects around the globe, of which the biggest threat is sea level rise (Jacobo, 2021). Sea level rise from melting and continued climate change would consequently intensify coastal erosion, causing floods in areas that had previously never seen flooding, and increase inland flooding as the salty ocean waters change groundwater tables and inundate freshwater resources, according to scientists (Jacobo, 2019).

The continued inaction and noncommittal approach by developed economies to effectually control their greenhouse gas emissions remains the number one factor that contributes to rising sea levels, and especially endangering island nations and low-lying countries to being submerged by rising sea water. This is despite the fact that leaders from the countries most at risk of rising sea levels, appealed to rich nations to act more forcefully against a planet that was warming rapidly at the United Nations general assembly held in 2021 (Psaledakis & Nichols, 2021).

Dystopian fiction cautions us not to act lightly when faced with environmental disasters, and highlight the compounding disparities across cultural divides. Under the 2015 Paris Agreement on climate change mitigations, countries had agreed to commit towards restricting the increase in global temperatures to 1.5 degree Celsius, the threshold that scientists believed would deter the worst effects of global warming, however this would require an overall reduction of global emissions by 50 percent by 2030 and to net-zero by 2050 (Psaledakis & Nichols, 2021). Since the 2015 Paris Agreement, there have been regressive actions on the part of the US to uphold their commitments. President Trump had taken to reversing a number of initiatives agreed upon by his predecessor, Obama, and in terms of climate policy, President Trump justified United States' withdrawal from the Paris agreement citing negative impacts to the US economy and employment sector. This is a major step back by the Unites States, one that would impact the clean energy plan, exit from the Paris Agreement, and a return to conventional energy policies (Yu, 2018).

Subsequently, there has been a change in the United States government which saw President Biden elected to office in 2021, and there have been efforts by China and the US, two of the world's largest polluters to commit to a cooperative approach to better climate management in which they agreed to reduce methane emissions, protect forests and phase out coal. These announcements were made in 2021 at the United Nations Climate Change Conference (COP26) in Glasgow (Al Jazeera 2021).

CONCLUSION

In Orwell's *1984*, the purpose of the Ministry of Truth was to rewrite history, by altering any actualities which did not fit in with party doctrine. In a distressingly alarming case of life imitating art, Russia's president Putin is doing exactly that today with the sudden invasion of Ukraine which he termed as "Military action." The impact of this invasion is yet to be ascertained, but suffice to say that the escalation of attacks on civilian lives renews painful memories of conflicts and ignites the chilling prospect of yet another long, drawn-out war that could potentially draw other countries into the equation. This chapter has sought to demonstrate that there is a delicate balance between achieving security or happiness in the domestic sphere while the external environments remain fragmented through uncontrolled dominance and power play politics, and that nations and populations must come together and stand guard against constricted politics and autocratic leaders who could destroy the tenuous normalcy that we take for granted.

REFERENCES

Broich, John. 2017. 2017 isn't '1984'—it's stranger than Orwell imagined. *Independent*. Retrieved March 10, 2022 from https://www.independent.co.uk/ news/world/politics/2017-isn-t-1984-it-s-stranger-than-orwell-imagined-a7555341 .html.

Buchanan, Larry, Bui, Quocktrung, & Patel, Jugal K. 2020. Black Lives Matter May Be the Largest Movement in US History. *The New York Times*. Retrieved February 20, 2022 from https://www.nytimes.com/interactive/2020/07/03/us/george-floyd -protests-crowd-size.html.

Al Jazeera. 2020. China and the US announce deal to boost cooperation on climate change. Retrieved February 25, 2022 from https://www.aljazeera.com/news/2021 /11/10/china-launches-enhanced-climate-action-plan-with-us-envoy.

Boyle, Harriet. 2022. "Huxley's warning about technology in *Brave New World*." University of Canterbury. Retrieved from http://dh.canterbury.ac.nz/engl206/2015 /06/04/huxleys-warning-about-technology-in-brave-new-world.

Cohen, Martin, & Tidman, Keith. 2022. The dangers of social media's insinuation into our lives, Retrieved February 20, 2022 from https://www.courant .com/opinion/op-ed/hc-op-social-media-insinuation-into-our-lives-20220209 -npkqbgp5azhu5n6gbrey7zyfx4-story.html.

Dimoch, Michael, & Gramlich, John. 2021. How America Changed During Donald Trump's Presidency. Pew Research Center. Retrieved February 24, 2022 from https://www.pewresearch.org/2021/01/29/how-america-changed-during-donald -trumps-presidency.

Gopnick, Adam. 2017. Orwell's "1984" and Trump's America. *The New Yorker*, January 27, 2017. Retrieved March 2, 2022 from https://www.newyorker.com/ news/daily-comment/orwells-1984-and-trumps-america.

Hartnett, Meghan. 2018. The Future of Racial Classifications: Exploring Race in the Critical Dystopia. In BSU Honors Program. Theses and Projects. Item 283. Retrieved March 2, 2022 from http://vc.bridgew.edu/honors_proj/283.

Huxley, Aldous. 1932. *Brave New World*. London: Harper Perennial Modern Classics.

Jacobo, Julia. 2021. Melting Artic ice will have catastrophic effects on the world, Retrieved February 25, 2022 from https://abcnews.go.com/International/melting -arctic-ice-catastrophic-effects-world-experts/story?id=81588333.

Kalafut, Marlena G. 2019. "It's not the end of the world: an analysis of the similarities in dystopian literature and their shared refletion of the innate fears of humanity." Honors Program Projects. 98. Retrieved February 20, 2022 from https://digitalcommons.olivet.edu/cgi/viewcontent.cgi?article=1110&context=honr_proj.

Miller, Derek D. 2011. Brave New World and the Threat of Technological Growth. *Inquiries Journal/Student Pulse* 3 (04), Retrieved February 10, 2022 from http://www.inquiriesjournal.com/a?id=509.

Psaledakis, Daphne, & Nichols, Michelle. 2021. 'Death sentence': low-lying nations implore faster action on climate at U.N. Retrieved February 15, 2022 from https://www.reuters.com/business/environment/death-sentence-low-lying-nations-implore-faster-action-climate-un-2021-09-23.

Ricks, Thomas E. 2017. What Orwell Saw—and What He Missed—About Today's World. Retrieved February 15, 2022 from https://www.politico.com/magazine/story/2017/05/23/george-orwell-1984-modern-day-215177.

Seaton, Jean, Crook, Tim, & Taylor, DJ. 2017. Welcome to dystopia—George Orwell experts on Donald Trump. *The Guardian*. Retrieved February 20, 2022 from https://www.theguardian.com/commentisfree/2017/jan/25/george-orwell-donald-trump-kellyanne-conway-1984

Shames, Shauna, & Atchison, Amy. 2020. Are we living in a dystopia? *The Conversation*. April 29, 2020. Retrieved February 20, 2022 from https://theconversation.com/are-we-living-in-a-dystopia-136908.

Stillman, Peter G. 2003. Dystopian Critiques, Utopian Possibilities, and Human Purposes in Octavia Butler's Parables. *Utopian Studies*, Vol. 14, no. 1: 15–35 Retrieved February 20, 2022 from https://www.jstor.org/stable/20718544.

Stock, Adam. 2019. Modern Dystopian Fiction and Political Thought: Narratives of World Politics, Routledge: London.

Razaq, Samar. 2020. Covid-19, Orwell, and the media, *British Journal of General Practice* 2020; 70 (698): 451. https://doi.org/10.3399/bjgp20X712397.

Whiting, Kate. 2019. 6 dystopian novels that resonate today. Retrieved February 22, 2022 from https://www.weforum.org/agenda/2019/10/6-dystopian-novels-that-resonate-today.

Yu, Hongyuan. 2018. The US Withdrawal from the Paris Agreement-Challenges and Opportunities for China, *China Quarterly of International Strategic Studies*, Vol. 4, no. 2: 281–30. Retrieved February 22, 2022 from https://www.worldscientific.com/doi/pdf/10.1142/S2377740018500100.

World Social Report-Inequality in a Rapidly Changing World. 2020. PDF retrieved February 22, 2022 from https://www.un.org/en/file/71229/download?token=cylubVd_.

Chapter Nine

The 19th Century American Socialism

A Vision of a Future Utopia

Majed S Al-Lehaibi, Jazan University, Saudi Arabia
Bernard Montoneri, Independent
Researcher, Taiwan

Bellamy's utopian novel *Looking Backward: 2000–1887* (1888) was published in a time of protest and reform. Edward Bellamy (1850–1898), an American author, journalist, and political activist born in Massachusetts, intended to criticize the social ills and injustices of America's Gilded Age (1870–1900). His utopia is the result of the tension between the ideal world and the status quo. To begin with, the whole trajectory of Bellamy's criticism and vision of the nineteenth century is summarized in this passage:

> In place of the dreary hopelessness of the nineteenth century, its profound pessimism as to the future of humanity, the animating idea of the present age is an enthusiastic conception of the opportunities of our earthly existence, and the unbounded possibilities of human nature. The betterment of mankind from generation to generation, physically, mentally, morally, is recognized as the one great object supremely worthy of effort and of sacrifice. We believe the race for the first time to have entered on the realization of God's ideal of it, and each generation must now be a step upward (Bellamy 2007, 170–171).

Looking Backward is futuristic in its outlook. It gives hope of resolution. It is the reflection of the time's desires, hopes, and aspirations projected into the future. *Looking Backward* is a temporal utopia (uchronia), not a spatial utopia (co-temporally with the lives of their authors, but in a distant part of space).

Its setting is an actual location, Boston, in the year 2000. From that future time, the novel looks backward to 19th-century Boston society. It conveys hope and a belief in progress (the idea that the future will always be better than the past) to the people of the nineteenth century; the Golden Age of society lies in the future, and the chaos of the day is necessary for progress.

BELLAMY, HIS LIFE AND WORK

Edward Bellamy is an American author, journalist, and political activist born in Chicopee Falls, a manufacturing village near Springfield, Massachusetts in 1850. His father, Rufus King Bellamy, was a Baptist minister and his mother, Maria Louisa Putnam Bellamy, was a Calvinist. Her father, Reverend Benjamin Putnam, sent her to a female academy, where Maria learned Latin and Greek and developed conservative religious beliefs. Edward's younger brother, Charles, was born in 1852. Edward went to school in his hometown and then to New York before spending one year in Europe, notably in Germany.

Edward Bellamy worked as a journalist and wrote hundreds of editorials during his career. Bellamy's cousin, William Packer, helped him obtain a position writing editorials for the *Evening Post of New York* (Gilman 1889, 51). He then worked as an assistant editor for the *Springfield Union*. In 1880, Edward and his brother Charles published a triweekly paper called the *Penny News*. Years later, Edward published a weekly newspaper, *The New Nation* (1891). As his health deteriorated, publication stopped in 1894.

As an author, Bellamy wrote twenty-three short stories published in various magazines between 1875 and 1889, including *To Whom This May Come* in 1889, and several novels, notably *Six to One: A Nantucket Idyl* (1878), *The Duke of Stockbridge* (1879), *Doctor Heidenhoff's Process* (1880), and *Miss Ludington's Sister* (1884). He developed tuberculosis at age 25, making Bellamy's life difficult and painful; in 1877–1878, he spent a year in the Hawaiian Islands to improve his health condition. He married Emma Augusta Sanderson in 1882 and had two children, Paul born in 1884 and Marion in 1886. Edward took part in raising his children ("except diapering and feeding" according to his daughter; Bellamy Earnshaw n.d., 10, 12) and read stories to them. He died of tuberculosis, age 48, in his hometown. Bellamy's fame rests in the publication of his best-seller published in 1888, *Looking Backward: 2000–1887*.

LOOKING BACKWARD, GENERAL PRESENTATION

Bellamy explained in 1889 that at first, he chose the date of A.D. 3000: "Instead of the year A.D. 3000, that of A.D. 2000 was fixed upon as the date of the story" (Bellamy 1889, 4). In the first draft, he also chose to set the story in Asheville, North Carolina, instead of Boston. Concerning the plot, he adds:

> Instead of a mere fairy tale of social perfection, it became the vehicle of a defi- nite scheme of industrial reorganization. The form of a romance was retained, although with some impatience, in the hope of inducing the more to give it at least a reading (Bellamy 1889, 3).

Bellamy began to work on *Looking Backward* in 1886. Contemporary events, such as the bloody Haymarket affair in 1886—a bombing at Haymarket Square in Chicago on May 4, during a rally in support of workers—surely had a significant impact on the writing of the novel, even though he yearned for a peaceful social reorganization and had little sympathy for the anarchists and Marxists (McClay 1994). The memory of the bloodshed during the Paris Commune (1871) was still fresh and daunting. The following big strikes in America, in 1877, 1886, and 1892–94, became known as the infamous "Three Earthquakes" (Schiffman 1953, 731).

Short Summary

The protagonist Julian West, a Boston entrepreneur, falls into a hypnotic sleep in 1887 and does not awaken until September 10, 2000. Dr. Leete and his daughter Edith take care of him and explain the changes that have occurred in the 113 years that he has been sleeping. Bellamy's Boston of 2000 is a wonderful place. He envisages a more comfortable, pleasant, and peaceful world. All citizens have a college-level education, and most people work until the age of forty-five. The national wealth is distributed equally to all citizens, and there is no ownership of goods and capital. People are free to choose their career and every worker is paid the same salary. Society is peaceful, therefore prisons and criminal institutions are not needed anymore.

Main Characters

Julian West: The protagonist is a thirty-year-old man born in an aristocratic family named Julian West. He is engaged to Edith Bartlett, a pretty Boston aristocrat. On May 30, 1887, Doctor Pillsbury, a skilled mesmerist, is treating the young man because he suffers from insomnia, a psychological symptom most likely caused by the growing social unrest. Julian has built a soundproof vault in the basement of his house, where he can relax and rest. Doctor Pillsbury has already helped Julian fall into a hypnotic sleep several times. On September 10, 2000, another doctor, Doctor Leete, finds Julian in the base-ment of his house, still young and in suspended animation.

Doctor Leete: After Julian is hypnotized, a fire starts and burns almost everything except the room in the basement where he is sleeping. Everybody, his fiancée included, assumes he is dead. In the year 2000, Leete finds Julian while building a laboratory and revives him. He offers to be Julian's guide and together, they visit Boston, a city that has become clean and prosperous. Dr. Leete is a rational and sympathetic man. He introduces this new world to Julian with kindness and logic.

Edith Leete: She is the daughter of Doctor Leete. She gives Julian emo-tional support, and they eventually fall in love. Julian then learns that she is the great-granddaughter of his 19th-century fiancée, Edith Bartlett, who kept Julian's love letters and eventually agreed to marry another man after a period of mourning.

Influence

In Germany, one of the most famous novels inspired by *Looking Backward* was obviously *Something Later! A Continuation of Bellamy's Looking Backward from the Year 2000*, published by the devout Catholic Phillip Laicus in 1891. Phillip Laicus keeps the idea of the nationalization of the industries, but insists on marriage and morality.

Bellamy's novel was translated into Chinese in 1891. Liang Qichao (1873–1929) wrote an unfinished novel titled *The Future of New China* (1902), set in 1962. As to Wu Jianren (1866–1910), he wrote *The New Story of the Stone* in 1905, which was "almost certainly inspired by Edward Bellamy's 1888 American novel" (Huters 2005, 151), a fantasy story designed as the sequel of Cao Xueqin's great classical novel *Dream of the Red Chamber* (first printed edition: 1791). In the novel, Jia Baoyu is transported to Shanghai of 1900 and explores China in the 1900s. The male protagonists of *Dream of the Red Chamber*, Jia Baoyu and Xue Pan, wake up "in contemporary Shanghai after a hibernation of some 150 years" (Huters 2005, 158). In 1910, Lu Shi'e published *Xin Zhongguo* (*New China*), longer title: *Lixian sishi nianhou zhi Zhongguo* (*China, forty years after the establishment of the constitutional monarchy*). The protagnist wakes up in Shanghai in 1950. Men and women have the same rights, there are no foreign concessions, and people are prosperous.

Despite receiving bad reviews in Russia, *Looking Backward* inspired many writers. Nikolai Shelonsky, a Russian writer and journalist of the late 19th and early 20th centuries, was the first, with the publication of *In the World of the Future* in 1892, even though he was more interested in technological progress—such as a television called "telephot," photo printing, and victory over gravity—rather than in a socialist utopia. The protagonists, four Russian scientists, fall asleep in a cave in India and wake up one thousand years later in a utopia with no meat and no weapons.

According to SFE, "Brazilian Proto SF is being slowly rediscovered in the last decades" (SFE The Encyclopedia of Science Fiction 2021). *São Paulo no ano 2000, ou, Regeneração nacional* (*São Paulo in the Year 2000, Or, National Regeneration*) was published in 1909 by Godofredo Emerson Barnsley (1874–1935) with his hero, Jeremias Serapião, as the counterpart of Julian West.

DISCUSSION

Bellamy's Utopia and Social Darwinists

Bellamy's utopia demonstrates the liberal idea that history is progressive and that the future will always be better than the past, hence the apparent superiority of the novel of 21st-century society over the 19th century. The Golden Age is in the future, and it is possible when the government becomes the primary employer through the general consolidation of all industries. The 21st century no longer suffers from socioeconomic instability, crime, and other tragedies of the past. Bellamy describes this utopian vision:

> *Looking Backward* was written in the belief that the Golden Age lies before us and not behind us, and is not far away. Our children will surely see it, and we, too, who are already men and women, if we deserve it by our faith and by our works (Bellamy, 2007, 197).

Bellamy conveyed a belief in unplanned or random evolution, similar to the Social Darwinists, who believed that everything in nature, including human society, has evolved from simple to more complex forms, just as we see in organisms. Like the Social Darwinists, Bellamy conveyed a sense of linear evolution. West, in *Looking Backward,* notes that evolution in the nineteenth century was happening and now it "is all so plain in the retrospect that a child can understand it, but not being prophets, we of that day had no clear idea what was happening to us" (Bellamy, 2007, 9–10).

Darwin's theory of evolution and natural selection were understood by social Darwinists to suggest that struggles in human societies are comparable to and part of the struggle for survival in nature, that social conflicts and social struggles resemble the struggles in nature. As a social Darwinist and a classical liberal American scientist, William Graham Sumner (1840–1910) believed in social progress. However, it was a selective sort of progress. He assumed that only the "fittest" could thrive in the social and economic life, and that society is organized best when organized under something of a meritocracy. Those who are the best will succeed and in succeeding, they will pull everyone along with them and drive social progress. Therefore, the government should not get in the way of evolution by intervening to help the poor who fail in the economic competition because to do so would contravene the laws of nature. Sumner held that government should stay out of individual competition; otherwise, it limits the freedom of individuals to achieve or excel on their own. The notion that society follows the laws of nature became a very important theme in the late nineteenth century. American historian and public intellectual Richard Hofstadter (1916–1970) noted that the social Darwinists believed that "competition was glorious. Just as survival was the result of strength, success was the reward of virtue (in the form of the accumulation of capital)" (Hofstadter 1992, 57).

For social scientist William Graham Sumner, competition is the very catalyst of progress. He stated:

> We can take the rewards from those who have done better and give them to those who have done worse. We shall thus lessen the inequalities. We shall favor the survival of the unfittest, and we shall accomplish this by destroying liberty. Let it be understood that we cannot go outside of this alternative: liberty, inequality, survival of the fittest; not-liberty, equality, survival of the unfittest. The former carries society forward and favors all its best members; the latter carries society downwards and favors all its worst members (Ruse 2021, 116).

In contrast to Sumner, Bellamy held that cooperation constituted the very foundation of progress. Eventually, it guarantees absolute equality, not just equality of chance, which is deficient and leads to inequality since it is based on competition. This concept of cooperation means that all will survive comfortably, not just the elite. This is basically the goal that New England intellectual, activist, and preacher, Orestes Augustus Brownson (1803–1876) wants promotes in the essay, *The Laboring Classes* (1840). For Brownson and Bellamy, the belief of Social Darwinists that helping the unfit impedes progress was unacceptable. They rejected the idea that humanity is part of nature and not otherworldly, linked to a higher realm, that human beings are simply a type of animal with a larger brain. Such an assumption took away the dignity of the human, who, Bellamy believed, has elements of divinity. Brownson and Bellamy believed in the innate divinity of man and his being formed in his creator's image. Sumner argues that "There can be no rights against nature or against God. [. . .] But, now, if men have rights by birth, these rights must hold against their fellow men and must mean that somebody else is to spend his energy to sustain the existence of the persons so born" (Ruse, 2021, 119). Bellamy and Brownson believed that all human beings are endowed with natural rights and believed in "the actual condition of all men that equality between man and man, which God has established between the rights of one and those of another" (qtd. in Ekirch 1964, 71).

Brownson and Bellamy argued that social and economic forces create the underclass. It is the inefficiency of the system that creates those who Sumner branded as the unfit. Both thought that this system was immoral and needed to be replaced. Evolution was the solution for Bellamy, but Brownson thought that the capitalist system was past saving:

> Now, the great work for this age and the coming is to raise up the laborer, and to realize in our own social arrangements and the actual condition of all men that equality between man and man, which God has established between the rights of one and those of another. In other words, our business is to emancipate the proletaries, as the past has emancipated the slaves (Brownson, 1840, 13).

Brownson saw it to as necessary to equalizing the actual economic conditions of all men to create political and social equality in America. Brownson believed that could not happen without a revolution . . . Still, he thought that the revolution is a matter for the future because "we are not ready for this measure yet. There is much previous work to be done" (Brownson, 1840, 24). Bellamy agreed with Brownson's view of social disorganization, contrasting the Boston of 1887 to the happier world of 2000. For Bellamy, American society was coming to resemble:

> . . . a prodigious coach which the masses of humanity were harnessed to and dragged toilsomely along a very hilly and sandy road. The driver was hunger, and permitted no lagging, though the pace was necessarily very slow. Despite the difficulty of drawing the coach at all along so hard a road, the top was covered with passengers who never got down, even at the steepest ascents (Bellamy 2007, 6).

Bellamy agreed with Brownson that society was divided between rich and poor. In his analogy of the coach, neither class is comfortable; the rich are in constant danger of losing their position while the poor work hard with no reward. The tug-of-war between the two leads to strikes by the workers.

However, Bellamy disagreed with Brownson's radical solution, demonstrating a profound distrust of the ruthless capitalists and of ignorant labor agitators. While agreeing with Brownson's diagnosis, he has a different idea about the cure; believing that strikes would cause a social apocalypse, Bellamy preferred evolution to revolution. Therefore, in *Looking Backward*, there is a sense that Bellamy represented the appeal of society's upper ranks to the middle and lower classes for nonviolent change. His main character, Julian West, says,

> I myself was rich and also educated, and possessed, therefore, all the elements of happiness enjoyed by the most fortunate in that age. Living in luxury, and occupied only with the pursuit of the pleasures and refinements of life, I derived the means of my support from the labor of others, rendering no sort of service in return. My parents and grand-parents had lived in the same way, and I expected that my descendants, if I had any, would enjoy a like easy existence (Bellamy 2007, 5).

The Labor Question and the Workers' Condition

Bellamy preferred a peaceful answer to the "labor question" (Bellamy 2007, 36). First of all, he considers "excessive individualism" (24) fatal to brotherhood and the common interest, with the result being wealth spent on private luxuries instead of on the welfare of the whole society. These miserable conditions of the status quo will be ended by means of evolution. Evolution for Bellamy leads to cooperative progress. This is in striking contrast to Sumner's sense of evolution, which is progress made possible only by competitive struggle and the attainment of material wealth. Therefore, Bellamy proposes a reconstructed theory of evolution leading to a utopia of equality and cooperation. In *Looking Backward*, he notes that "each generation must now be a step upward" (171). He considers that evolution moves from the simple to the complex. From Bellamy's perspective, this increasing complexity, if applied to society, will lead to higher stages of civilization. He sees social evolution as a gradual and peaceful progression towards harmony, solidarity, and ultimately a better world.

In Sumner's case, there is no limit to progress, but to make his point, Bellamy starts at the end as if all the past was leading up to this end. While Sumner talks about the present, Bellamy describes a point in the future that is inevitable, evolved without a plan. Bellamy refers to a kind of paradigm shift led by evolution. If evolution is progressive, "the betterment of mankind from generation to generation, physically, mentally" (194), then much of the human misery in 19th-century society was "caused by our [temporal] misplaced emphasis upon selfhood (this is basically the critique of the social Darwinist world view)" (McClay 1994, 79). As McClay argues, "Bellamy offer[s] . . . a[n] image of new paradigm of social organization, coupled with a searing critique of the dissociated, inhuman conditions of postbellum nineteenth-century industrial America" (McClay 1994, 75).

Industrialization prompted enormous social changes. It created great disparities in wealth between the workers and the owners; it led to a rise of cities organized around commercial and manufacturing activity. Immigrants and people from rural areas flooded into cities to fill manufacturing jobs. They worked long hours, often for low wages, with little medical care available for the kinds of injuries that were likely to occur in factories. Workers demanded better working conditions, higher wages, and shorter hours; in short, they strove to improve their position in society. Economic inequalities undermined political equality. The gulf between the rich and the poor grew; the capacity for the poor man to influence government diminished substantially.

Economic inequality grew wider from the middle of the nineteenth century. Panic and depression were common, while labor actions, mostly strikes, hit industries that were increasingly nationalizing, causing a ripple effect throughout society. As industrialization grew, an alternative explanation for human relations developed. Reformers urged government to alleviate the problems that resulted. Social Darwinism arose in response to these contextual factors.

In his 1859 book *The Origin of Species,* Charles Darwin formulated a theory of biological change. Darwin concluded that natural selection determined whether organisms could adapt to environmental changes. Those that succeed in adapting to their environment survive; those that do not die out. Once accepted by the biological sciences, the theory began to filter into the social sciences as well. Herbert Spencer first applied this notion of evolutionary biology to human conduct in *First Principles*, which was published in the 1860s. It understood evolution to mean progress and so it suggested that human struggles for progress was comparable to the struggle for survival in nature. Social Darwinists believed that society is organized best when organized under something of a meritocracy. Those who are the best will succeed. In succeeding, they will pull everyone along with them and drive progress in society.

Sumner perceived those who wanted to use government to alleviate social ills as the enemies of society. In *What Social Classes Owe to Each Other*, he questioned the motives and the responses of these people. The way he framed it in the introduction is:

If, then, the question is raised, What ought the state to do for labor, for trade, for manufactures, for the poor, for the learned professions? etc., etc.—that is, for a class or an interest—it is really the question, What ought All-of-us to do for Some-of-us? But Some-of-us are included in All-of-us, and, so far as they get the benefit of their own efforts, it is the same as if they worked for themselves, and they may be cancelled out of All-of-us. Then the question which remains is,

What ought Some-of-us to do for Others-of-us? or, What do social classes owe
to each other? (Summer 1883, online).

Framing the question this way lays out the differences among the Darwinists,
Sumner, and the reformers. The response to that question by reformers such
as Edward Bellamy and Orestes Brownson was that the wealthy have a moral
obligation to aid those who are less fortunate or are suffering from physical
maladies. They argued that social and economic forces create the underclass.
Therefore, the well-to-do and government have an obligation to improve the
condition of those who are less well off. This contrasts with Sumner's conten-
tion that such action would lead to ruin.

While Sumner justifies the socioeconomic conditions of the time through
the logic of Social Darwinism, Bellamy and Brownson were more futuristic
in outlook. The growth of large corporations brought not only tremendous
profit for corporations and their owners, but also a wave of workers' strikes.
Looking Backward is the reflection of the desires, hopes, and aspirations of
the times projected into the future. Bellamy's utopia demonstrates the liberal
idea that history is progressive, and that the future will always be better than
the past, hence the apparent superiority in the novel of 21st-century society
over the 19th century. Like the Social Darwinists, Bellamy conveyed a sense
of linear evolution. West, in *Looking Backward,* notes that evolution in the
nineteenth century was happening, and now it

> . . . is all so plain in the retrospect that a child can understand it, but not being
> prophets, we of that day had no clear idea what was happening to us. What we
> did see was that industrially the country was in a very queer way. The rela-
> tion between the workingman and the employer, between labor and capital,
> appeared in some unaccountable manner to have become dislocated (Bellamy
> 2007, 9–10).

Unlike Brownson, who thought that the capitalist system was past saving,
Bellamy represented the appeal of society's upper ranks to the middle and
lower classes for nonviolent change. From Sumner's perspective, men are
rational calculators of their own good. This is the nature of man: self-inter-
ested-again, I want "X," I will do the things to get "X"; and I am free to act
on those impulses. Man "should be left free to do the most for himself that he
can, and should be guaranteed the exclusive enjoyment of all that he does"
(Summer 1883, online).

The autonomous individual acting out of self-interest is the beginning and
end of Sumner's analysis. The core of individuality is self-reliance, individual
responsibility. To Sumner, one's station in life is the sole responsibility of the
individual. Unlike Sumner, who praises inequality as a fact of life that should

be encouraged, both Bellamy and Brownson believed in natural rights. The class division that Brownson drew was clear cut: the nonworking men (the bosses) and the proletariat. This is what divides society. The rich provide the jobs, which, become the means of exploitation.

Sumner agreed that society should guarantee equality of chances, and in that way help a man find a job and become a productive member of society. However, in Brownson's diagnosis of working conditions, the government should use its powers to alleviate the condition of workers and regulate owners. A paternalistic government that is concerned with the welfare of its citizens is needed to fix the ills of society.

For Brownson, it is useless to fix the status quo, and revolution is the only solution. In contrast, Bellamy finds that salvation lies ahead in time. The image of society, then, is going to be an organic one. It will be "as a family, a vital union, a common life, a mighty heaven-touching tree whose leaves are its people, fed from its veins, and feeding it in turn" (Bellamy 2007, 149). He espoused a kind of communal patriotism, in which "rational devotion to the father land convinced people to lay aside competition: "By making the native land truly a father-land, a father who kept the people alive and was not merely an idol for which they were expected to die" (Bellamy 2007, 149). Bellamy imagines a caring and responsive nation. The nation evolves or grows like a tree. The people are the leaves of that tree; they have no reason to compete for resources, as all depend equally on the health of the common trunk, the government. Bellamy refers to his project as "nationalism" rather than socialism to distance himself from the opprobrium and violence associated with socialism. His project gave rise to 165 nationalist clubs throughout the United States to spread Bellamy's ideas (McClay 1994, 75). Gilman notes: "Mr. Edward Bellamy, a novelist by profession, is the recognized father of the Nationalist Club" (Gilman 1889, 50). Bellamy refers to his project as "nationalism" rather than socialism to distance himself from the opprobrium and violence associated with socialism.

Bellamy "[made] the cause of the victims of society his own" in his utopian vision. His response to the observation of Jesus that "The poor ye have always with you" was:

Somewhere else I believe Christ tells his disciples that two duties sum up all the law and the prophets: one being to love God wholly, the other to love one's neighbor as one's self. Now, how long do you think, if everybody loved his neighbor as himself, there would be left any who were poorer than his neighbor? . . . if there is any such thing as blasphemy it surely consists in quoting the great apostle of human brotherhood against the abolition of poverty" (Bellamy 1938, 65–66).

Bellamy critiques Sumner's ideas, considering "excessive individualism" fatal to brotherhood and the common interest, with wealth being spent on private luxuries instead of on the welfare of the whole society. These conditions that Brownson criticized and Sumner defended will change by means of evolution. Evolution for Bellamy leads to cooperative progress. This is in striking contrast to Sumner's sense of evolution, which is progress made possible only by competitive struggle and the attainment of material wealth: "Capital . . . is the force by which civilization is maintained and carried on" (Sumner 1883, online). Therefore, Bellamy proposes a reconstructed theory of evolution leading to a utopia of equality and cooperation. In *Looking Backward*, social evolution is equated with biological evolution. All Darwinists, social and biological alike, considered that evolution moves from the simple to the complex. From Bellamy's perspective, this increasing complexity will lead to higher stages of civilization if applied to society. He sees social evolution as a gradual and peaceful progression towards harmony, solidarity, and ultimately a better world. Like Brownson, Bellamy answers the "labor question." However, unlike Brownson, Bellamy has a peaceful solution.

In Sumner's case, there is no limit to progress, but to make his point, Bellamy starts at the end, as if all the past was mounting up to this end. While Sumner talks about the now, Bellamy describes a point in the future that is inevitable, evolving without a plan. Bellamy refers to a kind of paradigm shift led by evolution. If evolution is progressive, "the betterment of mankind from generation to generation, physically, mentally" (Bellamy 2007, 171), then much of the human misery in the nineteenth century was "caused by our [temporal] misplaced emphasis upon selfhood (this is basically the critique of the social Darwinist world view)" (McClay 1994, 79). *Looking Backward* offered " . . . a compelling image of new paradigm of social organization, coupled with a searing critique of the dissociated, inhuman conditions of postbellum nineteenth-century industrial America" (McClay 1994, 75).

In *Looking Backward*, Bellamy describes a system by which poverty is eradicated. The system has become so efficient that all blights on human existence have disappeared "as fleeting as a dream" (McClay 1994, 100). There is no war, no class conflict, and no commercialism. When these things disappeared, all their attendant apparatuses disappeared—lawyers, armies, politicians, banks, money, and merchants. This situation is the result of what Bellamy calls the final consolidation of private capital and the social engineering of means of production. All profit has been peaceably absorbed by the government and placed in "The Great Trust" (Bellamy 2007, 33). Bellamy creates a context to present his social ideas in an unthreatening way. In chapter 5, Julian asks Dr. Leete about the labor question. Dr. Leete responds: "As no such thing as the labor question is known nowadays," replied Dr. Leete, "and there is no way in which it could arise, I suppose we may claim to have solved it" (29). Leete tells Julian,

> You must, at least, have realized that the widespread industrial and social troubles, and the underlying dissatisfaction of all classes with the inequalities of society, and the general misery of mankind, were portents of great changes of some sort (Bellamy 2007, 29).

The revolution that Brownson thought was coming did not come. The labor question was settled through natural evolution. As capital became increasingly aggregated and more concentrated and its control more centralized, trusts built up, swallowing smaller entities until the government absorbed all of them. Capital ended up in the control of the state. This was not violent; it was the product of natural evolution from a small-scale agrarian economy to vast concentrations of wealth. Leete explains that

> . . . the organization of labor and the strikes were an effect, merely, of the concentration of capital in greater masses than had ever been known before. Before this concentration began, while as yet commerce and industry were conducted by innumerable petty concerns with small capital. . . . Moreover, when a little capital or a new idea was enough to start a man in business for himself, workingmen were constantly becoming employers and there was no hard and fast line between the two classes. Labor unions were needless then, and general strikes out of the question (Bellamy 2007, 30–31).

The Great Trust

That evolutionary progression led to the Great Trust. The old capitalist system, which Sumner defends, led to corporate tyranny that caused societal instability. People felt threatened by unemployment, the collapse of the labor market, tragedy, and illness. Once the government took over the capitalist monopolies, the profits were shared by the entire nation to improve society. In the resulting social stability, each citizen was guaranteed maintenance and ample provision. In great contrast to Sumner's perfect world as one in which government gets out of the way in order to allow the capitalist system free rein in the marketplace, Bellamy assumed that total control of the market by the government was the only way his utopian vision might be achieved.

Bellamy contends that this is the end of social evolution. History and conflict end with the establishment of the Great Trust. In a conversation, Reverend E. F. Bisbee asked, "Mr. Bellamy, you do not consider the social state pictured in *Equality* the end of human progress, do you? Oh, no,' he replied with what I felt to be almost a touch of impatience: it is only the beginning. When we get there we shall find a whole infinity beyond" (qtd. in Morgan 1944, 420).

There is no disagreement among the people because the source of disagreement, which is always material, has been removed. Political parties no longer exist. Because individuals are no longer in search of private wealth, corruption is eliminated:

> The small capitalists, with their innumerable petty concerns, had in fact yielded the field to the great aggregations of capital, because they belonged to a day of small things and were totally incompetent to the demands of an age of steam and telegraphs and the gigantic scale of its enterprises. To restore the former order of things, even if possible, would have involved returning to the day of stage-coaches (Bellamy 2007, 32).

There was a prodigious increase in efficiency, creating vast wealth at a rate that appears phenomenal in hindsight. Organizational change, change in capital, concentration of wealth, creation of vast resources by the capitalist engine, and technological changes increased human comfort, thus Bellamy's evolution occurred during the conduct of business.

With aggregations of capital, the tendency toward monopolies, which had been resisted so desperately, was recognized at last as necessary to complete this evolution toward the golden future of humanity. The evolution comes to fruition by the final consolidation of the entire capital of the nation. With this consolidation, the Great Trust becomes a mere manager and a distributor of goods and services.

Competition versus Cooperation

With the end of the evolutionary process and the end of history, the utopian vision is achieved. With want extinguished, self-interested behavior gives way to cooperation. Society supports all its members. The notion of competition is grounded in self-interest, which is a construct of liberalism. Bellamy argues that self-interested competitive behavior is a response to the structure of government, society, and the economy. If institutions reward self-interested behavior, people will behave in a self-interested way. If institutions reward cooperation, people will cooperate. As demonstrated by behaviorists like American psychologist and social philosopher B. F. Skinner (1904–1990), behavior is conditioned by cues in the environment. If changes in the rules of the system provoke changes of the behavior of those involved in the system. In short, it is after the Lamarckian—named after French zoologist, Jean-Baptiste Lamarck (1744–1829)—evolution by the force of habit: the repetition of habitual action produces an evolutionary change.

In Bellamy's utopian society, the distributional principle is in the social interest of all. After going through the necessary training and schooling, each citizen chooses a position in the industrial army (probably a Prussian-inspired, disciplined workforce) based on their interests and the number of hours of work a week that each job requires. Jobs are allocated based on their degree of odiousness. Those that are less attractive require one to work fewer hours per week. Those that are more attractive and intellectually fulfilling require more hours of work per week. This is one of the many aspects of society regulated by the managing trust. The efficiency of this system stems from the full individual choice of career. In this society, not all people will work as competently as others, but so long as one does their best, they have an equal claim on society. Even those in the "invalid corps" (Bellamy 2007, 76) offer what services they can.

Sumner wants to eliminate charity, that is, any giving without expecting anything in return. He wants people to help themselves, with the government guaranteeing equality of chances and fairness, but in Sumner's own words, "to lift one man up we push another down" (Sumner 1883 online). Bellamy agrees with Sumner in this regard, except that he wants to lift them all up. The striking difference between Sumner's world and Bellamy's is that in 19th-century society, one holds the umbrella "over himself and his wife . . . giving his neighbors the drippings" (Bellamy 2007, 89–90). In Boston of the year 2000, instead of putting up "three hundred thousand umbrellas [during the rain] over as many heads, and in the twentieth century they put up one umbrella over all the heads" (Bellamy 2007, 89).

In *Looking Backward,* Mr. Barton preaches that "equity left charity without an occupation" (Bellamy 2007, 167). There is no charity when the people in the community learn to work together. All people are entitled to a decent life just because they are human, not because of what they can contribute. "The amount of the resulting product has nothing whatever to do with the question, which is one of desert" (55). There is no conflict over wages because there are no wages. It is a different paradigm that does not understand the old-fashioned terms of wages and pay:

> But as soon as the nation became the sole producer of all sorts of commodities, there was no need of exchanges between individuals. . . . Buying and selling is considered absolutely inconsistent with the mutual benevolence and disinterestedness which should prevail between citizens and the sense of community of interest which supports our social system (Bellamy 2007, 51–52).

The individual is not motivated by fear of poverty or love of luxury, but by patriotism: "All men who do their best do the same" (55). Bellamy's system recognizes that "The Creator sets men's tasks for them by the faculties he gives them; we simply exact their fulfillment" (55). Everyone receives an equal share of the national product on his debit card. The amount of credit each person receives is, by and large, more than a person needs. Therefore, people's needs are always met. The nation "guarantees the nurture, education, and comfortable maintenance of every citizen from the cradle to the grave" (52). Each citizen chooses how to spend his allotment. In the economic sense, he is free. Bellamy's core principle is economic equality. Like Brownson, Bellamy saw equality and freedom in terms of the economy:

> The reorganization of society which is needed to render Christianity possible is an industrial economic reorganization. . . . Do not delude yourself with the idea that any amount of moral reformation can solve a problem which in basis is essentially economic . . . [first] clear away obstacles which have hitherto hindered the progress of Christianity and [you] will open to it a career such as the imagination of saint never pictured . . . (Bellamy 1938, 166–167).

For Bellamy, the underlying justification for economic equality is not tangible, as Brownson proposes, but moral. All humans have the same needs and desires, regardless of their talents. Therefore, every citizen receives the same share for his contribution to society. Dr. Leete says:

> Desert is a moral question, and the amount of the product a material quantity. It would be an extraordinary sort of logic which should try to determine a moral question by a material standard. The amount of the effort alone is pertinent to the question of desert. All men who do their best, do the same. A man's endowments, however godlike, merely fix the measure of his duty (Bellamy 2007, 55).

Sumner asserts that if society keeps supporting the poor, they will begin to regard it as a favor-granting institution and thus pillage the deserving, productive middle-class man. In Chapter 12 of *Looking Backward*, Dr. Leete suggests that the most unpleasant aspect of life in the nineteenth century was the inability of the society to care for those less fortunate. Sumner argues that man is self-interested. He reaps the benefit of his hard work, and he owes nothing to others. In this view, the poor are poor because they deserve to be poor. In response to this attitude, Dr. Leete laments to West that he is appalled by those who

> . . . could have had any heart for their work, knowing that their children, or grand-children, if unfortunate, would be deprived of the comforts and even necessities of life. It is a mystery how men with children could favor a system under which they were rewarded beyond those less endowed with bodily strength or mental power. . . . How men dared leave children behind them, I have never been able to understand (Bellamy 2007, 79–80).

While Sumner proclaims human nature to be self-interested and competitive, Bellamy believes that is essentially good: "The trouble with the present competitive system of business is that it will not let a man be good, though he wants to" (Bellamy 1938, 166–167). Human nature does not change; it is eternal essence, it has a spark from the divine. Julian West comes from the nineteenth century. His nature did not change, but once he is in the new cultural paradigm, he begins to adapt and take on qualities of the new man, a citizen of the utopia, and so he develops a new sense of human values. Julian, who once said of the strikers, "Caligula [third Roman emperor who ruled between AD 37–41] wished that the Roman people had but one neck that he might cut it off, and as I read this letter I am afraid that for a moment I was capable of wishing the same thing concerning the laboring class of America" (Bellamy 2007, 15), adopts Dr. Leete's views about the society of the nineteenth century. When Julian goes back to his time in dreams, he looks at the people with a new perspective. He is moved by what he sees:

> "I have been in Golgotha," at last I answered. "I have seen Humanity hanging on a cross! Do none of you know what sights the sun and stars look down on in this city, that you can think and talk of anything else? Do you not know that close to your doors a great multitude of men and women, flesh of your flesh, live lives that are one agony from birth to death? (Bellamy 2007, 190).

Bellamy describes his utopia as "the ideal, the possible face that would have been the actual if mind and soul had lived" (189). To achieve that vision, he changes not human nature, but the structure of society (structural change changes the incentives to which people respond). People can be cooperative. Different aspects of human nature emerge when economic circumstances change. With wealth shared, politics withers away. While Brownson wants to bring down the state, Bellamy wants the state to become the Board of Management. Since the country is one unified entity, "almost the sole function of the administration now is that of directing the industries of the country. Most of the purposes for which governments formerly existed no longer remain to be subserved" (122–123). The role of government evolves from interest-driven broker to manager of portfolios.

Bellamy considered his utopian vision of nationalism possible if conducted under the principles of efficiency and scientific management devised by Graham Taylor, an early leader of the Social Gospel movement, who founded America's first professorship of Christian sociology in 1892. As defined by the *Encyclopedia of Chicago*, the movement "can best be seen as an effort to use biblical and church historical themes as standards by which to measure modern urban industrial capitalist societies" (Martin 2005, online).

In this scenario, the whole nation becomes the sole employer, and the masses are organized in an industrial army; each member of which is required to contribute to the nation by doing their best. Therefore, a "utopian industrial social order might actually function did he perceive the full possibilities of the military model" (McClay 1994, 77). Bellamy's utopian vision of the nation, if applied on a smaller scale, will look almost like Taylor's factory. The nation becomes the sole corporation or sole employer, and all citizens are employees of the state. To Bellamy, the government is the Board of Management, and the masses are the workers. They share the idea that cooperation will lead to the good of both the nation/corporation and the masses/workers. According to Taylor, "Scientific Management, on the contrary, has for its foundation the firm conviction that the true interests of the two are one and the same" (1919, 10). Taylor holds that inefficiency in the system is the problem. The solution to inefficiency lies in devising a successful system of scientific management, not in finding the extraordinary worker. Taylor shares Bellamy's idea that changing to an efficient system will lead to a condition in which employer and employee alike will be better off. The scientific method of management will help workers perform better: "This close, intimate, and personal cooperation between the management and the workers is the essence of modern scientific task management" (Taylor 1919, 26).

There are three elements to Taylor's new method. Like Bellamy, whose system depends on the worker's interest and choice of career, Taylor wants to select the worker for each task scientifically. The allocation of work specifies "not only what is to be done but how it is to be done and the exact time allowed for doing it" (Taylor 1919, 39). As a result, "the man who is well suited to his job will thrive while working at this rate during a long term of years and grow happier and more prosperous, instead of being overworked" (39).

Like Bellamy, Taylor saw that establishing friendly cooperation between workers and management was important to the work. Finally, there must be a division of the work force into planning and execution. Cooperation means that management personnel help each workman; by knowing his needs and strengths, they can teach him better new methods. For example, management provides one group of skilled workers to help and guide the men in their work; they provide the workers another set of tool-room men who provide them with the proper implements and keep them in perfect order, and another group of trained men to plan the work in advance:

> No one bricklayer, then, can work much faster than the one next to him. Nor has any one workman the authority to make other men cooperate with him to do faster work. It is only through enforced standardization of methods, enforced adoption of the best implements and working conditions and enforced

cooperation that this faster work can be assured. And the duty of enforcing the adoption of standards and of enforcing this cooperation rests with the management alone (Taylor 1919, 82–83).

Like Bellamy, Taylor set differential rates for work performed, taking into consideration the need for special skills, training, or physical ability. Taylor believed in worker development and training because it is good for both the establishment and the worker. Once the employee is given the most favorable working conditions, a proper day's work, and his needs and desires are recognized and met, and through establishing the system of rewards for meeting the goals, the system has solved the problem of the workers whereby they "wear out their health, spirits, and morals, without becoming one whit better off than when they commenced labor" (Brownson 1940, 68).

Wages should offer the possibility, according to Brownson, that "by the time [the worker] is of a proper age to settle in life, he shall have accumulated enough to be an independent laborer on his own capital—on his own farm or in his own shop" (Brownson 1940, 71). Bellamy would add to that the engineering of "the leisure class." In Bellamy's utopia, the leisure class is unlike the "leisure class" of the warlike social structure, which failed "to take part in industry . . . [as an] expression of its superior rank" (White 1949, 82). Brownson considers the leisure class to be the non-working class that lives off the fruits of the labor of the working class.

Bellamy designed this class to be right for everyone who serves their nation until they are exempted "from further service to the nation after the age of forty-five" (Bellamy 2007, 115). The citizen of the utopia becomes an aristocrat not because of wealth or accident of birth, but because of the good service he has done for his nation. Dr. Leete explains that people devote themselves "to the higher exercise of our faculties, the intellectual and spiritual enjoyments and pursuits which alone mean life" (115). Moreover, *Looking Backward* has another dimension. While this utopia is full of material delights and comforts, Bellamy's economics is based on "That ye love one another" (*New Testament, John* 13:34).

According to Sumner, wealth is synonymous with virtue. Saving money is virtuous, and the savings bank depositor is a "hero of civilization [because] every social gain, educational, ecclesiastical, political, aesthetic or other" depends upon saved capital. He applauds wealthy individuals because they possess the best traits: "There is no other guarantee of good citizenship which is so simple and positive, and at the same time so far-reaching, as the possession of savings" (Sumner 1913, 347). Although that is a crude Social Darwinist perspective, which Bellamy clearly opposes, he may agree that virtue is child of comfort. His utopia "lies before us and not behind us, and is not far away" (Bellamy 2007, 197).

Bellamy and Millennialism

American paleontologist and evolutionary biologist Stephen Jay Gould (1941–2002) explains the difference between millenarianism and millennialism:

> Millennium is from the Latin mille, "one thousand," and annus, "year"—hence the two n's. Millenarian is from the Latin millenarius, "containing a thousand (of anything)," hence no annus, and only one "n" (Gould 1997, 112, note).

The Book of Revelation (20:1–4) states that Christ will bring peace and rule on earth for one thousand years. According to Mayer (2016), millenarianism generally refers to a more tragic and pessimistic view of the future that will be cataclysmic and destructive at first, while millennialism is more hopeful and optimistic: peaceful changes will bring a utopia. Theosophists (the Theosophical Society was founded in New York in 1875), such as Cyrus Willard and Sylvester Baxter from Boston area, were the first to respond positively to the publication of *Looking Backward* in 1888 and offered to create a Nationalist Club (Spann 1989, 192). Theosophists, preaching harmony and brotherhood, were particularly interested in Bellamy's vision of a utopia that would resolve the injustice and inequality of the 19th century. Jacob Dorn from Wright State University calls Bellamy's novel "Optimistic Millennialism" and states he "portrayed socialism in the year 2000 for millions of readers in his novels as applied Christianity" (Dorn 2002, abstract).

The novel shows Bellamy's fascination with the millennium. Many American evangelicals interpreted the biblical books of Daniel and Revelations to mean that Christ's second coming was imminent. There are dispensations, the belief that life on earth is divided into periods of time, each of which ends in a particular type of catastrophe. The first dispensation ended with the first sin and Adam and Eve's expulsion from the garden. Noah's flood ended another dispensation. The dispersal of people from the Tower of Babel and the creation of mutually incomprehensible languages ended yet another dispensation, as did the Crucifixion. In other words, in this view, humans are destined to go wrong despite their best efforts, and they are powerless to bring about great achievement on earth without God's direct intervention.

According to dispensational premillenarians, we now live in the sixth out of seven ages, the church age. This age is anticipated to end in the battle of Armageddon, the coming of the beast and the anti-Christ and the great conflict on earth. Christ then will return, reign, and bring peace for a thousand years. This was a useful explanation for evangelicals of what was going wrong in the world. Those who thought that urbanization led to the growth of various forms of crime could say that the world is plunging towards catastrophe. What is striking is that one could look at what is happening in the world as a sign that things are getting better, and another could construe it as evidence that things are getting worse. This is a matter of one's temperament.

This is a very literal interpretation of history in which each events taking place on earth are the playing out of a cosmic drama between earth and heaven. There is a sense of a world full of strife. Time, in millenarianism, is linear and moves to an end; it moves to a conclusion, to the end of time and end of history. Bellamy is "convinced that steady upward progress for the whole human race had been foretold in the Bible and that modern events inevitably would support such prophecy" (Schiffman 1953, 728). Bellamy believes in a friendly rather than hostile universe. He believes that "crisis in human life is correlated to the divine initiative to accomplish change for the appearance of the millennium" (Hopkins 1940, 14–20). So, the millennium leads inexorably to a great conflagration, the state of society that is the Kingdom of God. Bellamy wrote:

> There is no better . . . literature than the splendid poems in which Isaiah and the other Hebrew seers foretold an era when war and strife should cease, when every man should sit under his own vine and fig-tree, with none to molest him or make him afraid, when the lion should lie down with the lamb, and righteousness cover the earth as the waters cover the sea. . . . Did you suppose that because . . . [this] is called the millennium, it was never coming (Bellamy 1938, 66–67).

Bellamy believes the transformation from industrial capitalism to utopian Nationalism will be peaceful and caused by a sudden great awakening of the public. He sees people evolving toward a final goal: this state of "a paradise of order, equity, and felicity" (Bellamy 2007, 133), a place where there is no pain, no conflict, and plenty of food, a world where people live happily in harmonious rhythm. It is a world where people do not suffer.

The conflict of the nineteenth century revolved around work. Orestes Brownson argued that the working-class lives terrible conditions. When God thought of how to punish Adam and Eve, he could not come up with anything worse than work. Work is a form of punishment. Following the Calvinist tradition, Henry Ward Beecher considered poverty a sign of sin, a form of punishment caused by sin, just as Adam and Eve's punishment was caused by their sin. By the same token, the boon of God shows in righteous people in the form of material prosperity and success. This is the Protestant work ethic, where work is a religious routine. It is the idea of predestination, the notion that one is predestined to go to heaven or hell by God's decision. And so, being wealthy tells people that God has chosen them. Wealth is a sign of righteousness. This idea of predestination caused people to work very hard to prove to others that they had been chosen by God.

For Bellamy, what underwrites human inequality and associated suffering is "human folly and, moreover, folly that can easily be reversed" (McClay 1994, 99). Work is a religious routine because through continuous work and strife, one can eventually make oneself sinless and better off. If that happens collectively through working together in good will, it will lead to a gradual reorientation according to the principles of goodness, and society will become sinless and better off. This is the point when the "divine potential of human soul" (Schiffman 1953, 727) is achieved; it is the time when society progresses "ever onward and upward, till the race shall achieve its ineffable destiny" (Bellamy 2007, 4), when society progresses to the time when holy people inhabit the earth and humanity lives in peace and justice.

George E. McNeill writes in *The Labor Movement* that "Christ shall measure the relations of men in all their duties towards their fellows, in factory and workshop, in the mine, in the field, in commerce . . . the promise of the prophet and the poet shall be fulfilled . . . and peace on earth shall prevail . . . by the free acceptance of the Gospel that all men are of one blood" (qtd. in Schiffman 1953, 727). Bellamy's vision thus is primarily a religious and moral one. "Bellamy felt strongly about Christ's role in social history" (Schiffman 1953, 730). He saw Jesus as a divine social reformer, "Jesus Christ . . . a man seeking to wipe away tears and succor those in need . . . to suppose Christ God would be detached from his glory, would be to hold him responsible for the woe of humanity which, far from being responsible for he tried his best cure" (Bellamy's notes, qtd. in Schiffman 1953, 730). Bellamy considers religion the best moral guide for mankind. Therefore, to fix the ills of society, the Social Gospel says that we must do as Jesus did. He was attentive to those who were weakest, neediest, and suffering the most. George Herron asserts that it is our duty "to put the Christ life into social practice" (Herron 2007, 103). Mr. Barton, in *Looking Backward*, explains how the brotherhood of humanity governs the progress of a society:

> It is a pledge of the destiny appointed for us that the Creator has set in our hearts an infinite standard of achievement . . . men should live together like brethren, dwelling in unity, without strives or envying, violence or overreaching, and where . . . they should be wholly freed from the care for the morrow (Bellamy 2007, 169–170).

The Social Gospel movement's premise is that society now is in a state of illness, "the widespread industrial and social troubles, and the underlying dissatisfaction of all classes with the inequalities of society, and the general misery of mankind" (Bellamy 2007, 29), and the goal of curing it echoes Bellamy's assumption that when oppression is removed and replaced with love, society will be healed.

Bellamy "recognized in all people the presence of the Spirit of God. This Spirit would make all brothers and sisters" (Graham 1995, 113). In Chapter 28, Bellamy writes:

> Therefore now I found upon my garments the blood of this great multitude of strangled souls of my brothers. The voice of their blood cried out against me from the ground. Every stone of the reeking pavements, every brick of the pestilential rookeries, found a tongue and called after me as I fled: what hast thou done with thy brother Abel? (Bellamy 2007, 190).

Bellamy was one with the Social Gospel in seeking to solve the problem of poverty and servitude through brotherhood of men. The Social Gospel adherents believed in social evolution, with the role of humanity being to guide it down a benign path through cooperation. They found plenty of examples of such cooperation in nature, rejecting the Social Darwinist idea of natural selection that contends there always will be poor people, since such is the nature of the world: the bees and the ants cooperate with each other; the cattle do not fight each other for food, they live happily together. We, too, must cooperate to bring society forward in the spirit of the Gospel. Salvation is not a matter concerning individual souls; rather, it is a collective matter involving the interest of the whole society. Love is the source of order; it is the power that brings us together to generate harmony. Strife, conversely, is the source of separation and chaos.

In chapter 26, Mr. Barton's sermon emphasizes that competition, selfishness, and antagonism toward others were the driving forces of 19th century Boston society. He states that people have "seeds of the divine . . . [that] could flower only in favorable social soil" (Schiffman 1953, 732). The society was like "a rosebush planted in a swamp, watered with black bog" (Bellamy 2007, 168) and polluted with poisons, never able to produce blooms or live up to its potential. "The bush belonged to the rose family, but had some ineradicable taint about it, which prevented the buds from coming out," so it is "uprooted and burned" (168–169). When planted in new and "favorable conditions, the plant does better. These new and favorable conditions for evolution closer to God and heaven in the Boston of 2000, the holy city, are brotherhood, goodwill, education, and advancement of the world. If people of the nineteenth century could have imagined a society like this modern Boston, Mr. Barton says, "it would have seemed to them nothing less than paradise" (170).

Sumner, Brownson, and Bellamy reject the church as an institution for economic reasons. Sumner saw churches as tools of oppression. Brownson argued that organized religion oppresses workers and favors owners. In Bellamy's utopia, the absence of "churchly organization and machinery . . . [marks] the beginning of a world-awakening of impassioned interest in the vast concerns covered by the word religion" (Bellamy 1968, 264). Bellamy considers churches to be artificial barriers between people. So, they "were completely swept away and forgotten in the passionate impulse of brotherly love which brought men together for the founding of a new social order" (259).

Paul Edward Bellamy said that his father did not want him to go to church because "he felt the church failed to put the emphasis on religion where it belonged, namely on the translation of the Golden Rule into human relations; that it . . . did not denounce or attempt to correct evil and wickedness here below" (Morgan 1945, 84–85). In the utopia, one can hear the Sunday sermon in the comfort of one's home through telephone or electroscope, as there are no churches. Because of the power of one preacher to reach a huge number of people, the number of clergy is reduced, and worshipping in church becomes an obsolete ritual. Now they are closer to the historical origins of religion. Bellamy's utopia has fulfilled the prophecy of Jesus:

> The time has now fully come which Christ foretold in that talk with the woman by the well of Samaria when the idea of the Temple and all it stood for would give place to the wholly spiritual religion, without respect of times or places, which he declared most pleasing to God (Bellamy 1968, 258).

CONCLUSION

Looking Backward was a best-seller in its time, selling thirty-five thousand copies sold during its first year of publication (Brown 1988, 37), and has influenced many science fiction writers, including H. G. Wells. From the publication of the novel to the end of the century, 46 new utopian stories were published in America (McClay 1994, 75). Other authors, such as the British novelist and socialist activist William Morris (1834–1896), were "appalled by Bellamy's depiction of a rational, bureaucratized industrial state" (Britannica 2022). Morris wrote *News from Nowhere* (1890), a pastoral utopia and libertarian socialist response to *Looking Backward*. Like in most utopias and uchronias of the 18th and 19th centuries, the protagonist, William Guest, falls asleep and wakes up in a world where people enjoy working in nature, a world with common ownership, no private property and no class systems (Holzman 1984). As to *A Crystal Age*, first anonymously in 1887 and then with the author's name, William Henry Hudson in 1906 (Anglo-Argentine author and naturalist, born in 1841), it is a "significant S-F milestone" (Suvin 1983, 33), in which the hero, Smith, wakes up in a pastoral advanced utopia, but with little technology; the protagonist falls in love with a girl named Yoletta, in a place where people have abandoned sexuality and romantic love.

Before he died, Bellamy published a sequel to *Looking Backward* titled *Equality* (1897). In this utopian novel, Julian West has become a citizen in this new world. He describes various technological advances, such as the electroscope, private air cars, and phonograph records. There is a universal language and people are all vegeterians. While some critics were not favorable, the book sold quickly and some famous authors and intellectuals praised the sequel: John Dewey (1859–1952) for example considered that *Equality* was "more populist and democratic" than "authoritarian" *Looking Backward* (Westbrook 1993, 454). The Pledge of Allegiance of the United States used nowadays was devised by Christian socialist Baptist minister and Edward's cousin Francis Bellamy in 1892.

REFERENCES

Bellamy, Edward. 1889. *How I Came to Write Looking Backward*. The Nationalist [Boston], vol. 1, no. 1 (May), pp. 1–4. Retrieved March 20, 2022 from https://ia600604.us.archive.org/20/items/HowICameToWriteLookingBackward-may1889/0500-bellamy-howicametowrite.pdf

_____ 1938. *Talks on Nationalism*. Chicago: The Peerage Press.

_____ 1968. *Equality.* Upper Saddle River, N.J.: Gregg Press.

_____ 2007. *Looking Backward 2000–1887.* New York: Oxford University Press.

Bellamy Earnshaw, Marion. n.d. *The Light of Other Days*. Marion Bellamy Earnshaw Collection, 1.

Britannica. 2022. *Science Fiction, Literature and Performance*. The Editors of Encyclopaedia Britannica. Article added to new online database: Jul 20, 1998. Retrieved March 5, 2022 from https://www.britannica.com/art/science-fiction.

Brown, Peggy Ann. 1988. "Edward Bellamy: An Introductory Bibliography." *American Studies International*, 26, no. 2: 37–50. Retrieved March 20, 2022 from http://www.jstor.org/stable/41280650.

Brownson, Orestes Augustus. 1840. *The Laboring Classes*. Boston: Benjamin H. Greene.

Dorn, Jacob H. 2002. An Optimistic Millennialism: Edward Bellamy's Vision of Socialism as 'Applied Christianity.' Expectations for the Millennium: American Socialist Visions of the Future, 1–17. https://corescholar.libraries.wright.edu/history/106.

Ekirch, Arthur. 1964. *Voices in Dissent: An Anthology of Individualist Thought in the United States.* New york: The Citadel Press.

Ferrara, Mark. 2007. A Religion of Solidarity: Looking Backward as a Rational Utopia. *Renaissance: Essays on Values in Literature*. Vol. 59, no. 2: 83–91.

Graham, William. 1995. *Half Finished Heavens: The Social Gospel in American Literature.* New York: University Press of America, Inc.

Gilman, Nicholas P. 1889. Nationalism in the United States. *The Quarterly Journal of Economics*. Volume 4, no. 1: 50–76. Retrieved March 22, 2022 from https://www.jstor.org/stable/pdf/1883001.pdf.

Gould, Stephen Jay. 1997. *Questioning the millennium: a rationalist's guide to a precisely arbitrary countdown*. New York: Harmony Books.

Herron, George. 2007. *The Christian State: A Political Vision of Christ*. Whitefish: Kessinger Publishing.

Hofstadter, Richard. 1992. *Social Darwinism in American Thought*. Boston, Beacon Press.

Holzman, Michael. 1984. Anarchism and Utopia: William Morris's News from Nowhere. *ELH*, 51 (3): 589–603. https://doi.org/10.2307/2872939.

Hopkins, Charles. 1940. *The Rise of the Social Gospel in American Protestantism, 1865–1915*. New Haven: Yale University Press.

Huters, Theodore. 2005. *Melding East and West. Melding East and West: Wu Jianren's New Story of the Stone. Bringing the World Home. Appropriating the West in Late Qing and Early Republican China. Honolulu*: University of Hawai'i Press: 151–172. Retrieved March 20, 2022 https://www.jstor.org/stable/pdf/j.ctt1wn0r4p.10.pdf.

Marty, Martin E. 2005. *Social Gospel in Chicago*. Encyclopedia of Chicago. Retrieved March 25, 2022 from http://www.encyclopedia.chicagohistory.org/pages/1158.html.

Mayer, Jean-François. 2016. Lewis, James R; Tøllefsen, Inga (eds.). "Millennialism: New Religious Movements and the Quest for a New Age." *The Oxford Handbook of New Religious Movements*. II. https://doi.org/10.1093/oxfordhb/9780190466176.013.30.

McClay, Wilfred M. 1994. *The Masterless: Self and Society in Modern America*. Chapel Hill, NC: University of North Carolina Press.

Morgan, Arthur Ernest. 1944. *Edward Bellamy*. New York: Columbia University Press.

_____ 1945. *The Philosophy of Edward Bellamy*. New York: King's Crown Press.

Ruse, Michael. 2021. *Philosophy after Darwin: Classic and Contemporary Readings*. Princeton, NJ: Princeton University Press.

Schiffman, Joseph. 1953. Edward Bellamy's Religious Thought. *PMLA*, vol. 68, no. 4: 716–732. Retrieved March 25, 2022 from https://www.jstor.org/stable/459794.

SFE The Encyclopedia of Science Fiction. 2021. *Brazil*. Retrieved March 20, 2022 from https://sf-encyclopedia.com/entry/brazil.

Spann, Edward. 1989. *Brotherly Tomorrows: Movements for a Cooperative Society in America 1820–1920*. New York: Columbia University Press.

Sumner, William Graham. 1883. *What Social Classes Owe to Each Other?* Mises Daily Articles. Mises Institute. Retrieved March 10, 2022 from https://mises.org/library/what-social-classes-owe-each-other.

Sumner, William. 1913. *Earth-hunger and Other Essays*. Edited by Albert Galloway Keller. New Haven: Yale University Press. Retrieved March 25, 2022 from https://en.wikisource.org/wiki/Earth-Hunger_and_Other_Essays.

Suvin, Darko. 1983. *Victorian Science Fiction in the UK: The Discourse of Knowledge and Power*. Boston: G. K. Hall.

Taylor, Frederick Winslow. 1919. *The Principles of Scientific Management*. New York: Harper and Brothers Publishers.

Westbrook, Robert B. 1993. *John Dewey and American Democracy*. Ithaca, United States: Cornell University Press.

White, Morton. 1949. *Social Thought in America: The Revolt against Formalism*. New York: Viking Press.

Chapter Ten

The Invention of Morel, a Projection on Dreams and Immortality

Miguel Ángel González Chandía, Fu
Jen Catholic University, Taipei

Adolfo Bioy Casares (1914–1999) is a worthy representative of Argentine writings in the context of fantastic literature. Of which several authors from the tradition of River Plate have stood out. Bioy Casares, heir to Jorge Luis Borges (1899–1986), follows the line of reflection on issues that involve the existence of being. For example, the subject of death, which is of great interest to Bioy Casares. In 1940, Adolfo Bioy Casares publishes *La Invención de Morel* (translated as *The Invention of Morel* or *Morel's Invention*), his first novel, if the author's decision to deny his previous books is respected. In the same year, along with Jorge Luis Borges and Silvina Ocampo, he released the *Anthology of Fantastic Literature* which, obviously, reveals the literary tastes and affinities of the compilers. Bioy Casares assumes responsibility for the prologue, a text that is also the expression of the poetics that distinguishes his narrative production. From that moment on, the literary relationship he establishes with Borges is also notorious, as it can well be seen in the works written jointly, and in the mutual readings and interpretations that they exchanged about his books. We quote the following from Mariano García's article: "Bioy y sus precursores: La tradición de la ciencia ficción en la narrativa de Adolfo Bioy Casares," 2017 ("Bioy and His Precursors: The Tradition of Science Fiction in the Narrative of Adolfo Bioy Casares").

The prologue, by Jorge Luis Borges, is written from the friendship between the renowned Argentinian writer and his countryman Bioy Casares. This statement values the work of Casares, which undoubtedly marks a starting point in Latin American Literature. In the first place, it expresses the essence of the novel as a type of adventure narrative through the intellectual order. Secondly, he mentions famous intellectuals, for example: the renowned Scottish novelist Stevenson, and the no less famous Spanish philosopher Ortega y Gasset. From the years of 1882, in the case of the critic Stevenson, and 1925, for Ortega y Gasset, readers were reluctant to recognize novels that were of an adventurous tone. As the prologue indicates, these readers inclined their tastes towards the psychological novel. It should be noted that in those years, including the forties, authors such as Balzac, Proust, De Quincey, Chesterton, Dante, Henry James, Kafka and León Bloy, among others, suffered, in the words of Borges, a division between good and bad authors. What matters to us is to recognize the adventure story. Borges, even in a trial full of irony and sarcasm, asserts that the psychological novel should be avoided, and recognizes the priceless value of the adventure novel (Bioy Casares 1982, 85).

In Borges, there is a sense of appreciation for empirical characters. That is to say, in the middle of the 20th century, that the public complains about the inability of authors to weave plots that are interesting. For this reason, Borges enhances the way in which Bioy Casares approaches the narrative. The praise he attracts encompasses and elevates him in his role as a writer, mentioning works such as *The Turn of the Screw*, *Der Prozess* and *Le Voyageur sur la terre*. The prologue justifies a plot full of mystery, in addition to the novel by Bioy Casares, which illustrates reasonable facts. To achieve this reality, he utilizes symbols, and allusion through illusions leading the avid reader to plots that circulate in fantastic narratives. This term is not the equivalent of the supernatural. Borges refers to theories that are fully inserted in the concept of Science Fiction. My interest in reading *The Invention of Morel* lies in my preference to take a critical look at the scientific factor that occupies many of its pages: the story of Morel's memoirs. This is a story that seems reasonable to me from the point of view of Science Fiction today. Finally, Borges affirms that the work of Bioy Casares recreates a new genre in the world of literature. In his words, he considers that this novel is, without a doubt, the perfect work (Bioy Casares 1982, 86).

In the novel, death is something deeply feared by its main character. In accordance with him, the end of life is a reality that frightens many human beings. It is the ultimate and definitive reality that largely conditions the conscience of the author of the novel. Perhaps, there is the possibility of thinking that, in the depths of his being, the phrase that resounds is this one: 'In the end is the next beginning.' From the fugitive's point of view, the end of everything is what possibly indicates his existence, and that of the others in the ambiguity of his narrative. In other words, 'think everything through its end' summarizes his searching for an ultimate reason to existence. In this regard, Jürgen Moltmann (born in 1926) mentions that the ambiguities of history must, at some point, become unequivocal. History and its diverse interpretations can only be explained in a single sense, and without the possibility of doubt or mistake. For example, in critical literary history, a reality long enough to warn us of the transience of systems, is replaced by another over time. The concept of validity changes: "We exist in a context in which we ask ourselves the fundamental question, what is the end," if not the consequence that springs from the torment of history? Moltmann asserts it through the "intolerance of historical existence." This reality is formally evident through Moltmann's interpretation of a German proverb, "better a terrifying end than this endless terror" (1996, 10).

Our existence is caught throwing some light on events and experiences that display a high percentage of darkness and lack of intelligibility: suffering, pain, injustice, physical and psychical decline. On the other hand, however, those facts of experience refuse themselves to be rendered intelligible without a remainder; because the excess of clarity would rob them from their own particular character: that of an event which must be taken seriously in its own right, and which merits our human sympathy. Bioy Casares intends to provide one benevolent character of existence as a whole, even in the face of death, although turns out to be an impossible undertaking. For it deals with rendering intelligible painful data that one is not allowed to banalize. Or to put it differently: from the moment that a person's death and distress have been externally clarified with the help of comforting schemes of interpretation, one threatens to overlook the seriousness of the suffering person's situation. However, and this is the continuation of the dialectics (reconciling the Supreme Being with the existence of evil in all its forms), the suffering agent, by no means, wishes that his or her situation of suffering may be considered as something ultimate and unredeemed. The real experience of pain logically asks for the real release from it, even when the state of release is hard to be imagined in its matter of factness. This, again, points to the necessity of attaining some insight, at an existential level this time, in order to transform unbearable into bearable pain. A reflexive 'clarification' of, and dealing with, suffering and pain are by their own nature "antinomic." This means that the procedure of rendering the experience 'comprehensible' necessarily entails a dialectical approach, which has to focus on both the finitude of human existence, and on the means to render life-within-finitude meaningful. To this point, Kristian Depoortere affirms that the courage to be is the courage to accept the finitude of human existence with the evil that lurks invincibly in the possibility of building something human, and transforming the fallen humanity. With the understanding that an attitude of resignation corresponds to a dynamic response to suffering, we must bear in mind that we exercise our power in a limited way. However, Depoortere says resignation is not a negative attitude. There is in our being the necessary condition of struggle and rebellion against fatality. Undoubtedly, all this finds an echo in the discovery of the happiness that exists in our being, even if it is a limited creative activity (Depoortere 1994, 20).

The main character in the novel explains his attitude facing solitude, and the desires to find an answer from the place and the woman he observes every day in secret. The main character in the novel explains his attitude facing solitude, and the desires to find an answer from the place, and the woman he observes every day in secret. The protagonist finds the memories and the reading that will help him, in his reflection, in the acceptance and production of the future. His narration announces the objectivity of his observation of the events that occurred on the island. He is aware of a tiredness that he repeats over and over again, like a disease that plagues him. He is installed on a partly fictional island. He is a human being who exists in the midst of artificial things, rather false. Even in his monologue, he indicates the routine of a life that goes on from day to day, watching the sky as he points it out until six in the evening. In the passing of his daily life, he dreams of the company of the desired woman, and the alienation, and strangeness of the events that take place around him. In the midst of that noise and struggle, his thinking divides into three dimensions: death, which is a focal point in our reflection throughout these pages; the company of Faustine, that is, a deep sense of pain that accompanies the narrator; and finally, the horrific injustice of it all, from which he cannot escape in his future on the island. Perhaps, loneliness must always accompany him (Bioy Casares 1982, 113).

Previously, we consider suffering within a dialectical approach. And a classical model of this dialectical way of thinking is found in the philosophy of Immanuel Kant (1724–1804). His starting point is that the human beings are caught up in a world of temporal and material boundaries, which in one way or another limits the success of their enterprises. And he goes on saying, the very experience of this limitation gives rise to a deep yearning that prompts one to 'postulate' the perspective of a superior fulfillment ahead of the actual situation. The fugitive is not an exception regarding his attitude concerning his life. We interpret that Kant indicates that the more the moral agent experiences the deficient character of his acts, the more he feels the necessity of assessing them in the light of some ultimate (but not yet attained) global completion. In other words, the rational concept (or idea) of one's final completion provides one with the energetic force that allows him or her to go on working for attaining a more perfect ethical life.

Adolfo Bioy Casares penetrates the labyrinths of human existence. In a search for immortality, dreams, love, life, and death. His work, *Morel's Invention*, navigates through these themes whose narrative context is a vision of the future. It is for this reason that the primary reflection is to open a door to Science Fiction. The narrator wanders looking for a machine that cuts through the future that can become a perfect world. Achieving this goal is not an easy task. The author of the novel tries to go beyond the suffering that surrounds in an important part the course of life. How to avoid suffering? How is it possible to escape suffering? In other words, how can we become less vulnerable? Without a doubt, that the price to pay for the solutions to these questions is a substantial part of reality. There is a certain possibility that he becomes less sensitive to suffering and, at the same time, becomes less sensitive to love.

THE SEARCH FOR IMMORTALITY

In the context of fantasy literature, *Morel's Invention* points to an interpretation of the fantastic. That is to say, in a time where it sounds impossible to rationalize this work. And by pointing out this idea of the use of reason to combine it with a style in which the narrative interacts with an adventure play. However, we are interested in a study of metaphysical elements that roam this novel. That said, the search for the meaning of things and human existence are inserted in the combination of Science Fiction and fantastic art. We can affirm that it occurs in the mixture between reality and unreality; the sick protagonist wanders in the unreality that arises around him. Perhaps, his feverish state informs the unexplained phenomena he encounters. It is possible that they are attributed to dreams that inevitably occur during his stay in the island. It is a question that we can ask ourselves when the protagonist walks between reality and unreality that he faces on a daily basis. But he lives with the discoveries he makes, and places described near him, which resemble a bomb shelter in the basement of one of the buildings. In an image that the author recreates and explains through the narrative, for example, an atmosphere pervades suspension of which influences the facts in the surroundings, various fantastic elements, and especially working of the recording machine. To rephrase it, the narrative flourishes in a climate of exploration, reveals ultimately, Science Fiction. The narrator explores elements of science new to him. However; the impression remains that the quest for immortality navigates in the context of Science Fiction. At least, it is our proposal of what a reading of Casares's work suggests. In current terms, in our postmodern society, it appears in scientific circles only as an amalgamation of the selfish desires of a large majority of human beings. Personally speaking, in several moments while reading the novel, we are left with the feeling that its author continues to offer an ironic point of view about the aforementioned "ridiculous" desires that he has about life (Bioy Casares 1982, 98).

The fugitive tries to rationalize what he discovers and appears in front of his eyes. Especially, the figure of a woman, who is revealed in the middle of the secret observation that he carries out. In the reality that looms in front of him, he describes the figure of this woman. The fugitive's description of the woman shows her with physical or material elements: she wears a colored scarf on her head, and hands together on her knees as well. The narrator describes the color of the woman's hair, and the contours of her figure, and compares her with visions of art, of a past that has remained in his memory. We must say that the plot of this romance refers to the key reason for the protagonist's self-devastation. This, it seems, is love; a love that is both devastation and a form of salvation. The narrator considers that this deep affection can bring happiness, or the certain possibility of revenge as well (Bioy Casares 1982, 100).

The thought of the protagonist and his monologue is the clear and vivid description of the suffering that overwhelms him. There is the fact of having been unjustly condemned to live on an island. The narrator attests to it. He writes his memoirs, beyond the hope that he finds in his love for Faustine, since she still is a new reason in life for a persecuted fugitive. He hates the world so much, because it is a world in which he has been unjustly condemned. However, due to the circumstances—wanted by the police for political reason—in which the protagonist finds himself, it is inevitable that he has a negative view of the woman of his dreams. There is a possibility, he thinks that this woman will turn him over to the police. His thinking and rationality are focused on challenging the status quo. With governments and authorities corrupt, in his own words, everything has turned into hell for the persecuted everywhere. It's a destiny that mortifies him, and yet he maintains a sense of hope. The reality of his emotions and analysis is mixed with fear and doubt. He is persecuted, and even so because of the complete loneliness that surrounds him. He has to continue living on this island as the only place left for his existence, a location with its unique history, and built approximately in 1924 (Bioy Casares 1982, 89–90).

A destiny that mortifies him, and of which he maintains hope. Although, this reality is mixed with fear and doubt. Around the time he spent on this solitary island, he owned different places explored every day, for instance, a museum, a chapel and a swimming pool. The protagonist waits for her in the afternoons near the rocks on the beach. He approaches the woman and intends to establish a useless conversation after all. He prepares and decorates the garden with flowers and recites romantic words that he hopes will deeply move her. Although, all these efforts are in vain because she shows no interest in him and ignores his presence at all times (Bioy Casares 1982, 90).

All this contextualizes him in his most sensitive side, of the infatuation he feels for Faustine. She is an important part and hope to emerge from the shadows of death, in the imaginary prison of the island. The fugitive's description of Faustine confirms his deep admiration for the woman. The woman keeps showing up every day. She rests on the beach like she always does. The narrator describes the routine and different details of the woman who daily observes the movement of the sea and the horizon. She walks freely in front of the garden. In the narrator's eyes, she pretends that he has not seen that place he has prepared with so much attention and dedication. In the reader's thoughts, the fugitive is irritated by this fictional world where Faustine seems to live. Especially since all the attention he demonstrates to the woman looks unimportant to her. In the end, he feels more comfortable between the images he has found and a peaceful way of living with these representations (Bioy Casares 1982, 95).

Apparently, Faustine's very presence offers him hope beyond the sentiment of a conviction that he considers by all means unjust. However, all his effort is in vain, because apparently, she has no interest in him. The fugitive has discovered a place, a corner where he can atone for her presence, without her noticing. He suddenly finds himself facing Faustine. He thinks it is the right opportunity and seizes the moment to declare his love for her. In this situation, he begins to realize the inexplicable events that happen with Faustine. The fugitive's presence is invisible to her eyes. The text mentions it as if he were invisible. He witnesses a strange repetition of Faustine's movements and dialogue. Even she always appears and disappears so suddenly for reasons he does not know. It is as if she were a holographic image of the desired woman in his presence (Bioy Casares 1982, 108).

The protagonist lives in that constant questioning about what is real. He wonders, if what he sees and experiences around him is authentic. He also tries different answers or possible explanations to everything that is happening on this island. There is actually this island and its inhabitants. It is possible that he only refers to an island where madness is the best description of everything. And he lives in that doubt or skepticism the whole narrative. It is the possibility of entering the world of images and, thus, achieving Faustine's love and immortality. In any case, doubts persist and emerges more and more as a menace. He has never stopped pursuing every effort and pursuit it by all means in order to win her love. He does not want to miss the last probability to reach his goal. He declares out loud his feelings for her. The decorated garden does enhance for a special occasion in its favorite place. However, he is interrupted by other members who accompany Faustine. Nevertheless, following the group's steps through the museum, he concludes that she is an image projected by Morel's machine. The pain that overwhelms him is growing, and he wonders how to create a little corner where he can swear eternal love to her. However, the only consolation he has left is to think that this garden is his creation. It is not something unreal; on the contrary, it is visible to his eyes and all his senses (Bioy Casares 1982, 115–16).

The protagonist collects them in his diary. A life diary that recounts the details of his experiences on the island. The fugitive continues to write down every fact that appears in his life, with the remote possibility that one day those who find such annotations may help to fulfill his unfulfilled wish. The future that the fugitive thinks leads him through the vicissitudes of one of the main themes that concern us in this chapter. We have already indicated the theme of the company of women, also identified as loneliness. Perhaps the fugitive realizes that the most important thing will be to give life in exchange for immortality. From the beginning of Morel's story, we find Faustine's reactions and thoughts that only belong to the supposition of the fugitive mind. In this reality, actions or scenes of interaction between the characters in the woman's environment are not only described; they are also a projection of the narrator's thoughts and consciousness. These are projections of the main protagonist as well. The novel's readers may interpret the path which the fugitive reveals and follow the track that he wants to impose on us at the recognition of these themes. Faustine's thoughts are only an image of a mystery unraveled. However, it is not necessary to establish greater complexity to the story, though exploring the fugitive's mind and life is a difficult task. His monologues recreate a climax that is living permanently in the world of Faustine. In this way, the narrator can achieve happiness; these images are part of his daily thoughts (Bioy Casares 1982, 113).

In this regard, Kant has spelled out this insight in his *Critique of Pure Reason* (1781), where he investigates the nature of scientific research. And to place Morel in this context, we interpret that Kant tells us that, on this level, nobody will be able to endure the unsuccessful attempts at understanding, unless he or she firmly believes in the eventual happy outcome of his intellectual enterprise. The rational belief in the idea of the eventual good result constitute, in Kant's eyes, the in-built thrust that steers the actions of the cognitive faculty. It is interesting to note that Kant expands this insight to the ethical practice of man and woman. The *Critique of Practical Reason* (1788) and the work *Religion Within the Limits of Reason* (1793) both elaborate the existence of volitional "schemes" (or "ideas") operative in the ethical agent and offering him or her, (in our case Morel) some rational faith in the eventual attainment of the 'good life,' in spite of the experience of failure. The more the moral agent puts energies into ethical concerns, the more the in-built (rational) persuasion grows that the disappointments. Pain and suffering that accompany the moral act are to be seen in the light of their eventual decrease and defeat. This rational projection of victory is, in Kant's eyes, a necessity: it helps the moral agent to overcome Morel disappointment, and to go on striving after the good life as some hoped for reality. It is in this context, too, that one may understand Kant's reflections on man's immortality. For instance, the striving after the good life in the face of adversity triggers off the idea (or persuasion) that our experience of time must be finished if we are to attain at our final goal. No adversity, not even death, will be capable of putting an end to our dream of eventual accomplishment.

The protagonist tells in his diary the function of his creation, a machine that, through the projection of images, which last a week, will capture permanent love (immortality). Everything started from the moment he has captured the image of the woman in the island. The fugitive thoughts rejoice in his condition of the living dead, like a zombie who refuses eternal rest; he emphasizes the theme of love. This feeling worries humanity in the dimension of immortality. That is to say that in this life, he refuses to die, and love is the solution to eternal life. It is interesting to place this statement in a Christian context, which states the following: Of the three so-called theological virtues, faith, hope, and love, the most important of these is love. We do not dare to continue this reflection too extensive.

However, we are only at the limit of what Bioy Casares' story argues about love in the context of the novel. The love for Faustine drives away the feeling of rebellion that blinded the fugitive. The main reason the narrator's mouth awakens the dead in a literary context is that it was impossible not to stop having hope with the woman he loved. The fugitive recognizes his love for Faustine, beyond using rationality to explain the fantastic phenomena in the novel. Faustine brings the fugitive back to life, and the homage he dedicates in an inscription on the flowers in the garden enhances a convincing admiration and timid praise to love.

The fugitive narrator is willing to sacrifice his life. In the novel's last pages, he reaffirms his desire to live forever in an ideal world with his beloved Faustine. Everything should be in order to gain immortality. Nevertheless, ironically, he has to die first in the real world, a man innocent and only guilty of loving the woman of his dreams. This decision to sacrifice itself demonstrates that human desires are superior to the very value of their existence. For instance, a further reflection tells us what we are experiencing in this postmodern age; where desires motivate us and push us to achieve the dream of a better life. The fugitive's passion goes beyond a passion for science, which does not mind sacrificing human lives (Bioy Casares 1982, 114).

This tribute by the protagonist acquires special trims. Incidentally, he decides to sacrifice his life to achieve immortality. He is a real human being living in one island somehow not real, because many of the things in it are artificial, rather, they are false. All these points out through the narration of the strange events that happen in front of him. On the other hand, in this context, the reader focus on the story that mentions other individuals, people characterized by the fugitive as human beings accompanying Faustine. He records the miracle of the appearance of people who walk through the buildings and the beach in different facets. He focuses critically on the description of these people: Dora and Alec, Faustine's companions, several abominable intruders—the narrator thinks. There are also various fishers and one bearded tennis player. All of them are secondary characters, and the narrator asks himself the following question: how is it possible that these people came into the island? Who brought them to this place? He cannot understand, especially in the middle of a storm striking the island overnight (Bioy Casares 1982, 106).

Suddenly, they appear in the hotel. The narrator did not see them some minutes before, in a place so lonely and total silent. To him, this island was abandoned and uninhabited. After all, these people or images always appear or disappear in extraordinary circumstances in such targeting. Amidst what will describe as hallucinations and extraordinary phenomena, they appear abruptly in each narrative segment. In the novel, according to the observation of the protagonist, they are illusions or the possible presence of aliens. Otherwise, this one is something not easy to believe and to confirm. These presences are holographic representations like the woman. Ultimately, they may be hallucinations imposed in some way on the fugitive's consciousness. The protagonist begins a series of perceptions of appearances repeated, where his judgment and mind begin to doubt the reality of their existence. They must be dangerous people who put his life in constant danger. He does not know the identity of each of them and does not intend any contact. It is possible to argue that not knowing the identity of those people; they are inventions only in the mind and thinking of the fugitive. Furthermore, he probably has invented their identities. In addition, he reflects and considers one possible answer: most of these people are police officers. They are unknown on a desert island, and better to keep them in this way. Otherwise, they are a threat to his life. Moreover, probably, they are members of the secret police constantly chasing this fugitive (Bioy Casares 1982, 106).

The protagonist insists with his protest and acceptance of the reality he received. Kristian Depoortere says on this regard that life should not admit the existence of suffering. That suffering is "meaningless." However, it finds sense in acceptance that it is the courage to fight suffering in a society impregnated by evil. "It is our conviction that suffering is meaningless . . . To use the word 'meaningless' is to indicate that suffering should not exist." He continues saying: "This affirmation is of capital importance because an overhasty attribution of meaning to suffering leads to a cease-fire in the battle against suffering, and to a kind of approval or justification of suffering." He then adds: "The immediate attribution of meaning and the insensitivity to concrete suffering constitute a vicious circle" (Depoortere 1994, 21).

The fugitive uses his disappointment in the face of death in the next monologue. The contrast of his struggle has in mind the restlessness of fear and dismay. The fugitive is scared. He watches the inhabitants who share the island with him appear and disappear. He senses the threat looming around him, and he immediately hides. However, he expects that they will come at any moment. Does he wonder that there is there any chance he could run away? He is not willing to be captured. However, the fear is so much present and real. Thinking of fleeing to another uninhabited island is not an option. The plot continues in suspense through the novel's pages. That is the feelings, the emotions that accompany the fugitive. However, after all, he sits in a place that resembles a safe building. He thinks and calculates each step, each decision with tact and skill at all times. After all, his love for Faustine is the key to continuing living on the island (Bioy Casares 1982, 106).

People call into question man's self-justification in creating social structures that oppress (or eliminate) those at the underside of history. Kenneth Surin mentions the oppression of the downtrodden (Jews) identified in the darkness of suffering. He follows Sartre argument on the victims of history and the unjustifiable suffering of citizens:

> Chateaubriant, Oradour, the Rue des Saussaies, Tulle, Dachau, and Auschwitz have all demonstrated to us that Evil is not an appearance, that knowing its causes does not dispel it, that it is not opposed to Good as a confused idea is to a clear one, that it is not the effect of passions which might be cured, of a fear which might be overcome, of a passing aberration which might be excused, of an ignorance which might be enlightened, that it can in no way be turned, brought back, reduced, and incorporated into idealistic humanism. . . . We heard whole blocks screaming and we understood that Evil, fruit of a free and sovereign will, is, like Good, absolute . . . (Sartre 1948, 635).

Sartre's concern is about those who find themselves in the darkness of suffering, feeling unable to appreciate the Good that might come out from their desperate situation (not even for the future generations). The position of Theodore Adorno is even more radical. His indignation over the "wounds of senseless suffering," explained away by the systematic thinking and its magic belief in general progress, casts a new light on the problem of suffering. Those who are summoned to account for their acts, are the "bearers" of the systematic thinking that oppresses the victims of history. While they cannot exactly be identified, these persons are being denounced, in an attempt at changing the oppressive structures. The fugitive writes in his diary the experiences of an oppressive system that brought him to the island. A place that is synonymous with the prison that has trapped him. In this way, it is related by the chronicle that brings together his experiences, his emotions. All of them are the result of the lack of freedom in which he has been condemned. However, beyond the horror of suffering the lack of freedom, the persuasion is that the suffering which is caused by inter-human deeds ought to be redeemed by some inter-human endeavor, too. This persuasion is profoundly rooted in the moral indignation that calls for some radical action binding on the true "believers." This is, at least, the core of Adorno's message. *The Invention of Morel* emphasized the thoughts of the fugitive. In most descriptions of him, the narrator stresses the environment around him. Therefore, he tries to write down his testimony. He knows that he is under persecution, and what will happen is the sensation of a death foretold. Impossible to think that he can get out of the hell in which he is condemned. It is also the sensation that his consciousness evokes at every moment. Morel's plot inscribed in his memoir leaves the reader with a world that wanders through madness and dreams. At this point, the reading opens interpretations about this dimension of a confusing place, in its colors, sounds, contacts, pains, temperatures, and the construction of an imaginary world; in which Bioy Casares's uses some scientific or philosophical theories. They are the basis of a fantastic place that reveals his literary invention. Without a doubt, it represents an open window to a place other than what our senses and reason can describe. The narrative abounds in this sense in philosophical and scientific possibilities (Bioy Casares 1982, 89–90).

The reflection of the fugitive and his sense of immortality is interesting. We can contextualize from his monologue, the scope of his interpretation. Moltmann affirms: "The history of European thought offers us tow images of hope in the face of death: the image of the immortal soul, an image cherished by the ancient world; and the Bible's image of the resurrection of the dead" (Moltmann 1996, 58). However, Morel argues that his idea of immortality also evokes the ancient world. In this way, it is cited in the footnote of the novel by Bioy Casares (the story of Isis and Osiris). Immortality is going to become possible in all souls. The ancient story says that Isis and Osiris were sons of Gheb and Nut and brothers of Seth. Seth, jealous of Osiris, locked him in a chest and threw him into the Nile. Isis and Osiris's wife managed to rescue him from it. Nevertheless, Seth seized Osiris again and dismembered him. The body, torn into small pieces, was distributed throughout the country. Isis, with great sorrow, went through Egypt and managed to find and gather all the remains and bring Osiris back to life (Bioy Casares 1982, 154–55).

Moltmann indicates that every doctrine about the immortality of the soul begins with Plato (Moltmann 1996, 58). He notes that Plato describes the death of Socrates to to highlight what the immortality of the soul is. In his first argument, Plato assumes that life and death are opposites, like waking and sleeping, and that they come into being from the antithesis between them. He also considers that

The second argument is the cognitive one: our learning is nothing other than recollection. All cognition is a re-cognition. Because like is only known by like, what the soul perceives in the world after birth must already have been implanted in it before birth (Moltmann 1996, 58).

The projection of dreams and immortality also include the process of being through suffering. In a world that is not "the best possible worlds" as it was argued by Gottfried von Leibniz (1646–1716). In spite of this optimistic outlook, one ought to be realistic. Indeed, the best possible world, which is ours, will never acquire the degree of happiness that is natural to God, the Creator. However, happiness is a form of life that includes several sensitive gratifications. Leibniz philosophical mysticism argues that the essence of this mysticism lies in the soul's capacity of mirroring and reflecting the infinite. In our view, it mirrors Love as an absolute virtue. Additionally, our existence searches for the ultimate prize in this best possible world among many worlds.

SUFFERING AND HOPE

Morel, in this situation of powerlessness, intents to generate its own schemes of dynamic strength, when the continuous dynamic and creative impulse of life seems to be fatally interrupted. Is it possible to argue that his experience of the absence of meaning can, in fact, only be clarified intellectually? If one integrates it into the dynamic vision of one's not yet given (but hoped for) eventual conquest of meaning, and meaning can only be restored to misfortune and disillusion. If one succeeds in deriving a new sense of beauty and value from the future-oriented schemes of expectancy as far as they contain a vital promise of "new life." We summarize several points argued by Depoortere: First of all, this interpretation of suffering does not stand up to the test of reality. There is a possibility that an individual can grow up suffering (or grow through suffering), but the risk of not growing up is much greater. We recall the following example: In the year 1974, the center of Managua, the capital of Nicaragua, was destroyed by a violent earthquake; in that center, the brick and concrete buildings belonging to the upper and middle class could be found, whereas the poor majority of the citizens used to live in their shanties. After the earthquake, funds were raised worldwide, and gifts in kind were to flow into Nicaragua, but the dictator Somoza blocked them to fill his own pockets. Somoza attitude reveals the risk of not growing up. This social catastrophe continues happening in different places, and we helplessly witness this avoidable suffering. However, following Depoortere's line of argument, we point out: while some people are purified by pain, others are broken or bitter. Only if the challenge is not overwhelming and the person confronted is strong enough. Should a catastrophe serve as an alarm for another that happens to it? It is the kind of question that bothers us always. Besides, we do not find a solution to that. However, suffering makes people shrink and close in themselves. The vast majority are broken, bitter, or seriously hurt. The terrible thing about this story is that only some people are purified amid the pain of their fellow human beings (Depoortere 1994, 41).

Roberto Bolaño (1953–2003), in his novel *Nazi Literature in America* (1996), paraphrased Zach Sodenstern (1962–2012), a highly successful Science Fiction writer, referring to the story *A Little House in Napa*, which introduces the Gunther O'Connell saga (1987). We find it interesting to read Bolaño's view of this novel quoted as a succession only interrupted by the final word of unpleasant and aggressive situations. At first glance, it does not look like a Science Fiction novel. Perhaps one utopic vision or dreams and visions of the adolescent Gunther O'Connell paint her with a specific prophetic and fantastic veneer. There are no space flights or robots, or scientific advances; on the contrary, the society he describes seems to have regressed on the scale of civilization (Bolaño 1996, 112–13).

Concerning with this regression on the scale of civilization, we have to say that Bioy Casares alludes to *The island of Doctor Moreau* (1896) by H. G. Wells (1866–1946). First of all, it should be noted that Bioy Casares introduces in Morel's invention is a puzzling mystery of operations, the vast majority of them wander through the monologues of its protagonist. Where he tries to find a solution not supernatural but fantastic. On the contrary, in Wells fiction, the sinister doctor Moreau turned animals into men through sadistic operations. Finally, Moreau could not keep the humanization of the beasts unchanged. Little by little they reverted to animality. In any case, Bioy Casares, in his novel shows the image of the tropical island and the name of the inventor. For example, in *Plan de evasión* (1945), the experiments of doctor Castel with the prisoners of the Devil's Island emerge, which provide, at the same time, the common setting and the allusions of the plot. In *Dormir al sol*, Bioy Casares returns to Wells, in a much more literal way: Dr. Samaniego actually produces transfers between men and animals. In other words, while Wells places his fiction at the limit of what the science of his time might believe possible, Bioy Casares moves his fiction into the territory of pure fantasy. Dr. Samaniego only partially traffics in the bodies of men and animals; his true permutational science lies in the transfer of souls (Rodríguez 1974).

In *The Invention of Morel* his main character is an example of what modern society constitutes. The individual increasingly focuses on the importance of his or her personal existence, detached as it were from their natural subordination to the kinship-group and the patterns of order prevailing in the group. Wester's civilization is basically a civilization of individualism. Theodore

Adorno in the core of his message offers one thought to redemption from suffering and destruction of humanity. The persuasion is that the suffering which is caused by inter-human deeds ought to be redeemed by some inter-human endeavor, too. This persuasion is profoundly rooted in the moral indignation that calls for some radical action binding on the true "believers" (Adorno 1966, 201).

The regression on the scale of civilization is also, in the view of Adorno, the presence of the physical evil, which may as well be the culminating-point of some moral evil. The theology after Auschwitz evidences this new relationship. If in the contemporary life climate one agent sets out to torment the other physically (or morally), he will hardly stop before torturing him physically, too. The deportation program of the Jews in Nazi Germany provides the direct application of this insight. The hatred of the Jewish race had to find its expression not only in defamation campaigns and attacks on their civil rights (which make them suffer morally), it had to show itself in the form of bodily humiliations: slaughter in concentration camps, exhaustion through overwork in sub-human conditions of starvation, filthiness and not looked after diseases. Only the physically exhausted and emaciated person is effectively being tortured in his psyche according to the extreme suffering that the modern tormentor wants to expose him to. The moral suffering only attains its culminating-point, when it is sadistically accompanied by bodily practices of torture. Dorothee Sölle points out that the experience of affliction, wherein psychological pain, is not spared physical pain, is a rule accompanied by the awareness of some social suffering. In our modern, secular society this form of pain appears to be the most influential component that leads to the situation of global affliction. The suffering person lives 'in fear of social ostracism.' Affliction is ridiculous. Therefore, the lack of solidarity with the afflicted is the most natural thing in the world. It is natural for us more or less to despise the afflicted, although practically no one is conscious of it (Sölle 1975, 13–14).

Although Bioy Casares's narration emphasizes the invention of the perfect machine, which allows three-dimensional beings to be projected onto reality. Morel's invention is the machine that records his life and friends on the island for seven days. The fugitive mentions the sea and its tides activating its motors. In this way, the images of the characters are projected towards eternity. Therefore, the island inhabitants that the fugitive finds are mere images that are repeated in this circle of seven days. The machine accurately reproduces each individual with absolute perfection. Even activating one of its devices makes it possible to aspirate and smell every living being. It is also possible to caress the woman's hair as if he had her within reach of the touch. All his wide receivers reproduce the image of the woman, complete, identical. It is the holographic images extracted from mirrors, with sounds and resistance to the touch. Besides, that is the maximum empirically expression of the use of every sense (Bioy Casares 1982, 147).

However, we cannot ignore an essential fact that runs through the pages of the novel. If it is important to indicate the machinery that largely fulfills the dreams of the protagonist. But, we cannot forget that the emphasis is placed on that impossible love between the narrator and the woman, Faustine, who he used to find on his walks around the island. Hope keeps the narrator alive and expectant. His fight for Faustine's love is the reason for his existence. Even in the failed interaction that happens between the two of them (Bioy Casares 1982, 100). That is an expectant desire to pursue the woman around the island. When she goes through different places, for instance, the beach, the garden, the museum, he hopes to capture the image that will remain forever in the memory. The narrator does not expect much. In part, his steps follow the way that makes peace in the mind and soul. Faustine is the horizon that the fugitive pursues romantically. Even though she is the reason for self-destruction, it is love in two dimensions: devastation and salvation. One interpretation realizes the desired love, impossible to capture in the real world. Morel's machine creates a version of the world where the protagonist and Faustine can be forever lovers. The others people on the island are still immature in the face of love. They still do not understand how a human being can achieve this hope. We indicate that a desire exists in a society that seeks profound changes in the utopia of liberation from evil and its consequences. They have to work hard to reflect on this unavoidable suffering and evil. The rest of the people on the island must anticipate the encounter with their inner feelings and the longed-for love (Bioy Casares 1982, 100).

However, Faustine is made only of cinematic images. Images that the protagonist tries to reveal and project outside of his consciousness. The narrator suggests forms of communication and interaction with the woman. In a moment of almost unconsciousness, he tries to communicate even in terms that border on obscenities. However, calm returns to his spirit and looks at the sunset. Likewise, someone awaits to share time, and the woman appears calm. In the monologues, the climate that accompanies the protagonist interrogation is not of absolute tranquility after all. On the contrary, he strives to control his outbursts of passion. Moreover, he tries to lower his voice, and again insults and shouts emerge throughout the innumerable pages. The fugitive's request finds no echo in the woman. She does not respond to the insults that cry out for dialogue. The silence that surrounds the woman is profoundly annoying him. He thinks that verbal contact is the possibility of being human. The possibility of a relationship between them could be a way of liberation. The voice of the fugitive tries very hard, but only a long silence remains as an answer. The silence that surrounds them is a reality that dislodges the protagonist. Finally, only the incommensurable love is real, namely the inner and interior side (silence) of things, their character of an entity and a soul and conscience (Bioy Casares 1982, 108–9).

The story behind the machine indicates that, when the protagonist discovers it, discovers it and learns to operate it, he films himself. In such a way that his images match hers. He pretends to create dialogues, which allude to an erotic understanding. And it is love that sustains all the fugitive's inner monologues. It is the fiction of love that the protagonist proclaims. According to Bioy Casares, what is essential beyond the perfect machine is the invention of love that Morel communicates. A love that goes beyond the description of a scientific reality which proposes Morel in his narrative. He practices how to film his image, in such a way, that his image should match hers. Furthermore, he pretends allude to an erotic understanding of his deep feelings through dialogues. The fugitive inner monologues are signs of love in absolute terms. He deals with the relationship of the finite (soul) and the infinite (love) in a very particular way. In all of its parts, the whole of reality (in the fugitive conscience) is inhabited by infinite love, the sense of a real presence and an accurate and necessary psychical fulfillment. Moreover, dealing with the relationship of the finite (soul) and the infinite (love) in a very particular way. In all of its parts, the whole of reality (in the fugitive conscience) is inhabited by infinite love, the sense of a real presence, and an accurate and necessary psychical fulfillment. What is more, this routine is always an essential part of daily life; perhaps a time being in touch in a mystical search. The fugitive touching the woman horrifies him and raises the following statement: is it possible to be in danger of touching a ghost? The answer is Morel's image shared with the reader about powerless love (Bioy Casares 1982, 109–10).

Morel memoirs suggest the possibility to encounter the weakness and the impotence of love. However, we find this purifying experience by combining the concepts of power and love as one attempt to consider. Under the condition of the experienced human solidarity, he will continue to resent the brutal facts of lack of humanity. In our understanding, Morel's invention helps reflect the power of love. Moments of personal crisis, therefore, unresolvable as they may seem, confront the dramatic hero (the fugitive and Morel) with some more profound level of truth that surfaces even amid personal 'darkness' (absolute and inexplicable silence, science, and horror). This deeper level tells them it is wrong to think that suffering is irredeemable. The fugitive's suffering lends itself to be transformed into the liberating experience of surrender via the path of the catharsis of the soul.

Perhaps, the image that Morel wants to share with us is the powerless love. Depoortere suggests the following:

> If we attempt to combine the concepts of power and of love and to discover something like a power of love, the first thing we encounter is the weakness

and the impotence of love. It is only through this purifying experience that the specific power of love is manifest (Depoortere 1994, 78).

It is important to mention that Morel and his invention help us to reflect on the power of love. Beyond the contact with the religious message, the author discloses an additional dimension of "meaning," not to be found in what we explain in Kant schemes of expectancy and of ultimate human completion before. The essence of this additional dimension is love, as distinguished from hope. Indeed, the worshipping and praying "believer" will be able to project towards the future some "horizon of meaning" that draws the light of its promise from a practice of love and praise of the universe. Love praises the goodness of the finite existence as well as the goodness of the Creator of the universe. However, in order to discover (or to keep in touch with) this specific dimension of love, the meditating person will, practically speaking, have to make his advantage from the texts of a religious tradition, by dealing with this topic. In a religious context is possible to affirm (as the interiorization and the suggestive message of the biblical narratives with regard to the praise of the Creator and his creation) that the believer will succeed in expanding his in-built structure of hope towards the practice and the worship of a universal love.

If the loving affirmation wins the victory over pain, suffering and disillusion, this very option for love and praise produces and 'excelling potential' of strength and affirmation (yes to life) which is different from the pure retrieval of one's lost 'dynamism,' construed in terms of some repeatable, identical human capacity of hope. To be sure, Kant and his Inventive schemes of expectancy allow us to better understand the dynamics of hope that emerge from the roots of human existence, a description that particularly appeals to the mind set of citizens of the Enlightenment. In addition, they indirectly clarify the 'model' of a love that reaffirms (and fortifies) itself through pain and misfortune. Yet, at a decisive point, they fail to explain the essence of love and praise, taken in a religious perspective. This expansion or 'intensification' of the energetic potential of love, now, is the vivid source that recreates suffering (which in itself lacks any ground of meaningfulness) into an 'assumed' suffering; it is then converted into a positive element that reinforces, in turn, the basic energetic impulse of love's vivifying 'strain' and 'intensification.' This makes us, finally, understand the content of the 'greater good' that transcends its antecedent forms of goodness. Indeed, the more intense 'straining' of love's energetic potential (the greater good) would not have been possible without the assumed pain (whereby the element of 'assumed' pain reveals the transformation of 'meaningless' pain into love's excelling meaningfulness.

CONCLUSION

Bioy Casares uses scientific or philosophical theories as the basis for the construction of imaginary worlds that reveal his narrative inventions. Interpretations by Immanuel Kant and others allow us to elaborate a plausible interpretation. Critical reflection that is an open window to an imaginary world with an invention of what the author calls: "the perfect machine." In this chapter we attempt a reflection on the way in which Bioy Casares opens an invisible door towards imaginary and aesthetic possibilities of philosophical and scientific theories. This chapter focused our attention on interpreting some of these philosophical elements, which are born from the protagonist's narration. There is one possibility among many to critically analyze the author of the novel *Morel's Invention* perception of reality. For instance, in a passage in the novel, the main narrator synthesizes that perspective in a reality (his world) that is presented as an indeterminate flow, a kind of compact current, a vast flood where there are no people or objects, but confusingly smells, colors, sounds, contacts, pains, temperatures. It is possible to point out that Morel's world wanders through madness and dreams. For example, the protagonist may be an invisible being, on an island of madmen. Where everything is a dream. And that doubt remains in the reader, in the uncertainty that surrounds the novel from the beginning to the end. Morel's discovery of the perfect machine is a possible certification of this doubt and uncertainty (Rodriguez 1974).

It is interesting to highlight what the author places in his author's narrative: a narrative voice takes the reader through the reading in an interpretation of the fictional universe as the guiding and semantic thread of the story is told; a modality in its dialogic character of the fantastic as a way of writing that introduces a dialogue with the 'real.' The incorporation of this element is a fundamental part of its essential structure. In our day, this vision whets the appetite of the reader avid for the fantastic and scientific in nature. Nothing new if we take into account the time and generation that we have to live and experience. In the novel there is the search for love and immortality. Both realities that must go through periods of suffering and pain. A "brave new world" is possible as Aldous Huxley indicates in his novel of the same name. It does not seem to us a blunt affirmation of what we observe and experience in our time, and that it is expressed in this way. On the contrary, we are witnessing a world and society where dehumanization has been growing by leaps and bounds. And for which, it is not easy to develop a positive response. We have written these reflections with the hope of changes that augur a different reality. However, what appears to us shows otherwise. Morel's imaginary world recreates the madness of desensitization, the lack of solidarity, the search for an impossible love, in a cyclical and equally ambiguous world.

Roberto Bolaño recreates an ambiguous and uncertain society and universe in some of his novels. His novel is published posthumously in *2666* (2004). In it, he describes characters, events and dark realities that prophesy an increasingly terrifying world of ours. It is also a story where whispers and small details flow, full of hidden structures and intuitions that seem too ephemeral, or too terrible to be put into words. It is an example of tragic exuberance, of metaphysics and endless in the production of it. Like the novel *The Savage Detectives* (2010), which describes stories that are unfinished; in addition to being the image of a violent, provocative society, of a dark and equivocal future. Morel's world and his perfect machine is the scientific ability to capture for eternity the image of a group of friends and that of its inventor who, in his projections, repeats the acts performed by all of them during a certain number of days. It is the synthesis of a world in its perfect realization through technology. However, the image we capture from this projection is different. It is the perception of a limited future in human interactions, a definite world of liquid relationships.

Perhaps a day will come when a happy age, looking back at the past, will see in this suffering and shame one of the paths that led to peace. It is possible that the protagonist of *Morel's Invention* captures in the perfect machine the peace for the future generations. [. . .] that he may succeed in putting the natural forces and resources into de service of civilization, and that he will build up a new world where the maximum of happiness will befall to as many citizens as possible (Russel 1930, 114). One may say, the work of Morel reaches the goal of diminishing the pain and suffering. However, we are not on the side of history already made. We were situated in such a way that every lived minute seemed to us like something irreducible. Therefore, in spite of ourselves we came, to the conclusion, which will seem shocking to lofty souls: "Evil cannot be redeemed," even with the discovery and existence of the perfect machine (Surin 1983, 231).

REFERENCES

Adorno, Theodore. 1966. *Negative Dialektic*. Frankfurt: Suhrkamp Verlag Publishers.
Bioy Casares, Adolfo. 1973. *Dormir al sol*. Buenos Aires: Emecé Editores.
_____ 1975. *Historias de amor*. Buenos Aires: Alianza Editorial.
_____ 1982. *La invención de Morel*. Madrid: Cátedra S. A.
_____ 1945. *Plan de evasión*. Buenos Aires: Emecé Editores.
Bolaño, Roberto. 2004. *2666*. Barcelona: Anagrama S. A.
_____ 1993. *La literatura nazi en América*. Barcelona: Anagrama S. A.

_____ 2010. *Los detectives salvajes*. Nueva York: Vintage Español.

_____ 2010. *Nocturno de Chile*. Nueva York: Vintage Español.

Depoortere, Kristian. 1994. *A Different God: A Christian View of Suffering*. Leuven: Peeters Press.

Galeano, Eduardo. 1971. *Las venas abiertas de América Latina*. Madrid: Siglo XXI Editores.

García, Mariano. 2017. "Bioy y sus precursores: la tradición de la ciencia ficción en la narrativa de Adolfo Bioy Casares." *Revista Iberoamericana* 83 no. 259–260 (abril-septiembre): 449–464. https://doi.org/10.5195/reviberoamer.2017.7512.

González Chandía, Miguel Ángel. 2018. "Roberto Bolaño y el apocalipsis: salvajismo y carnaval." *Fu Jen Studies*, 51 (summer): 104–121.

Houekkebecq, Michel. 2015. *Sumisión*. Barcelona: Anagrama Editorial.

Huxley, Aldous. 1932. *Un mundo feliz*. Scotts Valley, California: CreateSpace Independent Publishing Platform.

Jay, Martin. 1973. *The Dialectic Imagination: A History of the Frankfurt School and the Institute of Social Research 1923–1950*. London: Little Brown and Company Publishers.

Kant, Immanuel. 1781. *Critique of Pure Reason*. Cambridge: Cambridge Edition.

_____ 1960. *Religion within the Limits of Reason*. Translated by T. Green and H. Hudson, New York: Harper & Row Press.

Kübler-Ross, Elizabeth. 1975. *Death: The Final Stage of Growth*. New Jersey: Prentice Hall-Englewood Cliffs.

Moltmann, Jürgen. 1966. *The Coming of God: Christian Eschatology*. Minneapolis: Fortress Press.

Orwell, George. 1949. *1984*. London: Secker & Warburg.

Peursen Van, Cornelis Anthonius. 1969. *Leibniz*. Baarn: Faber and Faber Publishers.

Rodriguez Monegal, Emir. 1974. "La invención de Morel." Retrieved February 11, 2022 from https://www.cervantesvirtual.com/obra-visor/la-invencion-de-bioy-casares/html/b452088e-3c86-4487-b286-4fb834c33c88_2.html.

Russel, Bertrand. 1930. *The Conquest of Happiness*. London: George Allen and Unwin LTD Publishers.

Sartre, Jean-Paul. 1948. *Literature in Our Time*. Section IV. *Partisan Review*, XV, no. 6: 635 ff.

Surin, Kenneth. 1983. "Theodicy." Harvard Theological Review 76, no. 2 (April): 225–247.

Sölle, Dorothee. 1975. *Suffering*. London: Longman, Todd Publishers. Wells, Herbert George. 1896. *The island of Dr Moreau*. United Kingdom: Heinemann.

Appendix

Non-exhaustive List of Titles in Science Fiction, Utopias and Dystopias

375 BC

Plato, *The Republic*

360 BC

Plato, *Timaeus* and *Critias* [fragments]

9 BC

Titus Livius, *Ab Urbe condita*

5 AD

Tao Yuanming, *Taohua Yuan Ji* (*Peach Blossom Spring*)

1516

Thomas More, *Utopia*

1602

Tommaso Campanella, *The City of the Sun*

1626

Francis Bacon, *New Atlantis*

1638

William Godwin, *The Man in the Moone*; or a *Discourse of a Voyage Thither* by Domingo Gonsales

John Wilkins, *The Discovery of a World in the Moone*

1657

Savinien de Cyrano de Bergerac, *L'Autre Monde ou les États et Empires de la lune* (*Voyage dans la lune*)

1659

Jacques Guttin, *Epigone, histoire du siècle futur*

1665

Robert Hooke, *Micrographia*

1686

Bernard de Fontenelle, *Entretiens sur la pluralité des mondes*

1703

David Russen, *In the Iter Lunare; or, a Voyage to the Moon*

1705

Daniel Dafoe, *The Consolidator; or, Memoirs of Sundry Transactions from the World in the Moon*

1722

Daniel Dafoe, *A Journal of the Plague Year*

1726

Jonathan Swift, *Travels into Several Remote Nations of the World* (*Gulliver's Travels*)

1752

Voltaire's *Micromégas*

1741

Ludvig Baron von Holberg, *Nicolai Klimii iter subteraneum*

1765

Marie-Anne de Roumier, *Les Voyages de Milord Céton dans les sept planettes*

1771

Louis-Sébastien Mercier, *L'An deux mille quatre cent quarante*

1781

Nicolas-Edme Restif de la Bretonne, *La découverte australe par un homme volant*

1805

Jean-Baptiste Francois Xavier Cousin de Grainville, *Le dernier homme*

1818

Mary Shelley, *Frankenstein, or The Modern Prometheus*

1820

Adam Seaborn, *Symzonia: a Voyage of Discovery*

1826

Mary Shelley, *The Last Man*

1834

Felix Bodin, *Le Roman de l'avenir*

1836

Louis Napoléon Geoffroy-Château, *Napoléon et la conquête du monde—1812 à 1832—histoire de la monarchie universelle*

1840

Vladimir Fyodorovich Odoevsky, *4338-i god: Peterbugrskie pis'ma*

1846

Emile Souvestre, *Le Monde tel qu'il sera*

1859–1862

Martin R. Delany, *Blake; or, The Huts of America* (first African American utopian and science fiction novel published in serialized form)

1862

Nikolai Gavrilovich Chernyshevsky, *Chto delat*

1864

Jules Verne, *Voyage au centre de la terre*

1865

Jules Verne, *De la terre à la lune*

Achille Eyraud, *Voyage à Venus*

1868

Edward S. Ellis, *The Steam Man of the Prairies*

1869

Jules Verne, *Autour de la lune*

Jules Verne, *Vingt mille lieues sous les mers*

1874

Jules Verne, *L'Île mystérieuse*

1882

Albert Robida, *Le vingtième siècle: Roman d'une parisienne d'après-demain*

1884

Edwin Abbott, *Flatland: a Romance of Many Dimensions*

Mathias Villiers de l'Isle-Adam, *L'Eve future*

1885
Nilo María Fabra, *Cuatro siglos de buen gobierno*

Richard Jefferies, *After London*

1886
Enrique García y Rimbau, *El Anacronópete*

Robert Louis Stevenson, *The Strange Case of Dr. Jekyll and Mr. Hyde*

1887
W. H. Hudson, *A Crystal Age*

Albert Robida, *La Guerre au vingtième siècle*

Camille Flammarion, *Lumen*

1888
Edward Bellamy, *Looking Backward 2000–1887*

1890
Ryukei Yano, *Ukishiro Monogatari*

Ignatius Donnelly, *Caesar's Column*

1891
William Morris, *News from Nowhere, or An Epoch of Rest*

1893–94
Eugene Richter, *Pictures of a Socialist Future*

Camille Flammarion, *La Fin du monde*

1894
Arthur Machen, *The Great God Pan*

1895
H. G. Wells, *The Time Machine*

1896
H. G. Wells, *The Island of Doctor Moreau*

1897
Kurd Lasswitz, *Auf zwei Planeten*

Edward Bellamy, *Equality*

H. G. Wells, *The Invisible Man*

1898

Garrett P. Serviss, *Edison's Conquest of Mars*

Leopoldo Lugones, *El Psychon*

Leopoldo Lugones, *La Meta Música*

H. G. Wells, *The War of the Worlds*

1899

Leopoldo Lugones, *La fuerza Omega*

Leopoldo Lugones, *Acherontia atropos*

1900

Leopoldo Lugones, *Yzur*

1901

H. G. Wells, *Anticipations*

H. G. Wells, *The First Men in the Moon*

1905

H. G. Wells, *A Modern Utopia*

1906

H. G. Wells, *In the Days of the Comet*

1909

Filippo Marinetti, *Il manifesto del futurismo*

1911–12

Hugo Gernsback, *Ralph 124C 41 +: A Romance of the Year 2660*

1912

Edgar Rice Burroughs, *Under the Moons of Mars* (in book form: *A Princess of Mars*, 1917)

1915

Charlotte Perkins Gilman, *Herland*

1920

Karel y Josef Čapek, *R.U.R. (Rossum's Universal Robots)*

Yevgeny Zamiatin, *We*

David Lindsay, *A Voyage to Arcturus*

61923

Anonymous, *Shi Nian hou de Zhongguo (China in Ten Years)*

Aleksey Tolstoy, *Aelita*

1924

Konstantin Fedin, *Cities and Years*

1926

H. P. Lovecraft, *The Call of Cthulhu*

1927

H. P. Lovecraft, *The Colour out of Space*

1928

H. P. Lovecraft, *The Dunwich Horror*

1931

H. P. Lovecraft, *At the Mountains of Madness*

Yan Leopoldovich Larri, *Strana schastlivih (The Land of the Happy)*

H. P. Lovecraft, *The Shadow over Innsmouth*

1932

Aldous Huxley, *Brave New World*

1934

H. P. Lovecraft, *The Shadow Out of Time*

1935

Olaf Stapledon, *Odd John (El extraño John)*

1936

Juza Unno, *Chikiu Tonan (The Stolen Earth)*

1938

C. S. Lewis, *Out of the Silent Planet*

1941

Jorge Luis Borges, *La biblioteca de Babel*

Isaac Asimov, *Nightfall*

1943

René Barjavel, *Ravage*

Antoine de Saint-Exupéry, *Le Petit Prince*

1949

George Orwell's *Nineteen Eighty-four*

1950

Jack Vance, *The Dying Earth*

Ray Bradbury, *The Martian Chronicles*

1953

Arthur C. Clarke, *Childhood's End*

Ray Bradbury, *Fahrenheit 451*

1954

Isaac Asimov, *The Caves of Steel*

1961

Stanislaw Lem, *Solaris*

1962

Arkadi Natanovich Strugatsky and Boris Strugatsky, *Stazhery*

Anthony Burgess, *A Clockwork Orange*

Aldous Huxley, *Island*

1963

Pierre Boule, *La Planète des singes* (*The Planet of the Apes*)

1964

Stanislaw Lem, *Bajki robotów*

Arkadi Natanovich Strugatsky y Boris Strugatsky, *Trudno Bit Bogon*

1965

Frank Herbert, *Dune*

Philip K. Dick, *Do Androids Dream of Electric Sheep?*

1968

Arthur C. Clarke, *2001: A Space Odyssey* (2001 series)

1969

Ursula K. LeGuin, *The Left Hand of Darkness*

Kurt Vonnegut Jr., *Slaughterhouse Five*

Michael Crichton, *The Andromeda Strain*

1970

Joanna Russ, *And Chaos Died*

Ion Bing, *Det Myke Landskapet*

John Sladek, *The Müller-Fokker Effect*

1971

Gérard Klein, *Les seigneurs de la guerre*

Tor Age Bringsvaerd, *Sesam 71*

Stanislaw Lem, *Dzienniki gwiazdowe*

1972

Tor Age Bringsvaerd, *Blotkakemannen & Apache-pikene*

Roman Johanna Braum and Günter Braum, *Der Irrtum des Grossen Zauberers*

Arkadi Natanovich Strugatsky and Boris Strugatsky, *Piknik na obochine*

1973

J. G. Ballard, *Crash*

Sakyo Komatsu, *Nihon Chinbotsu*

Michel Jeury, *Le Temps Incertain*

Arthur C. Clarke, *Rendezvous with Rama*

1974

Roberto Vacca, *La morte di Megalopolis*

Michel Jeury, *Les Singes du Temps*

Joe Haldeman, *The Forever War*

Ursula K. Le Guin, *The Dispossessed*

Roman Johanna Braum and Günter Braum, *Unheimliche Erscheinungsformen auf Omega XI*

1975

Ernest Callenbach, *Ecotopia: The Notebooks and Reports of William Weston*

1979

Barry B. Longyear, *Enemy Mine*

Frederick Pohl, *Getaway*

1982

Agustín de Rojas, *Espiral*

1984

William Gibson, *Neuromancer*

1985

Orson Scott Card, *Ender's Game* (Ender series)

Kurt Vonnegut, *Galápagos*

Bruce Sterling, *Schismatrix*

1986

Iain M. Banks, *Consider Phlebas* (Cuture series)

1987

Octavia E. Butler, *Dawn* (Xenogenesis series)

1988

Frederick Turner, *Genesis*

1989

Dan Simmons, *Hyperion*

1990

Michael Crichton, *Jurassic Park*

1991

Neal Stephenson, *Snow Crash*

1992

P. D. James, *Children of Men*

1994

Gabriel Bermúdez Castillo, *Salud mortal*

1995

Andreas Eschbach, *Die Haarteppichknüpfer*

Keizo Hino, *Hikari*

Greg Egan, *Permutation City*

Neal Stephenson, *The Diamond Age*

Ken MacLeod, *The Star Fraction* (Fall Revolution series)

Huang Yi, *Xun Chin Ji*

1996

Paul Di Filippo, *Ribofunk*

César Mallorquí, *El coleccionista de sellos*

William Gibson, *Idoru*

1998

Paul J. McAuley, *Ancients of Days*

Kim Stanley Robinson, *Antarctica*

Bruce Sterling, *Distraction*

Michel Houllebeq, *Les Particules élémentaires* (*The Elementary Particles*; other translation: *Atomised*)

1999

Vernor Vinge, *A Deepness in the Sky*

Neal Stephenson, *Cryptonomicon*

Greg Bear, *Darwin's Radio*

2000

Javier Negrete, *Buscador de sombras*

Ken McLeod, *Cosmonaut Keep*

Nalo Hopkinson, *Midnight Robber*

Ursula K. Le Guin, *The Telling*

2001

China Miéville, *Perdido Street Station*

Ted Chian, *Hell Is the Absence of God*

2002

Harry Norman Turtledove, *Ruled Britannia*

Gavin Menzies, *1421. The Year China Discovered America*

Greg Egan, *Schild's Ladder*

Elizabeth Moon, *The Speed of Dark*

2003

Issui Ogawa, *Dairoku Tairiku*

To Ubukata, *Marudoku Skuranburu*

2004

Joe Haldeman, *Camouflage*

Vandana Singh, *Three Tales from Sky River: Myths for a Starfaring Age*

2006

Cormac McCarthy, *The Road*

2007

Michael Chabon, *The Yiddish Policemen's Union*

2009

Paolo Bacigalupi, *The Windup Girl*

2011

Ernest Cline, *Ready Player One*

2013

Samantha Shannon, *The Bone Season*

2015

Michel Houellebecq, *Soumission*

Margaret Atwood, *The Heart Goes Last*

2019

Margaret Atwood, *The Testaments*

2020

Suzanne Collins, *The Ballad of Songbirds and Snakes*

Index

Absurdism, 119, 126
Adorno, Theodore, 221, 225
Afro-Diaspora, 81, 82, 84
Afro-Pessimism, 79, 80, 83, 86
Apocalypse, 5, 119, 127, 133, 134–135, 138–141, 189,

Bastille prison, 3, 9, 16–17
Black Dystopia, 4, 68
Black Utopia, 4, 67–75, 79, 84–85
Blake; Or, The Huts Of America, iv, 4, 67, 72
Borges, Jorge, Luis, 211–212

Capitalist, 45–46, 56, 61–63, 70, 78–79, 102, 148, 151, 162, 189, 192, 195–196, 199
Censorship, 3, 5, 9, 12, 14, 20, 119, 135–137
Chaos, xiii, 111, 119, 129, 184, 205, 239
Colonialism, 16, 22, 149
Collapse, 5, 59, 114, 119, 137, 166, 177, 195
Commerce, 59–61, 79, 139, 195, 204
Control, 5–6, 15, 76, 78, 94, 106, 119, 133, 135, 137, 154, 172, 174–175, 179, 195, 226
COVID-19, 146, 156, 167, 173–174

Dehumanization, 45, 63, 80, 229
Destruction, 5, 57, 72, 110, 119, 123, 125, 134–140, 225–226
Disappearance of electricity, 5, 47, 119, 125–126, 133
Distance learning, 145, 164–166
Dreams, 7, 24, 55, 71, 104, 129, 199, 211, 214–216, 219, 222–224, 226, 229
Du Bois, W. E. B., 4, 68, 73–74
Durability of love, 5, 119, 141
Dystopia, 4–5, 15, 46, 48–49, 53, 55, 58, 63, 68, 75, 97, 109–110, 114, 145, 147, 152–155, 162, 166–168, 171–172, 177–178

Economic Colonization, 63
Electric chair, 4, 56, 129, 130
Exodus, 86, 125–126
Extrasensory perception, 110

Fahrenheit 451, 5, 119, 135–137, 239
Fantasy literature, 37, 215
Futuristic novel, 4, 24, 46

Genre, ix, 31–32, 34–36, 38, 40–41, 50, 91, 97, 114, 123, 139, 171–172, 178, 212, 246; Subgenre, 3, 31, 38–39, 41
Glasnost, 95

Hard Science Fiction, 3, 38–41
Harwell, David, 3, 38, 41
Homo aquaticus, 96, 104, 110, 112
Human-animal hybrid, 5, 91, 96
Human-nonhuman hybrid, 94–96, 107
Hypothesis, 33, 38–40, 48

Immortality, 7, 214–215, 217–219,
    222–223, 229
Industrialization, 57, 138, 154, 191
Infernal machine, 5, 119, 139
Internet, vii, 56, 134, 156, 158,
    164–165, 174
Irony, 35, 47, 119, 126–128, 166, 212

Kant, Immanuel, 214, 218, 228–229

Labor Question, 7, 190, 194–195
Liquid relationships, 230

Moltmann, Jürgen, 213, 222–223
Morel's memoirs, 212
Marronage, 76, 78
Mass Consumerism, 61
Mechanization, 63
Meritocracy, 25, 188, 191
Millenarianism, 202–203

Nationalism, 7, 86, 193, 199, 203
Nationalist Club, 193, 202
New man, 92–94, 199
New Provence, 5, 119, 138

Object recognition, 161–162
Objects of perception, 163–167
OGPU (Russian United State Political
    Department), 94–95, 100, 102, 106

Palace of Versailles, 3, 9, 16, 19
Pandemic, 5, 147, 156, 167–
    168, 173–174
Perestroika, 95
Philistine culture, 4, 46, 61

Proletariat, 92, 151, 193
Proto science fiction (proto SF), ix, 3,
    9, 11, 187

Racism, 3, 5, 70, 119, 140
Red Movement, 92
Remedy for premature aging, 92

Scientific knowledge, 39–40, 77
Sexism, 3, 5, 119, 140
Sight and hearing, 160, 162–163, 167
Slavery, 3, 10, 16, 22–24, 69–71, 73, 75,
    77, 79–83, 85, 108
Social Darwinists, 7, 187–188, 191–192
Social Gospel, 199, 204–205
Speratti Piñero, 32
Sturm und Drang, 23, 26
Supreme Being, 213
Suvin, Darko, 3, 35–36, 40, 206

Technocratic hubris, 5, 119, 137
Technology, 1–3, 5–7, 9, 38, 45, 49–50,
    52, 56–57, 61–63, 71, 112, 119, 128,
    133–135, 142, 146, 148, 151, 153,
    155–158, 161–162, 167, 172–173,
    178, 206, 230
The Great Terror, 106
The Great Trust, 7, 194–196
Theosophical Society, 32, 202
Time Travel, vii, 2–3, 5, 9, 15, 119, 122
Totalitarian Soviet Union (totalitarian
    leadership), 106
Tribal War, 5, 119, 139

Uchronia, 14–16, 25–26, 183
Utilitarianism, 59, 63
Utopia, 4–5, 7, 9, 15, 24–26, 45–46, 49,
    53–56, 58, 67–73, 75, 79, 84–85,
    103–104, 109, 114, 126, 139, 140,
    147, 150, 152–153, 167, 183, 187,
    190, 192, 194, 199, 201–202, 205–
    206, 226, 233

Vernian Society, 61

White Movement, 92

Women's Rights, 3, 10, 20–21, 25

Xenotransplantation, 104, 112

About the Editor and Contributors

Dr. Bernard Montoneri, Independent Researcher, Taiwan

Bernard Montoneri earned his Ph.D. (History, Languages, and Literature) and his BA in Chinese from the University of Provence, France. He is an Associate Professor and has taught Literature and languages for almost 25 years. He is now an independent researcher. He has around 60 publications and was the co-founder and editor-in-chief of the IAFOR Journal of Education until 2017. He is now the editor-in-chief of the *IAFOR Journal of Literature and Librarianship*. His research interests include Literature, Translation Studies, French and English Writing, Teaching and Learning Evaluation, Data Envelopment Analysis, Networking, Plagiarism, and Fake News. Dr. Montoneri wrote a chapter titled "Plagiarism and Ethical Issues: A Literature Review on Academic Misconduct" in *Ethics, Entrepreneurship, and Governance in Higher Education*, IGI Global, USA (2018). In 2020, he edited a book titled *Academic Misconduct and Plagiarism: Case Studies from Universities around the World* with Lexington Books and authored the chapter titled "Fake News and Fake Research, from the Cave to the Light: Critical reflection and Literature Review").

E-mail: bernardmontoneri@protonmail.com

ABOUT THE CONTRIBUTORS

Dr Fernando Darío González Grueso, Tamkang University, Taiwan

Fernando Darío González Grueso earned his PhD (Theory of Literature and Comparative Literature) from the Autonomous University of Madrid, and his MA (Comparative Literature) and his BA in Hispanic Philology from Alcalá de Henares University, Spain. He is an Associate Professor and has taught Literature and Spanish language for more than 21 years. He has published 4 peer-reviewed books and around 15 indexed articles, and is the co-founder and co-editor-in-chief of the series of books Estudios Hispánicos in Taiwán (EHT). He is now member of the editorial committee of *IAFOR Journal of Literature and Librarianship* and *SinoELE*. His research interests include SF, Theory of Genres, Horror and Terror Genres, and Traditional Oral Literature, including urban legends. Dr. González Grueso has written a book on Science Fiction and Mythology, entitled *La ficción científica. Género, Poética y sus relaciones con la literatura oral tradicional: El papel de H. P. Lovecraft como mediador*, in addition to three articles on the same genre. He is currently working on another book on SF, *Horror and Terror and Its Interrelations*.

E-mail: dariog@mail.tku.edu.tw

Dr Murielle El Hajj, Lusail University, Qatar

Murielle El Hajj holds a PhD in French Language and Literature from the Lebanese University, Lebanon. She is currently Assistant Professor at Lusail University, Qatar. She is also Associate Editor of the IAFOR Journal of Literature & Librarianship and the IAFOR Journal of Education: Language Learning in Education issues, The International Academic Forum (IAFOR), Japan, as well as Editorial Board Member of In Analysis, revue transdisciplinaire de psychanalyse et sciences, Elsevier Masson SAS, France. Her domain of research focuses on psychoanalysis of literature, the perspective on the unconscious in literary study, the roles of the instances involved in the analytical/critical praxis, and the relation between literature and psychoanalysis. Her research interests include analysis of written narrative structure and focalization; comparative studies of literary genres; discourse analysis and semantics; French linguistics, literature, modernism, and postmodernism studies; gender studies; literary semiotics and semiology; psychoanalysis; psychoanalytic criticism and textoanalysis; rhetoric and stylistics; and schizoanalysis. She has published peer-reviewed book chapters and articles, as well as book reviews and poems in international journals.

E-mail: murielle.elhajj@hotmail.com

Dr Michaela Keck, Carl von Ossietzky University, Germany

Dr Keck is senior lecturer at the Department of English and American Studies at Carl von Ossietzky University in Oldenburg in Germany. She received her doctorate degree in American Studies at Goethe University in Frankfurt and has taught at universities in Taiwan, Holland, and Germany. Her research foci include nineteenth-century American literature and culture at the intersections between literature, visual culture, gender, the reception of myth, and the environment. Further research interests include captivity narratives and African American literature and culture. She is the author of *Walking in the Wilderness: The Peripatetic Tradition in Nineteenth Century American Literature and Painting* (2006) and *Deliberately Out of Bounds: Women's Work Classical on Myth in Nineteenth Century American Fiction* (2017). Among her research articles, which have been published in various peer-reviewed European and international journals, are studies of North American women writers, ranging from Louisa May Alcott to Margaret Atwood (for more information, see https://uol.de/en/michaela-keck?type=0).

E-mail: michaela.keck@gmail.com

Dr Anna Toom, Touro University, USA

Dr Anna Toom is associate professor of psychology in Graduate School of Education at Touro University, New York, USA. She earned her M.S. in Computer Science from Moscow Institute of Radio Engineering, Electronics and Automation (Russia, 1972), her M.S. in Social Psychology from Moscow State University (Russia, 1978), and her PhD in Industrial Psychology from Moscow State Academy of Management (Russia, 1991). Dr Toom has been working as a university researcher and psychology teacher for about forty years. Within the last fourteen years, her primary scientific interest concerns teaching and learning in virtual environment which is based on informational technologies. Dr Toom's pedagogical interests focus on creating new methodology for teaching online psychology courses with the use of the fictions and film arts. Dr Toom is an author of forty-four publications in the fields of psychology and education, presented in refereed journals, monographs, and conference proceedings in English, Russian, and Spanish.

E-mail: annatoom@gmail.com

Dr Akiyoshi Suzuki, Nagasaki University, Japan

Akiyoshi Suzuki is professor of American literature, world literature, and East-West Studies at Nagasaki University, Japan. He has held positions such as English Test Design Commission of the National Center for University Entrance Examinations in Japan, guest professor at Suzhou University of Science & Technology in China, and so forth, and now he is president of Katahira English Literature Society, chief-in-editor of Japan Society of Text Study and Japan Society of Stylistics, an editorial board member of the International Association for East-West Studies (U.S.A.), and others. Dr. Suzuki has published around 50 books and 70 articles and introduced innovative and inventive readings of literature, such as 3-D topographic reading of Haruki Murakami's fictions (*IAFOR Journal of Literature & Librarianship*, 2[1]), resistance against identity-centrism reading of Henry Miller's fictions (*Delta* 7), and so on. His current project is to examine the nature of literature and promote peace in the world by finding affinities of expression and imagination in world literature.

E-mail: suzu-a@nagasaki-u.ac.jp

Dr Beena Giridharan, Curtin University, Malaysia

Professor Beena Giridharan is Dean for Learning and Teaching at Curtin Malaysia, after completing a five-year tenure (2016–2021) as Deputy Pro Vice-Chancellor at Curtin University, Malaysia. In her role, she reports to the Pro Vice-Chancellor, and provides academic leadership to Curtin Malaysia, with a particular focus on academic operational efficiency. Her research and academic interests include: vocabulary acquisition in ESL, educational administration and leadership; higher education practices, transnational education (TNE), and ethno-linguistic studies in indigenous communities. As a member of an OLT (Office of Learning and Teaching, Australia) funded project entitled 'Learning without Borders' she has investigated leadership roles in Trans-National Education (TNE) and internationalization of the curriculum. Beena Giridharan is a Fellow of the Curtin Academy, at Curtin University. Beena Giridharan is also a fellow of the Higher Education Research and Development Society of Australasia (HERDSA) since 2006. Beena Giridharan won the 2006 Carrick Australian Award for University Teaching, and the 2006 Curtin University, Australia, Excellence in Teaching and Innovation award, and was a visiting professor at the Virginia

Commonwealth University, Richmond, Virginia. She is a recognized global leader in higher education.

E-mail: beena@curtin.edu.my

Dr Majed S Al-Lehaibi, Jazan University, Saudi Arabia

Dr Majed S Al-Lehaibi is professor of American Literature and Intellectual History at Jazan University, Saudi Arabia. His key areas of interest include the 20th Century Novel, American Social and Political Literature of the 1930s, American Culture and Intellectual History of the 19th and 20th Centuries; and African American Literature. He is currently working on a project investigating Industrialization, Urbanization, Immigration and the Bifurcation of Literature into "highbrow" and "lowbrow" in the late 19th and early 20th century America. Among his published works are a paper entitled "The New Human: Robot Evolution in a Selection from Asimov's Short Stories," one on "Hemingway and Dos Passos: The 1930s" and one on "The Metropolis and the Modern Self."

E-mail: mallehaibi@jazanu.edu.sa

Dr Miguel Ángel González Chandía, Fu Jen Catholic University, Taipei

Dr Miguel Ángel González Chandía earned his PhD in Systematic Theology at KULeuven-Belgium, and his BA in Theology, from the Pontificia Universidad Católica of Santiago, Chile. He is a full professor at Fu Jen Catholic University, Taipei. He has taught Latin American Literature and languages for almost 17 years. His courses include Spanish Writing and Reading, Oral Expression, and Drama. He has some 20 publications, and was a co-editor of the *IAFOR Journal of Education* until 2020. His research interests include Literature, Contemporary Latin American's women writers: and studies in Isabel Allende, Marcela Paz, and the *Papelucho short stories*, Marcela Serrano, Jorge Edwards, and the works of Roberto Bolaño, especially *2666*, *Los detectives salvajes* and *Nocturno de Chile*. Dr. González has published a chapter titled "Una visión apocalíptica de Roberto Bolaño y su *Nocturno de Chile*" in Estudios hispánicos en Taiwán, colección Universitas Taiwanesa, Ediciones Catay, Taichung-Taiwan (2020). In 2021, he published "Isabel Allende y su novela *Paula*: enfermedad, muerte y esperanza" in *Fu Jen Studies Journal*.

E-mail: 064929@mail.fju.edu.tw

Lightning Source UK Ltd.
Milton Keynes UK
UKHW010951111122
411996UK00003B/13

9 781666 918137